BORN TO BE A BAGGIE

A WEST BROMWICH ALBION SUPPORTER'S 50-YEAR ODYSSEY

Dean Walton

AMBERLEY

Dedicated to Mom – Elizabeth 'Betty' Walton – 05-04-29 to 31-07-98
and
Dad – Harold Walton – 09-09-27 to 18-10-09.

Cover illustrations:
Front top: My parents (centre) on their way to Wembley for the 1954 FA Cup final.

Front and back bottom: The final whistle has just been blown at Fratton Park, Portsmouth, in 1994. Albion had avoided regulation to the old Third Division following our 1-0 victory, most of the 12,000 Baggies have invaded the pitch in celebration.

First published 2016

Amberley Publishing
The Hill, Stroud
Gloucestershire, GL5 4EP

www.amberley-books.com

British Library Cataloguing in Publication Data.
A catalogue record for this book is available from the British Library.

ISBN 978 1 4456 5857 5 (print)
ISBN 978 1 4456 5858 2 (ebook)

Typesetting and Origination by Amberley Publishing.
Printed in the UK.

Contents

Foreword by Tony 'Bomber' Brown
(574 appearances, 218 goals)

It was around the time that I was making my West Bromwich Albion debut in 1964 that Dean was attending his first game; it's incredible to think that he has rarely missed a home game since. Watching the Baggies at 150 grounds and in eighteen different countries shows amazing dedication and loyalty. As a former player I know how much we appreciated supporters like Dean.

There is a special feeling within this club and there has always been a strong bond between the players and the fans. When I first set foot in The Hawthorns, as a fifteen-year-old schoolboy from Oldham, I felt so instantly at home. I went on to have twenty great and very happy years with the club as a player. Since my career finished I have continued to live in the local area and now consider myself to be a genuine Albion supporter, still attending all games home and away.

I have always thought that the Baggies fans are unique, some would say barmy. To my knowledge the Albion supporters were the first to start dressing up at away games and they have created some magnificent sights over the years such as the beachwear parties and the Super Heroes at Queens Park Rangers.

It was at one of the end-of-season matches that I first met Dean; he was at St James' Park with his Mask-arade colleagues giving away 'Bomber Brown' masks to every Albion fan as they entered the ground. The gesture was in support of the so-called 'Newcastle Brown Day' and I must admit that I found it an extremely humbling experience.

During further conversations with Dean it turns out that we were both in the stands in Valencia for that legendary evening in 1978. I was unfortunately sidelined through injury that night, but was proud to sit with the fans and witness one of the best individual football displays that I have ever seen – Laurie Cunningham was on fire that night, and it was his starring role in Albion's excellent 1-1 draw which brought his talent to the attention of Real Madrid.

One of Dean's happiest memories is the promotion-winning game at Oldham in 1976, and, even though I scored the winning goal, a lot of the credit must be given to the Albion fans. They took over Boundary Park that day and turned it into a home game. I'll never forget the scenes on the motorway and the roads into my birthplace; everywhere was just a sea of navy blue and white or yellow and green. How could we possibly lose with backing like that?

Another game where the fans ensured an Albion victory came at Fratton Park, Portsmouth, in 1994. The Baggies needed a win to avoid returning to the dark days of the old Third Division. Some 12,000 fans poured down the A34 from the Midlands, taking over two thirds of the stadium to roar the lads to victory.

A similar occurrence was at the previous season's play-off semi-final against Swansea. We needed to overturn a 2-1 deficit from the first leg and it was one of those nights, when everyone pulled together under The Hawthorns' floodlights and made sure that it was Albion who progressed to the final at Wembley.

I am proud of the many records that I broke in my playing days, including the most goals scored and most appearances made by any Albion player in the history of the club. I was fortunate to play in some great sides alongside and against some marvellous players. My best friend was the Albion supporters' hero Jeff Astle, known as The King by the Brummie Road Enders; I know how much Jeff adored the fans and greatly appreciated the support he received, so much so that he too ended up as a supporter when he hung up his boots. Jeff is sadly missed at the club, but I know that all his family are eternally grateful to the Albion fans who continue to chant his name and support the Jeff Astle Foundation, by raising money for such a worthwhile cause. The 'Astle Day' against Leicester in 2015 was very special.

I am honoured to write the foreword for this book, I still love the club and thank every single Albion fan for their friendliness and continued support.

Foreword by 'Super' Bob Taylor
(377 appearances, 131 goals)

I signed for the Albion in January 1992, and although I had played against the Baggies a couple of times, I have to admit that I didn't know much about them. Luckily I got off to a good start. I was soon scoring goals regularly, and the fans took to me right away. It became a privilege to follow in the footsteps of some great goal-scorers from Albion's past like Ronnie Allen, Tony Brown, Jeff Astle and Cyrille Regis.

It didn't take long to settle into the area, which was very similar to the North East where I came from. The supporters turned out to be the same as the people that I had grown up with in my home town; real people with working class values, a sense of humour and loyal to the cause. They told me about the history of the club and the reputation that Albion have always had for exciting attacking football.

The Baggies fans have always made me welcome, even when I played for Bolton (against Albion) they still chanted my name and applauded me at the end of the game. It was great to return to The Hawthorns for a second spell and score the goal that clinched promotion to the Premier League in 2002. The run-in leading up to that game was unbelievable and the fans played a huge part in helping us catch and then overtake Wolves. The support at Coventry, Nottingham Forest and that memorable afternoon at Bradford will live with me forever.

After all these years spent living in the Midlands, I now consider the Black Country as my adopted home and the Albion fans as my friends. I have now become a supporter myself and love to join the Albion fans on their travels. I've even been known to dress up for the end of season theme parties!

It is no surprise that some of those fans show such dedication to their club that they are prepared to follow them all over the world. This book is a testimony to that fact and I am sure that all you 'Baggies' will enjoy reading about Dean Walton's travels both home and abroad and that it will bring back a lot of memories, good and bad.

As for me, I remember that amazing night in the snow at Brescia. Of all the games I played in, that has to be one of the most bizarre. I wonder which game you will recall.

Foreword by Adrian Chiles
(Television and Radio Presenter and West Bromwich Albion Supporter)

However committed you are to your football team, however authentic you feel as a fan, there will always be someone to make you feel a bit inadequate. Dean Walton is that man for me. Reading this book it turns out he's seen about four matches for every one I've been to, and I've not missed many. And, while I have impeccable middle-class credentials having been raised west of Birmingham in Hagley, Dean boasts a proper Great Barr upbringing, with parents sporting proper working-class names like Betty and Harold. And he can remember watching the 1968 cup final on the television. I envy him all these things.

We first met properly, at some terribly early hour, at Luton Airport one summer morning. We were boarding a flight operated by a Polish budget airline to Zagreb. Albion were playing in Croatia, you see, in an essentially meaningless pre-season friendly at Varazdin. I wanted to be there because I have family in Croatia. Well, that was my excuse. Dean had no excuse whatsoever. Neither did he have any clue, as I remember, how he was going to get to Varazdin from Zagreb. Luckily for both of us, as you'll read, a friend of mine, a football journalist in Zagreb, was on hand to drive us both there. There was a minor farce in my friend's flat involving changing a door on his new fridge – I remember Dean with a spanner in his hand – and then off we went to Varazdin. On the way, the three of us stopped for a bite in a restaurant on a hill. My Croatian friend, you see, is one of the country's leading eaters and drinkers, with a physique to match. He ordered Olympian quantities of food and drink, but Dean was equal to everything thrown at him in this ad hoc episode of man versus food.

There we sat, the three of us, outside a charming restaurant in Croatia with the sun on our faces and our bellies heaving with meat and strong liquor. It was bromantic, I promise you. And I believe the Albion didn't even lose, though my memory of the rest of that day is sketchy at best.

Dean's memory of that day, and every other Albion day, turns out to be crystal clear. Enjoy sharing them with him.

1

Baggie by Birth

I entered this world on 24 November 1960, born at home in Green Lane, Great Barr, opposite the Hamstead Pub. Albion did not herald my arrival in any style. Two days later, they lost 2-1 at home to Spurs despite a goal from Don Howe.

I really didn't have a say in my football allegiance. My parents, Betty and Harold Walton, were born a few doors away from each other in Oak Lane, West Bromwich, and were staunch Albion fans; as was my older brother Alan, who was five when I was born. My mom's best friend was my dad's sister, so that's how they were introduced. However, just as romance was blossoming, Dad was called up for the army and posted to Singapore and Malaysia. As he was leaving the house to serve his country, my grandad called him back, he said 'Here you are son, you're a man now,' and gave him a packet of ten cigarettes! Over the next couple of years, Mom and Dad's relationship was conducted long distance, through letters only, then, after Dad was demobbed, they married at All Saints Church, West Bromwich, on 3 March 1951.

My aunties, uncles and cousins were also dyed-in-the-wool Baggies and many of them were season ticket holders. Dad's twin sister, my Auntie Barbara, actually met her future husband 'Maltese' Tony Falzon, on one of Dad's coaches going to an away game. My grandparents were also regulars at The Hawthorns, (and possibly Albion's pre-1900 Stoney Lane ground) I remember Grandad telling me about the great Jesse Pennington and the League Championship winning team of 1920.

Dad held a senior position in the Albion Supporters Club. His main responsibility was to organise the coaches in the late 1940s and early 1950s. Mom was fanatical and always travelled on Dad's hired 'charabanc', together with my aunts and uncles. Some excellent photographs from that era taken by my father on various trips are among my most prized possessions. I used to love hearing stories from these adventures, such as the time my parents joined the snow-clearing effort at St James' Park in an attempt to get the fourth-round FA Cup tie against Gateshead played in 1952. It proved to be a losing battle, but they still had an enjoyable weekend as members of the Newcastle United Supporters' Club provided them with a bed for the cold night.

Uncle Arthur loved to tell the story of my dad's embarrassment on a trip to Portsmouth. In the vicinity of Fratton Park, the coach pulled over and Dad shouted to a local chap: 'Oi, Jack (as in Jack Tar – British Army slang for sailor), could you tell me where the nearest fish and chip shop is?' The Pompey fan was not impressed and answered: 'How did you know my name?' Feeling pleased with himself, Dad replied: 'I just guessed.' 'Jack' then had the last word by responding: 'Well, guess where the f***ing chip shop is then!'

Many programmes and match tickets from the 1930s, 1940s and 1950s have been handed down to me. One of the most treasured items is Mom's home-made rosette, which she wore at the 1954 FA Cup final, fully embroidered around a 1954 penny.

The sixties

Sadly, I can't recall the first game that I watched, but it would have been around 1965. I would go with whoever would take me – Dad, Mom, my uncle or various neighbours. I just loved it. I was fascinated by everything – the crowd, the chanting, the smells but, most of all, those magnificent navy blue and white stripes.

Mostly, I would go with my neighbours. We would catch the No. 6 bus from the top of Hamstead Road, past the old colliery, through the Scott Arms to West Bromwich, and walk along the High Street, past the old Woolworths, the market hall and the Imperial cinema. I remember walking by a building site which was later to become the Queen's Square precinct.

Once inside the ground, I would be lifted up and sat on the wall just to the left of the goal at the Birmingham Road End, with my legs behind the advertising boards. I was in my element and, although only six or seven, would be perfectly happy on my own, with the neighbours or family friends checking on me at half-time, then lifting me off the wall at the end. At half-time, I would turn to the Woodman Corner to watch the scores being placed into the boxes of the scoreboard. Each match was marked by a letter of the alphabet, which had to be cross-referenced with the fixtures on the back of the programme.

I absolutely worshipped Jeff Astle. He seemed to score in every game! Following each goal, he would run towards the adoring Brummie Road Enders, arms aloft, often directly in front of me. He was and always will be my hero. I once spent my pocket money on a large poster of 'The King' from one of the sellers on the perimeter track. It stayed on my bedroom wall for years.

I vaguely remember looking towards the back of the Brummie and seeing 'Sammy', who used to climb on the barrier to conduct the crowd, leading the chant: '2-4-6-8, who do we appreciate? A-L-B-I-O-N ... Albion'

I can clearly remember certain home games from the 1960s, such as our 6-3 victory against Manchester United on 29 April 1968. We had beaten Birmingham City in the FA Cup semi-final just 48 hours earlier while United were on course to complete the League and European Cup double. I was with Mom on the Woodman Corner in a crowd of 45,992 to see us go 4-0 up through Astle (2), Ronnie Rees and Tony 'Bomber' Brown. Denis Law pulled one back from the spot before we scored another two in the space of a minute through Asa Hartford and Jeff. That completed his hat-trick. Brian Kidd knocked in two late goals for the bemused visitors, but it had been a great experience. I used to love watching us play United with Bobby Charlton, Dennis Law and, Mom's favourite, George Best – possibly because we used to hand them some right hidings!

Another memorable match was our 6-1 win over Coventry City in October, 1968 with another two goals from The King, a penalty from Bomber and one each for Hartford and Rees. An own-goal made it six. Our 1-0 FA Cup victory over Arsenal in February, 1969 is another game etched in my memory, with the ever-reliable Tony Brown thundering in the winner, this time watched by 45,354. I have always loved watching games under The Hawthorns floodlights, there is a special atmosphere when the pitch is illuminated.

For some reason, I stood in the Smethwick End for our 4-3 win against Spurs with goals from Bobby Hope, Astle (2) and Brown. We mingled with the Tottenham fans and all I remember is lots of good-hearted banter. Things were about to change.

Another big victory, this time a 5-1 roasting of Newcastle, is also clear in my mind. I was back on the Brummie Road wall to see five different Albion scorers: John Kaye, Hartford, Brown, Clive 'Chippy' Clark and Astle (of course).

I started school at Hamstead Infants in 1966. I'm pleased to say some of my colleagues from that first day are still good friends. Growing up football-mad, I spent every spare minute playing either opposite my house on the Hamstead pub car park, down on the school fields or in Red House Park. I lived at the top end of Hamstead and would be forever arranging games against the 'bottom enders' on the large patch of grass at the back of Langdale Road by the 'Golden Throstle' – an Albion supporters' club built on the site of the miners' shower block after the Hamstead pit closed down. On the odd occasion we didn't have a football, we would be out and about; building dens, messing about in the park or getting up to no good up the cut. I just can't relate to the kids of today spending hours indoors glued to the Playstation or Xbox. The last place I wanted to be was in the house. Fortunately, I could look out of my bedroom window and see which of my mates were congregating over the road. Within minutes, I would be playing with them, usually in a game of 'Three and in', 'Wembley' or a proper match but with 'rush-back' goalies if we were short of players.

My favourite all-time Christmas present was a set of junior goalposts complete with nets. What I didn't know is that my parents had colluded with my friend John Nash's parents (who lived in the Hamstead pub) to each buy a set of 'real goals'. As soon as our presents were revealed, we were both out on the pub car park, setting up and rounding up the rest of the Green Lane gang for an impromptu Christmas Day match. It wasn't quite like the trenches during the First World War, but you know what I mean.

I also loved climbing trees and was spoilt for choice as there were some massive beech and silver birches opposite the house. One day, after watching *Tarzan* on television, I convinced myself that I could swing on a branch from one tree to another. Of course, this was only possible in the movies and I came crashing down from about 30 feet. Unfortunately, I landed on my face and gashed underneath my bottom lip so that it resembled a second mouth. I ended up in Hallam Hospital for the first time, had to have six stitches and still have the scar.

Cup glory

I have no recollection of our 1966 two-legged League Cup final victory over West Ham. The only memory I have of 1967 is of Dad and Grandad returning disappointed from the first League Cup final at Wembley and cursing 'that bloody Rodney Marsh' after our agonising defeat to Queens Park Rangers. What I do remember is being heartbroken in 1968 when Dad could only get two tickets for the FA Cup final. He obtained them through his work colleague Walter Hickman, whose son Geoff was one of Albion's back-up goalkeepers.

Dad had taken Mom to Wembley in 1954 and Grandad in 1967, therefore it was my older brother's turn. Sadly, Alan's interest in all things football waned in his teens, so it still rankles that I wasn't there to see us win the FA Cup. Instead, I sat at home with Mom watching on television alongside my Action Man, who was appropriately dressed in his purpose-made Baggies kit. It was the first final to be broadcast in colour, but there was no such luxury for us. We had to make do with an old black and white set that you had to regularly bang on the top to stop the picture rolling. The game wasn't exactly a classic and, as the 90 minutes ended in a 0-0 stalemate, Albion boss Alan Ashman created history by replacing the injured John Kaye with Dennis Clarke, who became the first substitute to play in the Cup final. Then, just as the sun came out, Graham Williams and Doug Fraser combined on the left and the ball found its way to Astle. His first shot came back to him off Brian Labone and, with his weaker left foot, The King drilled it high into the net causing Everton 'keeper Gordon West to utter the immortal words 'What the f***in' hell was that?' as Astle's 94th-minute thunderbolt flew past his left shoulder. We had done it, Jeff had become the first player to score in every round of the competition and I couldn't contain my excitement. I ran outside to join my Green Lane-based Albion mates John Nash, Andy Payne and Andy Norton in a celebration dance on the Hamstead Pub car park, followed by our usual kick-around. Of course we all wanted to be Astle!

I wasn't going to miss the team bringing the cup back to West Bromwich, so Dad dropped us off really early next day, to enable Mom to perch me on the window-sill of Barclays Bank in the High Street as an estimated 250,000 Albion fans gathered to see each member of the team lift the Cup on the town hall balcony. The biggest cheer was reserved for Astle. My older brother, although only thirteen, was at the top of one of the tall trees, along with many others, outside the Halls of Remembrance.

I remember going to see John Osborne's house. He lived just around the corner from me, in Stanton Road and the front of his home had been decorated from top to bottom in blue and white bunting to welcome him back from Wembley. I actually got to hold the Cup when Graham Williams brought it to my school and I saw it again a few weeks later when Jeff Astle had it with him when he opened the new Amoco petrol station in Hamstead (sadly, no photos were taken).

I also went with my parents to admire the montage of flowers in Dartmouth Park, laid out to depict the FA Cup and the names of all of the players.

The following season, we reached the semi-final again. I wasn't allowed to go to Hillsborough (I was only eight) but I remember praying we would beat Leicester so I could go to Wembley. Unfortunately, it wasn't to be, thanks to Albion fan Allan Clarke's winning goal with just three minutes remaining. Little did I know then, that my time would come in less than a year?

1969/70

As the new season kicked off, I was now going to all the home games with Mom. Dad had fallen out with someone inside the club a few years earlier, resigned from his Supporters' Club duties and unbelievably stopped attending. I still have the letter from Supporters' Club President and ex-player Dave Walsh, asking him to reconsider. Mom and I had season tickets in the Halfords Lane paddock alongside Pat Beard, whose husband Stan was Albion's groundsman. Pat was later joined by her son David, who eventually followed in his father's footsteps and is the current head groundsman at The Hawthorns

Colin Suggett, Albion's first £100,000 signing, arrived from Sunderland and 'keeper Jimmy Cumbes joined us from Tranmere. Danny Hegan and Allan Glover also arrived.

Our form in the early part of the season was very inconsistent, with the only memorable home victories coming against Manchester United, Sheffield Wednesday and Manchester City. Fortunately, things were going well in the League Cup, where we started with a lovely 2-1 win at Villa Park. This was followed by a victory over Ipswich in a replay. Bradford City were next to fall, a 4-0 win at The Hawthorns putting us into the quarter-final. A 0-0 draw at Filbert Street brought Leicester back to our place, where an Astle brace sent us home dreaming of another Wembley appearance.

One of my favourite games was the second leg of the semi-final. After losing 1-0 in Cumbria, we swept Carlisle aside by a 4-1 margin. Goals from Bobby Hope, Colin Suggett, Tony Brown and Dennis Martin ensured our fourth final in five years. I was ecstatic in the knowledge that it was my turn to go to Wembley. I hadn't even contemplated the idea that we might not be able to obtain tickets. On this occasion, Dad managed to get a couple off young Asa Hartford. He was a regular customer at the petrol station that adjoined Churchfield Spring in Black Lake, where Dad was works manager. He often bumped into Asa and regularly got things autographed for me. Although Mom wanted to go, she insisted I went with Dad; she knew how much it meant to me.

Wembley, the first time

The day of the final, 7 March, soon arrived and off we headed down south in a mini-bus driven by my father and full of his work mates. I can still remember the M1 that day and seeing thousands of cars and vans clad in navy blue and white or the sky blue of our opponents Manchester City. I loved reading the witty slogans on the banners, my favourite was 'Jesus Saves ... but Astle gets the rebound'. We were all confident our name was on the cup as we had beaten City 3-0 at The Hawthorns a few weeks before.

Outside the Twin Towers, I nagged Dad to buy me every possible souvenir. I couldn't believe the size of the stadium and wanted to get inside as soon as the gates opened. Inside, the ground was even better, the atmosphere was spine-tingling and I sang along with the chants of 'Astle' and 'Albion'. The pitch was in a right state as a combination of heavy snow and the Horse of the Year show (held the previous weekend) had completely ruined it. So much for the famous Wembley turf – it was more like Red House Park!

In the fifth minute, Astle out-jumped the huge City 'keeper Joe Corrigan to put us 1-0 up. The King thus became the first player to score at Wembley in both the FA Cup and League Cup finals.

I was in dreamland and took great pleasure in ribbing the City fans during a trip to the buffet bar at half-time. I should have known better. I have since learned that Albion are inclined to let you down and, on this freezing afternoon, they did exactly that. Francis Lee was throwing himself to the ground at every opportunity to try and win a penalty or get an Albion player in trouble. Fortunately, the ref was having none of it but Mike Doyle inevitably equalised to take the match into extra time. I remember thinking: 'It'll be okay, this is when Jeff usually scores the winner.' Glynn Pardoe obviously hadn't read the script, he scored what turned out to be the winner and City duly lifted the cup. However, I wasn't there to witness it. On the final whistle, I was heartbroken and stormed out of Wembley with tears running down my cheeks, Dad running after me and trying to console me. 'It's okay,' he said, 'we'll probably be back next season and you can come again.' Little did we know that twenty-three years would pass and I would be a dad myself before Albion would return to the famous stadium. Could it have been Albion chairman Jim Gaunt's words that haunted us for all those years? After the 1970 final, he famously declared: 'I'm fed up with coming to Wembley. It's time we won the League.'

We went on to finish 16th that season, with Astle in magnificent form. He scored 30 League and cup goals on his way to selection for the England squad who set off for Mexico to defend the World Cup under Sir Alf Ramsey that summer. Jeff's scoring record over four seasons was phenomenal: 24, 23, 35 (the country's best) and 25. With that sort of tally, nobody could challenge his right to be included in the twenty-eight-man squad.

In the FA Cup, Tony Brown scored the finest goal of his career with his 'over the shoulder' half-volley at Hillsborough in our third-round 2-1 defeat against Sheffield Wednesday. We also lost there to Leicester in the semi-final the year before; the only time we had lost consecutive cup-ties on the same ground (other than The Hawthorns).

Our best win of the season was 4-0 against Nottingham Forest through goals from Astle, Bomber (2) and Glover. In typical Albion style, we followed up our best win with our worst defeat – a 7-0 thrashing by Manchester United. Everton were League Champions. The highlight of the season was without doubt Villa getting relegated to Third Division (snigger).

1970 World Cup

I had the World Cup to look forward to for my football fix in the summer. I only have vague memories of the 1966 competition. Being only five meant I wasn't really aware of the significance of it all. Also, I'm not even sure we had a television then. This time, I was glued to the TV in the hope that Jeff was selected. When he went on as a substitute for Francis Lee after 63 minutes against Brazil, I was praying he would score the winner. He nearly made a sensational World Cup debut; the first time he touched the ball, his header down created a chance that Alan Ball sadly miskicked. A couple of minutes later, Jeff was presented with an even easier opportunity. A defensive mix-up left him with only the Brazilian 'keeper to beat from about 12 yards. In Astle's words: 'I had all the time in the world. I could have taken the ball up to the 'keeper and slipped it past him. Instead, I blasted it straightaway and hit it past the far post.' Jeff will never be forgotten by non-Albion fans for that miss. The common misconception is that it got us knocked out of the World Cup. This is incorrect; England qualified from the group stages in any case and lost 3-2 to West Germany in the quarter-final after being 2-0 ahead. Curiously, Bobby Charlton's glaring miss in the same game never gets a mention. In fact, Sir Alf Ramsey was actually pleased with Jeff's performance against Brazil, so much so that he was selected to start in the final group match against Romania. Sadly, Jeff didn't have the best of games in a 1-0 England win. Jeff always maintained that England would have retained the World Cup if the players had not been so obsessed with the climatic problems of Mexico and the fear of running out of energy.

I was an active member of the Junior Throstle Club in the late 1960s and early '70s, entering all the competitions. Unfortunately, there were no mascot packages in those days so I never had the opportunity to lead that great team out onto the pitch. I did, however, win lots of JTC prizes, one of which regularly comes back to haunt me. In 1970, I won a competition to design a club mascot (years ahead of its time) and, for some strange reason I drew a wolf in a Wolves strip. What was I thinking? The good news was that I won a copy of the West Bromwich Albion Football Book autographed by the whole team. It just goes to show how insignificant Wolves were in Great Barr. Our rivalry has always been with a certain team from just down the A34 in Witton and, from my point of view, always will be.

I used to love to visit Dickens sports shop in West Bromwich, often adding to my Subbuteo collection. I also purchased Puma Top-Fit training shoes and a pair of Asa Hartford white boots. When I go into West Brom now, I still look at the Dickens building with great sadness. The bust on the upper floor of the outside wall is still there but the lovely old shopfront has been replaced by an Asian clothes store.

Quiz Ball was my favourite televison programme – it featured two teams of four, representing teams from the English or Scottish leagues. Albion actually won the trophy one year with John Osborne proving to be the quiz king.

Friday evenings were always Subbuteo nights. My parents would go to the Golden Throstle Club (later to become the Kings) in Hamstead to see up and coming acts like Charlie Williams and Ken Goodwin. In their absence, I was allowed to have my mates round for a Subbuteo tournament. I was always Albion, of course.

2

Back in the Brummie Road

As we entered the 1970s, I religiously attended every home game with Mom in the Halfords Lane stand. I absolutely loved it, with our wooden bench seats backing on to the gangway leading to the dressing rooms. Mom was never backwards in coming forwards and she had a favourite player in every visiting team; Alan Mullery (Tottenham), Bobby Moore (West Ham), Emlyn Hughes (Liverpool) and Jackie Charlton (Leeds) were a selection of the opponents she really liked. Each game, she would make a beeline for her favourite as he walked behind our seats, hand them my Soccer Stars sticker album and ask them to take it into the dressing room and get it signed by the whole team. It never failed, and Mom's chosen player would always return my album, fully autographed. I would sit there in awe as the likes of Bobby Moore would return to seek Mom out. I also collected autographs from the Albion players. My favourites were Tony Brown, Asa Hartford and, of course, Jeff Astle. I even got the autograph of Jeff's wife Laraine!

During the late 1960s and early 1970s, I also attended many away games, although sadly I don't remember which 'foreign' ground I visited first. Uncle Arthur used to take me to all the local ones, such as Stoke, Coventry and Nottingham Forest. If I couldn't go to the away game, I would go and watch the Albion reserves, who played at The Hawthorns on alternate Saturdays.

1970/71

The new season saw us sign John Wile from Peterborough to shore up our leaking defence. He was brought in to replace John Talbut, who was shipped out to Belgian club KV Mechelin. George McVitie also came in, from Carlisle, with Dennis Martin moving in the opposite direction.

We plodded along in mid-table with notable victories coming against Stoke (when we put five past England 'keeper Gordon Banks), Everton, who were thrashed 3-0, and Tottenham – on the wrong end of a 'Bomber' Brown hat-trick in December. On the down side, we shipped 21 goals in our first six away games. Our game against Wolves on 29 March was a disappointment. Despite goals from McVitie (known as 'Biscuit' to the fans) and Bomber, we lost 4-2 in front of 36,754.

The season will be most remembered for our game at Elland Road near the end of the season. With Leeds on course to win the League, we controversially won 2-1, ending a dismal run of twenty-seven away games without a victory. Referee Ray Tinkler allowed Astle's goal to stand despite every Leeds player stopping, claiming offside. All hell was let loose with several hundred Leeds fans invading the pitch and the game was close to being abandoned. On *Match of the Day*, commentator Barry Davies famously said: 'Leeds will go mad and they've every right to.' Thirty of the invaders were arrested and a linesman collapsed after being hit on the head. The result pretty much handed Arsenal the title.

In the FA Cup, a young Kevin Keegan turned up at The Hawthorns with Scunthorpe, where we won 3-1 in a replay. We bowed out against Ipswich in the fourth round by losing 3-0, again in a replay. We started off well enough in the League Cup, knocking out Charlton and Preston, before crashing out at White Hart Lane 5-0.

Tony Brown topped the First Division scoring charts with 28 goals, becoming the fifth Albion player to achieve this accolade.

1971/72

In the summer of 1971, ex-Albion and England right back Don Howe was installed as manager, replacing the popular Alan Ashman, who was on holiday abroad when told he was sacked. Things were never quite the same after that.

The pre-season Watney Cup remains firmly imprinted in my memory. After seeing off Wrexham and Halifax, we were paired with Colchester in the final at The Hawthorns. For a neutral, it was a cracker, with the Fourth Division side leading 4-3, then, up popped Jeff Astle with a last minute equaliser. Cue pitch invasion to celebrate with The King. Colchester eventually beat us on penalties, their 'keeper Graham Smith pulling off a string of fine saves and impressing Don Howe so much that he signed him shortly afterwards. Strikers Bobby Gould and Alistair Brown also joined us during the season.

The new boss set about breaking up the team, moving on some of our most popular players. Out went Bobby Hope, Graham Lovett, Graham Williams, Jimmy Cumbes and John Kaye.

Surprisingly, we won our first two games (against West Ham and Everton) before reality set in and we had to wait another ten matches for our next victory (at Crystal Palace). I attended the Texaco Cup game against Greenock Morton and distinctly remember a group of very noisy Scots in the 16,168-strong crowd for a game we lost 1-0 (1-3 on aggregate). I would love to see this competition resurrected, or some sort of tournament that enabled us to travel to grounds north of the border.

Good home victories over Liverpool, Manchester United and Chelsea (4-0) ensured we finished ten points clear of relegation, but we went out of both major cup competitions at the first stage for the first time ever, losing home games to Spurs (League Cup) and Coventry (FA Cup). Brian Clough's Derby County were League champions.

Junior school

As well as going to The Hawthorns every week, I was also playing for my school football team on Saturday mornings which prevented me from travelling to long-distance away games. I was a half-decent goalkeeper and gained a cup winner's medal playing for Hamstead Junior School when we won the Albion five-a-side trophy. We were fortunate to have a professional footballer helping us out. Walsall midfielder Nick Athey would come in every week and take us for specialist practice.

The headmaster, Jack Shipley, loved football and the whole school team had to stand on the stage for a special assembly when we reached the Harrison Cup semi-final. He conducted everyone in a rousing rendition of 'We shall not be moved'. Grandad used to come and stand behind my goal, offering advice and encouragement. He lived with us in Green Lane, so it hit me hard when he passed away suddenly in October 1971.

In March, 1972, Hamstead entertained St Oswald's school team from Liverpool. It made me proud to take them to The Hawthorns and stand on the Brummie Road terraces against Crystal Palace, Ally Brown scored on his debut in the 1-1 draw.

Looking back, it's hard to believe what we used to get away with. For our five-a-side games at Menzies school in West Bromwich, our PE teacher Mr Dimbylow would pack six of us, plus himself, the kit and the balls all into his tiny Triumph Spitfire – no health and safety rules in those days! On Saturday mornings, the usual routine involved throwing stones up at Warren Jones's bedroom window in order to wake him up to play for the team. 'Wozza' was the 'cock' of the school, a staunch Baggie and always getting into trouble; and to think he was only eleven at the time.

In September 1972, I moved to senior school, Dartmouth High in Great Barr, and immediately secured a place as goalkeeper in the school team, together with ex-Hamstead mates: Chris Chapman, Paul Tudor, Paul Hutchinson and Paul Affron. We made up the nucleus of a very good side, so much so that no fewer than seven Dartmouth players (myself included) went on to represent West Bromwich schoolboys in the Staffordshire League. During this time, I regularly faced Wayne Clarke, who represented Walsall Schools and would later go on to play for Wolves, Everton and Birmingham.

1972/73

I once again took my seat in the Halfords Lane paddock for the 1972/73 season. The game at home to newly-promoted Birmingham on 30 August was notable for three brothers playing in the same game. Our 'keeper was Peter Latchford and his brothers Dave and Bob both turned out for a Blues side wearing an unusual red, yellow and black strip. Bobby Gould and Colin Suggett grabbed our goals in a 2-2 draw. We had to wait until the eighth game of the season for our first victory, a 2-1 win over champions Derby. This triggered a mini revival, with four points coming from our next two games. There were only two points for a win in those days.

Don Howe concluded his only bit of decent managerial work when he signed winger Willie Johnston from Glasgow Rangers for a club record £138,000. He also recruited David Shaw from Oldham and Joe Mayo from Walsall.

We limped along playing boring defensive football, with a rare highlight coming in a 4-1 thrashing of Everton which gave us a glimmer of hope. Disappointingly, it was followed by four successive defeats and our fate was confirmed when we lost our last two home games – against Norwich and Manchester City. It didn't stop Mom and me travelling to St Andrew's for the last game of the season and the final death knell. We sat at the rear of the Railway End and I heard the Blues' fans rendition of 'Keep right on to the end of the road' for the first time. Despite goals from Astle and Wile, we lost 3-2 and that was that, the unthinkable had happened. Albion finished bottom and were relegated to the Second Division after twenty-four years in the top flight.

We didn't fare any better in the cups, although the FA Cup third round against Nottingham Forest was quite exciting. The first replay was abandoned because of snow, we drew two games before knocking them out in a second replay at Leicester. We won at home to Swindon before Leeds knocked us out in round five. After we beat QPR, Liverpool put paid to our League Cup campaign, by beating us 2-1 at Anfield in a replay.

I was now twelve and, despite the fact I loved keeping Mom company at Albion home games, I was craving to join my mates on the Brummie Road terraces. During the previous few seasons, I had spent half the matches watching the crowd to my left and wanting to be part of it. I loved the singing, the mass surges, the bouncing up and down, and saw it as my spiritual home.

In fairness, Mom was very understanding when I asked if I could relocate. It actually saved Dad a tenner as my new season ticket cost only £15. Mom continued to go, retaining her seat in the Halfords (equipped with obligatory tartan rug and flask) for another few seasons until ill health and a move to Rugeley prevented her attending; or could it have been Don Howe?

1973/74

My high school years began with Albion playing Second Division football. We got off to a good start, beating Blackpool away, then, in my first game as a Brummie Road season ticket holder, we edged Crystal Palace 1-0 with Glover scoring. We still didn't exactly set the division alight, but did find a bit of form and had eight wins in the bag before Christmas.

I loved standing on the Brummie Road, and together with my mates, we soon established our own space at the back on the right side. During the customary 'Knees up Mother Brown' and after each Albion goal, we would end up anything up to 20 feet further down the terraces as the crowd jumped up and down and surged forward. The singing would be non-stop and I was in my element. I remember the 'Zigger Zagger' chant and every goal scored by the visitors would be followed by the obligatory: 'You're gonna get your fu**in' heads kicked in!'

The highlights were our four wins over our arch enemies. It was the first time we had played Villa in a League match since 1967 (when they were relegated from the First Division) and I very nearly missed The Hawthorns meeting on Boxing Day. Although we both had season tickets, Andy Payne and I set off early in the morning and took our place in the queue at the Brummie Road turnstiles three and a half hours before kick-off. Whether it was the excitement of the game or over-indulging at Christmas, I don't know, but at around 1.00 p.m., and for the first and only time in my life, I fainted. The police telephoned Dad and allowed him to park on The Hawthorns pub car park. When I started to come round, I was violently sick, completely 'decorating' the back of the police car I was sat in. The officer and my old man insisted that I went to hospital but I was having none of it. I had waited so long for this game that I wasn't going to miss it for anything. I eventually convinced them that I felt better (I didn't) and we duly took our places on the terraces in a crowd of over 43,000. Although we won 2-0, the match was a bit of a blur for me and I was relieved to get home and go straight to bed.

For the return game, I agreed to accompany Mom in the seats but I really wanted to be with the massed ranks of Albion fans to our right on the old Witton End terrace. We again outclassed Villa and I was ecstatic when goals from John Wile and 'Bomber' (2) gave us a 3-1 win and further bragging rights at school.

Another memorable game came on 23 February, when Jeff Astle made his eagerly awaited come-back after he had been sidelined through injury since the previous April. Bristol City were the visitors and when The King put away our second goal, everyone went crazy. I managed to get over the perimeter wall and on to the pitch with hundreds of other Brummie Road Enders to celebrate.

We finished our campaign off with a 1-1 home draw against Luton. Having to watch their fans celebrating promotion in the Smethwick End made me green with envy. We had to make do with eighth place in a season marked by Tony Brown sensationally scoring seven goals against Nottingham clubs in seven days. 'Bomber' got a hat-trick against Notts County in the FA Cup third round and then managed four goals at Forest.

Willie Johnston was a new hero and netted his first goal in a 3-1 League Cup defeat at home to Exeter. He also became the first Albion man to be sent off in the FA Cup – a fourth-round replay at The Hawthorns against Everton which we won with a repeat of the 1968 final score, with Tony Brown on target this time. This match took place during the time of power cuts and a three-day working week, resulting in the programme containing only four pages.

The goalless draw at Goodison Park was the club's first Sunday game and it was there that Albion's anthem 'The Lord's My Shepherd' was supposedly first sung by the fans. Given the choice of day and the fact Goodison has St Luke's Church in the corner of the Gwladys Street End, our supporters started singing hymns and 'The Lord's My Shepherd' was the one everyone appeared to know the words to. I first heard it aired at a home night game shortly afterwards, along with other hymns such as 'Onward Christian Soldiers.'

I had never seen so many away fans at The Hawthorns as there were at the fifth-round clash with First Division Newcastle. There were Geordies everywhere in the 42,747-strong crowd, even in the Brummie Road End, and scuffles broke out everywhere inside and outside the ground. We were outclassed as Malcolm 'SuperMac' Macdonald and John Tudor ripped us apart in a 3-0 defeat.

Jeff Astle, scorer of 174 goals in 361 appearances in ten years, was released and joined South African side Hellenic. The last few seasons of my all-time hero had been plagued by injuries, but it was still a very sad day when he left. Jeff later toured the non-League clubs, turning out for Dunstable, Weymouth, Atherstone and Hillingdon before finally calling it a day in 1977. I was fortunate to see the great George Best pull on an Albion shirt; he turned out for Jeff's testimonial in 1975. I used to love to watch George play and we could always guarantee a full house when his United team were in town. His famous quote was a classic: 'I spent most of my money on booze, birds and fast cars. The rest I just squandered.'

Another one of my idols, Asa Hartford, joined Manchester City for £225,000, three years after his move to Leeds collapsed through the famous 'hole in the heart' revelation. Asa had apparently played with this condition for years and it had never been detected before. I had followed Asa's career since he made his debut and was disappointed to see him leave. A few years earlier, Mom and I attended his wedding to local girl Joy Francis in West Bromwich. We just turned up to see all the Albion players outside the church but, to our surprise, we were invited inside to witness the whole ceremony.

Senior school

The 1970s were also the decade when music became a big part of my life. I was a huge glam rock fan and would split my pocket money and paper round wages between Albion and the latest single by T. Rex, Sweet or Rod Stewart. I was a massive Slade fan and posters of Noddy Holder and the boys muscled in on my bedroom wall, which was covered in Baggies stuff. I loved the fact that Noddy's mother lived opposite my auntie and uncle in Bloxwich. I remember queuing outside Virgin Records in Birmingham for a copy of David Bowie's *Diamond Dogs* album the day it was released. My first live concert was Hot Chocolate at Birmingham Odeon in 1974 with my regular school girlfriend.

The highlight of the week (apart from the match) was going to St Bernard's disco every Friday. At the end of the evening, I would ask a girl for a dance when the DJ played 'Hey There Lonely Girl' by Eddie Holman. If I was lucky, I also got a snog!

Dartmouth School was a mix of Albion and Villa fans with a small sprinkling of Blues supporters. There were no Wolves fans whatsoever. The banter between us never stopped and still continues to this day. Whenever Albion played at Villa, we would catch the train from Hamstead station to Witton. The Joker and Beaufort Arms pubs would be heaving with Baggies fans and, at the station, there wouldn't be a Villa fan in sight, proving that Albion certainly ruled the roost on the Hamstead side of Great Barr.

I enjoyed my school years. The staff at Dartmouth took sports seriously, even appointing Leicester and England rugby player Les Cusworth as one of the PE teachers. I loved playing table-tennis and would actually go into school early to have a few games and listen to the latest LPs (long playing records).

Dartmouth was over a mile from my house so, more often than not, I would cycle there through Red House Park, finishing off my paper round on the way. I have never smoked, but on the odd occasion that I caught the school bus, I may as well have done. It was so thick with smoke, you could almost chew it.

I was very active in 'Fleming' house, always involved in things and raising money for a new football strip and a stereo music centre for our house room. I did this by organising 24-hour sponsored five-a-side games and house discos during lunchtimes. For this reason (and the fact I knew all the 'bad boys'), I was made Head Boy. It still didn't prevent me from getting the cane on a few occasions from Bellingham, Ackroyd or Lester – the head teachers commonly known as 'The Gestapo.' Educationally, I did okay but one report summed up my school years. It stated: 'If Dean would spend as much time concentrating on his school work as he does on his football, he would do very well.'

I had a great time with the West Bromwich town team on our 1974 tour of South Wales, playing against Cardiff and Swansea schoolboys. We also got to watch Cardiff City play at Ninian Park. Our accommodation was provided by Butlins at Barry Island during national schools week, where it's fair to say girls became a big distraction to us budding footballers!

1974/75

The club was at an all-time low. The fans were fed up with Don Howe's negative football and several players openly expressed their desire to leave. Supporter discontent was reflected in the attendance of only 11,425 for our first game of the new season – a 1-0 home defeat against Fulham. This was also in some part down to the fact that the price of a seat rose to a pound for the first time!

It was now time to start travelling to away games with my mates and visiting new towns and cities. It's hard to believe now, but my friends and I, although only thirteen or fourteen years old, would travel without adults, boarding either the HATS (Hawthorns Away Travel Service) Sealandair coaches from The Hawthorns Throstle Club or Global coaches picking up from the Malt Shovel pub on the Newton Road in Great Barr. We soon started to use Global more often, simply because we could book at the local ironmonger's shop. To fund my trips, I sold Albion lottery tickets outside the Hamstead pub in Green Lane. The pub was a regular haunt for the Albion players and I could always guarantee good sales to the likes of Len Cantello, Ally Brown and John Osborne.

My first unaccompanied trip was our second game of the season, at Hull. I remember standing outside a pub before the game, sending 'Millsy' in for drinks as he was the only one who looked remotely eighteen. We stood on the side at Boothferry Park in the terrace that backed on to the railway line. As a thirteen-year-old, I didn't really sense danger and remember walking round to the club shop (which was situated in the home end) with Chris O'Nyan to buy some programmes at the end. This wouldn't be so bad except we were wearing our Albion scarves and these were volatile times. It was probably the fact we lost 1-0 that saved us from a kicking. We also stood along the side on old wooden planks at Meadow Lane a few weeks later to witness our 0-0 draw at the world's so-called oldest football club, Notts County. I've never really understood this statement – who did they play in their first game?

Six wins out of our first eleven games saw us challenging, but we soon started to drop down the table and had to wait another seven matches before we gained another two points. My next away game was Southampton. The Dell was another new ground for me and lots of fighting to witness as Albion slumped to a 1-0 defeat.

London away matches were always an adventure. To prevent being 'bricked', the coaches would drop us off at Marble Arch and we were left to our own devices until our rendezvous back in the West End at 7.00 p.m. Along with my mates, I just followed the main gang of Albion fans on to the underground to make our way to the likes of Orient and Fulham. The Albion lads were wild and everything in the tube stations would be smashed up and Lord help any opposition fans that got in their way. During the trip to Orient on 23 November 1974 (the day before my fourteenth birthday) the big talking point was the Birmingham pub bombings two days earlier, when twenty-one innocent people lost their lives in IRA bomb attacks. In London, we bumped into a large gang of Birmingham City fans on their way to Tottenham. Normally, this could have been a dangerous cocktail, but the two sets of supporters joined together and, chanting anti-Irish songs, took out their anger on any mouthy Cockney.

Going to away games in the Second Division was the talk of the school and we would spend most of our spare time making plans for forthcoming trips. This included research into the opposition fans and discovering whether we might be in any danger. My normal match attire was a denim jacket covered in Albion sew-on patches, flared jeans, Doc Marten boots and silk scarves around my neck and on each wrist! West Bromwich Albion was a big name at that level and at away games it was usually the home fans that feared us. However, we did have to be careful at certain grounds. I remember getting in scrapes at Bristol City and Oxford United among others. Boundary Park, Oldham in January 1975 was the first time I experienced Albion fans 'taking' the home end. As impressionable fourteen-year-olds, we were easily led and when the talk among the older lads outside the ground was that we were all going into the Chadderton End. Who were we to argue? Sure enough, we paid at the turnstiles and gathered together with around 100 Albion fans just to the right of the covered terrace behind the goal. All of a sudden, the shout went up 'The West Brom!' and the Albion mob charged into the middle, forcing the Oldham supporters to scatter. The police got involved and, to my surprise, allowed us to stay put throughout the boring 0-0 draw, just forming a line to keep the fans apart. As a teenager, the adrenaline rush was incredible and provided me with a brilliant story to share with my mates at school on the Monday of 'how we took the Oldham End.' Similar adventures followed and we also shared the home end at the old Manor Ground, when we faced Oxford.

During the season, our home gates slipped to a meagre 7,000 as Don Howe's style tested even the most loyal fans. Also, the new threat of hooliganism gave people the excuse to stay at home. A glimmer of hope came on 8 March, when Ian Edwards made his debut and scored in our 4-0 win against Sheffield Wednesday. We left the ground rejoicing in the hope we had found a new 'Astle,' but it was a false dawn and he managed only another couple of goals before heading off to Chester.

I was enjoying the away games far more than the depressing atmosphere at The Hawthorns and further trips followed to Norwich, Bristol City, Villa, and Blackpool. Segregation was thin on the ground in those days and we got our comeuppance at the City Ground during the last game of the season. For some reason, we shared the side terrace, with a thin line of policemen separating us from the Nottingham Forest thugs. Although we lost 2-1, we were still easy pickings for the home fans as we exited the ground and I was lucky to get back to the coach with just a few bruises. No play-offs in those days meant our sixth-place finish kept us well out of the promotion places. To make things worse, those claret and blue vermin from down the road finished second and went up.

We whimpered out of the League Cup at Carrow Road, losing 2-0 to Norwich in a replay. In the FA Cup, we spanked Bolton 4-0 in a home replay in front of a rare 21,210-strong crowd. We still respected the FA Cup then. These days it drives me mad when manager's play weakened teams, particularly in the early rounds. It has devalued the best club cup competition in the world.

My ambition had always been to play professionally but I also wanted to follow the Albion home and away. After a couple of warnings, I finally lost my place in the West Bromwich schools' squad when I missed a Staffordshire Cup semi-final, choosing instead to make the early start to see Albion in an FA Cup fourth-round tie at Alan Ashman's Carlisle United who were then in the First Division. We lost 3-2 and as well as being out of the Cup, my personal football career at town level was effectively over.

The journey to Brunton Park seemed to take forever, but we still took a huge following. As we packed into the side terrace, the constant jumping up and down caused a crack to appear in the concrete steps. It could have been a major incident and the police had to cordon off the area to prevent more damage. We nearly ended up with the grazing sheep in the field behind the goal.

A personal taste of cup glory came in the 1975 Sandwell Schools' final played at the Birmingham County FA ground in Great Barr, where I kept goal in Dartmouth's 3-2 victory over Churchfields – our arch rivals from the other end of the Newton Road. Our win secured local bragging rights and there must have been over a thousand people watching a final that we edged 3-2 thanks to a Seamus Roche hat-trick that caused a mass pitch invasion by the Dartmouth kids.

3

Teenage Rampage

By now, everyone was fed up with Don Howe and his dull football and it was no surprise when he was relieved of his duties in the summer of 1975. Howe was replaced as manager by the 'Messiah' – Johnny Giles from the all-conquering Leeds team of the early 1970s. He was appointed as the club's first player-manager in a £48,000 deal and in what proved to be a new dawn for the Baggies. I was really excited about Giles being in charge.

The players would often train at the Aston University recreation ground, which was conveniently situated next to my school. Many a lunchtime was spent sneaking across the fence to obtain their autographs. I would also spend school holidays at one of the training grounds, either Aston University, Spring Road, Halfords Lane (Hopes's ground) or The Hawthorns itself. Along with my friends, I would collect autographs and take photographs of the players. We once turned up at the university to discover that training had been moved to Halfords Lane. Fortunately, Albion midfielder Allan Glover had made the same mistake and kindly gave us a lift in his Mini to the right location. On another occasion, we turned up at the ground to find that the players had gone to Sandwell Golf Club for the day, so off we went to track them down. Dave Foxall and I ended up caddying for Willie Johnston and Ally Brown. This was a massive coup for me as Willie was one of my heroes and provided another story for the classroom. They even gave us a fiver each for our services, which we would have happily provided for nothing.

1975/76

My brother Alan married in August 1975, but I was desperate to see Johnny Giles's debut, so, after attending the ceremony at St Matthew's Church in Walsall, Dave the best man gave me a lift to The Hawthorns, still suited and booted, just in time to see us draw with Mansfield in the pre-season Anglo Scottish Cup.

I was now attending the majority of away games and caught the train to Leicester to see us in another Anglo Scottish Cup tie. Although we lost 2-1 at Filbert Street, Giles was the stand-out player and scored a magnificent goal.

I couldn't believe that the new manager's first signing was Geoff Hurst from Stoke, the same Geoff Hurst of England who had scored a hat-trick in the 1966 World Cup final. When I heard the news, I immediately caught the bus to The Hawthorns, just in time for Hurst to arrive in his gold Rolls Royce. I managed to get his autograph. Sadly, this was nine years after Hurst made football history and he managed just two goals during his short Albion stay.

My optimism following Giles's appointment was soon shattered when I went on the coach to see Southampton beat us 3-0 in the first League game. Fighting at matches was now taken for granted and there were numerous skirmishes outside The Dell and even more along Birmingham Road when Chelsea came to town in the midweek.

Our next away adventure was another nightmare. Fulham put four past us at Craven Cottage. Our form was very inconsistent and we certainly didn't look like promotion material.

Following the recruitment of two Republic of Ireland men, Mick Martin and Paddy Mulligan, and with Giles himself pulling the strings in midfield, things slowly started to click. I made my first visit to Blackburn Rovers in October for our 0-0 draw. Ewood Park was a throw-back to old-style football grounds and the classic turnstile block was used in the Hovis advert at the time. Blackpool away was always a good day out and Albion fans would travel in their thousands to turn the promenade navy blue and white. Our visit on 8 November, was particularly memorable. We shared the home end at Bloomfield Road, with the police keeping the two sets of fans apart. All sorts of missiles were been thrown backwards and forwards over the police line. I couldn't believe it when a dart narrowly missed me and stuck in the head of a Baggie next to me. To my total astonishment, he just pulled it out of his scalp and threw it back into the Blackpool fans! He just used a handkerchief to stem the blood flow. On a brighter note, I was proud to witness one of the best goals I have ever seen when Willie Johnston lashed in a screamer from 30 yards directly in front of us. It not only proved to be the winner but went on to win the ATV goal of the season award.

On 13 December, I chalked off another new ground. Kenilworth Road, home of Luton Town, is a very poor excuse for a stadium, hemmed in by houses. It really was a sorry old place. The Hatters were bankrupt, providing the travelling Albion hordes with plenty of ammunition for witty songs including 'la la la la Luton's got no money, la la la la la la la don't you think it's funny?' There was certainly no sympathy. Another chant to stay in my memory was instigated by the programme seller just inside the away end. He shouted (almost singing) 'Programmes 10p each'. As each visiting Baggie came through the turnstiles, they would join in with the seller. Once the 2,000 or so Albion fans had gathered on the terraces, the chant went up 'Programmes 10p each!' Even now, whenever I hear a programme seller shout 'Programmes', I can't help following it with '10p each.' The mercurial Giles was sent off in this game and we succumbed to a 2-1 defeat.

We had a brilliant day out at York City, which saw the Albion fans take over two stands at Bootham Crescent to urge the lads on to a 1-0 win thanks to an Ally Brown goal.

At the end of January, on a freezing cold Saturday, Chris O'Nyan and I caught the coach to Chelsea. This was to be nothing like our previous London trips to Orient and Fulham. True to form, we were dropped off at Marble Arch and made our way on the underground to Fulham Broadway. It was painfully clear that this time we were not the 'top dogs' and the tube carriage, jammed full of Chelsea maniacs, made us feel very nervous. We agreed that exiting the ground after the game would be even more terrifying, so we purchased tickets to sit with the home fans and try and look as inconspicuous as possible. To make our situation even more precarious, Tony Brown added to Mick Martin's earlier goal to give us a 2-1 win. It was the coldest I have ever been at a match and it was the first time I had ever seen players wear gloves and even tights. The Chelsea players were kitted out like ballet dancers, even so-called hard-man Ron 'Chopper' Harris went for these accessories, but there were no such thermals for Albion's team. Fewer than 16,000 were in Stamford Bridge, but I felt as though every Chelsea fan was looking at us suspiciously. We daren't open our mouths and just nodded at each other. After the game, we tried to blend in with the crowd as we walked through the Chelsea firm as they came out of the Shed End en route to the Albion fans in the away end. The tube was even worse. It was even more packed with Chelsea fans baying for blood. We were only fifteen and frightened to death but thankfully we made it back to Marble Arch in one piece. We were so relieved to actually be able to talk again that once we were off the tube and in the safety of the West End, we let out an almighty 'Yeeeesss!'

It was not uncommon in those days to return home on the coach with several windows missing and, in one case, without the windscreen.

A week after the Chelsea game, we dispatched Bristol Rovers 3-0 and the 'p-word' (promotion) began to be mentioned for the first time. A classic away day at Notts County saw a record number of Hamstead/Great Barr Baggies travelling, so much so that for the first time we filled a Global coach by ourselves, picking us up at the Malt Shovel. Several of the Hamstead lads were well into the hooliganism craze and on the shared terrace at Meadow Lane, I witnessed a County fan being sprayed with blue paint by one of our boys – hilarious at the time.

Despite a couple of blips, our form was good and results kept us heading in the right direction. There were no play-offs, so it was all about the top three spots. Sunderland led the way, followed by Bristol City and Bolton, with Albion coming up on the rails. On 9 April, I skived off school to board the coach for a Friday evening game at Charlton. Unusually, the coach took us directly to the ground and the travelling Baggies were on the open end behind the goal with the vast famous Valley terrace to our right. At half-time, it was chaos. For some reason, the toilets and food kiosk were situated half-way behind the main stand and shared by rival fans. I was making my way to get a pie when a roar went up and the two sets of fans steamed into each other with seemingly no police presence. It eventually calmed down and I resumed my position behind the goal (sadly without a pie). Despite Bomber's penalty, Charlton won 2-1 and the long journey home was spent wondering if we had blown our chances.

Consecutive home victories against Fulham and Nottingham Forest ensured that our hopes were very much back on track. A 0-0 draw at Orient on the Tuesday night meant that third spot behind Sunderland and Bristol City was in our own hands providing we won our last game, away to Oldham. If we failed, we had to rely on Bolton losing their match at Charlton. And so 24 April, 1976 was to become one of the most memorable days of my life.

On Saturday morning, the northbound M6 on the way to Greater Manchester resembled an Albion home game as every car, van and coach seemed to be decked out in navy blue and white or yellow and green as Giles's army converged on Oldham. Over 15,000 Albion supporters made sure that Boundary Park resembled The Hawthorns. We were all in it together with just one aim. Everyone sang and screamed themselves hoarse as we urged the team on. I remember well-known Albion fan Dave Bowie, wearing a Stetson and holding a massive flag, conducting the crowd with endless renditions of 'Come on you Baggies.'

At half-time, with the score 0-0, news filtered through that Bolton were 3-0 up at Charlton. We *had* to win to gain promotion. The script was written for Albion legend Tony Brown. Bomber was born in Oldham Infirmary, just down the road. He scored the promotion-winning goal with a superbly taken volley on 54 minutes, directly in front of our massed ranks. An agonising 36 minutes later, the referee blew the whistle. We had done it. A mass pitch invasion followed as everyone danced on the Oldham turf shouting for the team. The players eventually appeared in the main stand and Giles was hoisted aloft by jubilant fans. The journey back was spent dreaming of trips to Old Trafford, Highbury and Anfield. I arrived home just in time to watch the game again on *Match of the Day* and just when I thought the day couldn't get any better, Mom informed me that I had got my ten homes up on the pools and had won £25 (aside from picking draws, another option on the Littlewoods coupon was to select ten games that would be won by the home team).

It had been an unforgettable season. Not only had we secured promotion but our reserves won the Central League title and our youngsters lifted the FA Youth Cup. I was one of the 15,558 at The Hawthorns to see the kids beat Wolves 5-0 on aggregate. The omens were good for our return to Division One.

1976/77

All through the red-hot summer of 1976, we eagerly awaited the new season and the fixtures confirmed that our first game back in the big time would be at Giles's former club Leeds United. We soon started making plans for my first visit to Elland Road. Together with the blue and white half of Hamstead and Great Barr, we booked with Global coaches, but were confused by the 8.00 a.m. pick-up time. Surely seven hours before kick-off was ridiculously early? All was revealed when we gathered at the Malt Shovel. Bang on time, along came an old green double-decker bus, commonly known as the 'Global Flyer.' We knew that it had been used for away games in the Midlands before, but was it really fit for a 108-mile journey to West Yorkshire? The bus coughed and spluttered along the M1, stopping numerous times to let the engine cool down. We were on the top deck and heard a huge thud that turned out to be somebody's head hitting the ceiling below as a valve blew under his seat.

Leeds was notoriously rough, so, as we entered the city, the steward told everyone to take their scarves and flags down from the windows as 'the buses in Leeds are also green, so no-one will spot us.' Fateful words; as we got closer to the ground, bricks started raining at the windows causing us all to dive down on the floor. How did they distinguish us from just another Leeds double-decker bus? When we eventually parked, it was clearly evident. There, in massive letters across the side of the bus, were the words 'Go with Global West Bromwich'. We were sitting ducks!

Inside the ground, in blistering heat, the atmosphere was fantastic, with Albion fans packed behind the goal in full voice. Giles's warm welcome from Leeds supporters' was short-lived as we surged into a 2-0 lead. Rumours were rife that Leeds fans had infiltrated our end and there were reports of scuffles underneath the stand. The game was eventually drawn 2-2 and then the fun really started; the walk back to the coach park was an absolute nightmare. We were surrounded by Leeds fans kicking the backs of our legs and, every few yards, we would witness an Albion fan getting a good beating on the floor. The walk was only a few hundred yards but it seemed like miles. At least our bus was easy to spot! Once at the coach park, we were able to regroup and stood in unison protecting our coaches (and bus). It was like a scene from 'Zulu' – the worst case of football violence I had ever witnessed. Welcome to the First Division.

The following Wednesday, we lost 1-0 to eventual champions Liverpool in our first home game in front of nearly 30,000. All the talk was about the Leeds bother and who had received the worst beating.

Our first victory came against Norwich on the Saturday, followed by a 1-0 defeat at QPR. Loftus Road, situated in Shepherds Bush, was another first for me and this time we didn't get dumped at Marble Arch. Instead, our coach parked in the old White City stadium car park. This old relic had been a 1966 World Cup venue, but was now just used for greyhound racing. It was sadly demolished in 1985. Inside Loftus Road, we shared a big open terrace behind the goal and again, with very little segregation, fights were breaking out all over the place.

Our first away win was a pleasing 1-0 against Birmingham City. This was the first time I had ventured to St Andrew's with my mates. We caught the bus into the city and walked through Digbeth to a ground in a massive state of disrepair. Few improvements had been carried out for years and the stands were literally rusting away. We were allocated half of the Tilton Road End with the massive Spion Kop to our left. Bomber hit a brilliant long-range winner to keep Blues' fans quiet. The walk back into town was a bit scary, though.

Another new venue on 25 September, Derby, where we thought a new hero had been discovered; Ray Treacy netted twice in our 2-2 draw. He had played for us in the 1960s and had just re-signed from Preston. After his Baseball Ground brace, he went on to score another four goals in the next ten games.

Our three home games in October were classics. Against Spurs, we recorded a tremendous 4-2 victory from two down, and managed an even better performance as goals from Giles, Ally Brown, Len Cantello and Treacy ensured a 4-0 thrashing of Manchester United. Back then, I used to catch the Hamstead 'football special' bus home. Unfortunately, so did every other Albion fan from the area, so I had to leave a few minutes before the end to guarantee getting on. On this occasion, the notorious United hooligans also left early and made their way round from the Smethwick End. They were all clad in decorated white butcher's coats, three-quarter length jeans, red, white and black scarves and polished Doc Marten boots. They formed a barricade across the Birmingham Road outside the old Throstle Club. I was covered in Albion scarves and could see my bus on the other side of the seething Reds. Should I turn around and walk back into town, or put my head down and run through the United fans to the bus? Stupidly, I went for option two and got a right good kicking, just about making it to the bus in one piece. Our excellent monthly treble was completed with a 3-0 win against West Ham.

We were soon brought down to earth at Portman Road. Paul Mariner, who we had nearly signed from Plymouth, scored a hat-trick as Ipswich put seven past us – the biggest defeat I had ever witnessed. This trip wasn't like any of the previous First Division games. There was no sign of trouble at all, which was a pleasant change. Apparently, Johnny Giles instructed the coach driver to pull over at a pub on the way back and told the players to have a few beers and get the result out of their system.

A Jack Russell terrier appeared on the pitch in our 3-0 home win against Everton, it ran around for a good 5 minutes and could have claimed David Cross's goal as it pushed the ball over the line with his nose. Derek Statham, a young left back, made his debut for us at Stoke in December, scoring a fine goal past England 'keeper Peter Shilton. I remember Hugh Johns on *Star Soccer* referring to him as 'Brian' Statham. John Trewick also scored in our 2-0 win.

It was now a regular occurrence for visiting fans to attempt to 'take' the Brummie Road End. This ritual was normally carried out a good half an hour or more before kick-off. West Ham and Spurs were the main culprits. Gangs of their hooligans would gather on one side of the stand, and a chant would go up, causing the Albion fans to initially scatter before regrouping to defend our territory. I saw some right battles in the late 1970s. In fact, I was caught in the middle of some of them. The police would eventually intervene, round up the visitors and escort them round the pitch to the adulation of the main body of their fans in the Smethwick End. I was proud that no away fans ever actually succeeded in 'taking' the Brummie Road.

I am certainly not trying to glorify football hooliganism. However, it was a big part of the match-day experiences in those pre-Taylor Report days. It would be impossible to recount my memories of that period without mentioning the tribal warfare that went with the football.

There was a significant signing in March, when Laurie Cunningham joined us from Orient in a £110,000 deal involving Joe Mayo. Cunningham was our first black player and created a real buzz around the club. There was a lot of racial tension about at the time and our new player certainly made a few Albion fans think twice about their prejudices. He scored our first goal in a 2-0 win at Tottenham on his debut. Goalkeeper Tony Godden, a bargain signing from non-league Ashford, also made his debut at White Hart Lane, replacing the thirty-six-year-old John Osborne. Another Cunningham goal followed in our revenge against Ipswich at The Hawthorns a few days later. He added to Bryan Robson's hat-trick in a brilliant 4-0 demolition.

I went on the train to Coventry on an April night and the walk through the park towards Highfield Road was highly eventful. It was 'going off' everywhere as numerous Sky Blues fans confronted us. We stood our ground and refused to be intimidated, so much so that a few thousand of us entered the home supporters' West End terrace. There we stayed with the police forming a barrier to keep rival fans apart throughout a 1-1 draw. Another rail journey took us to Leicester's old Filbert Street ground to see a fantastic Albion performance with Laurie in brilliant form and scoring again in our magnificent 5-0 victory.

Cup-wise, after knocking mighty Liverpool out of the League Cup in a home replay, we succumbed to lowly Brighton, a game remembered for Willie Johnston being dismissed for aiming a kick at the referee. In the FA Cup, I went to Manchester City for the first time. Dad came out of hibernation for this one, it was his first game for a number of years and he gave me a lift, but it was still rough. Maine Road was in the middle of Moss Side, one of the most run-down areas in the country. As soon as we pulled up, we were surrounded by little 'Mancs' offering to 'Mind your car for a pound Mister?' It translated to: 'Give me a quid or your car will be on bricks when you return.' Walking past the external wall of the huge Kippax terrace on the side of the ground, every turnstile except one was labelled 'home fans only'. And that was slap bang in the middle of the home fans' entrances. Next to the 'away fans' sign, the words 'WBA die today' were daubed in white paint. A rather ominous welcome! Willie spectacularly put us ahead and, if City hadn't equalised, I fear we would never have made it back to the car. City won the replay on a snowy night at The Hawthorns.

In May 1977, one of our best ever signings came in almost unnoticed, Cyrille Regis joining us from non-league Hayes for £5,000, on the recommendation of Ronnie Allen, then our chief scout. There were not many black players in football at the time, so to sign two in the space of just three months made national news. Graffiti appeared on a wall near to The Hawthorns: WBA – We Buy Africans. We didn't know whether this was the work of rival fans or racist Baggies.

At the end of the season, Giles left for Ireland and the player-manager's job at Shamrock Rovers. He had shocked us the previous summer by announcing he was dismayed with the state of English football and the restraints imposed on him at The Hawthorns. The news that he was definitely going broke in the spring and our final home game (against Stoke) was very emotional. We won 3-1 and with everyone on the pitch at the end, he appeared in the director's box to wave goodbye.

Our chants of 'Don't you leave us, don't you leave us, don't you leave us Johnny Giles' sadly fell on deaf ears. His mind was made up.

After the up-and-coming Graham Taylor turned us down, the board turned to a safe pair of hands in our legendary former forward Ronnie Allen.

The Queen's Silver Jubilee, 7 June 1977, is a day I remember for the wrong reasons. While everyone was enjoying street parties, I was in Hallam Hospital. The residents of Stanton Road, Great Barr had staged a 'best dressed' house competition and my friend asked if she could borrow my Union Jack flag, albeit depicted with the words West Bromwich Albion. Not only did I agree to help, I volunteered to fit it to the front of her house, which was next door to John Osborne's former home – the one that had been decorated in 1968. I shinned up the downpipe and leant across to tie a knot when the whole rainwater system became detached from the wall of the house with me hanging on to it. I bounced off the garage roof before landing unconscious on the front drive. I came round in hospital several hours later complete with a broken shoulder – not good news for a goalkeeper!

I left school a few weeks later. Hardly anyone I knew stayed on to the sixth form and I don't recall anybody from Dartmouth going to university. It wasn't the done thing then. The last day was celebrated by us pushing each other into the Red House Park lake fully clothed.

I wanted to work with my hands and, fortunately, Dad had contacts with a local building company so, in July 1977, I started as a trainee carpenter/joiner at Thorne Brothers builders in Great Bridge. My Great Barr accent soon developed a strange Black Country twang as I worked in the joinery shop and on sites across the region with various Tipton 'chippies'. My first wage packet was £21, which felt like a king's ransom compared to my £2.50 paper round money.

One of my early assignments was to help erect a large advertising hoarding on the side of a building in Wolverhampton town centre. Once installed, we had to coat the sign with primer and I thought it would be a good laugh to paint 'WBA' in massive letters. After I finished, we went for lunch, giving the letters time to dry. The subsequent painting of the whole sign would cover the letters. However, I was called in front of my angry boss next day as 'WBA' was still clearly visible! Surely I had improved Wolverhampton?

A regular wage enabled me to travel to more away games. The down side was that I also had to buy my own season ticket now I was employed. It cost me £20 back then, compared to £400 these days.

1977/78

The opening game brought an amazing sight at The Hawthorns. Punk rock was sweeping the country and London led the way. Chelsea were the visitors and I stood there gawping as hundreds of their fans celebrating the new craze walked down the Birmingham Road before the game. The Black Country was always a bit behind the times, so there we were in our donkey jackets and flares watching the Chelsea punks with their bondage gear, make-up and safety-pins. A comfortable 3-0 win gave us a perfect start to the season.

Cyrille Regis was unleashed against Rotherham in our second-round League Cup game. I was one of the 15,000 who saw the twenty-one-year-old steal the show with his raw aggression. With Albion already 2-0 ahead, we were awarded a penalty and the crowd urged the youngster to take it. He duly put it away and added another goal on a memorable debut. Despite leading scorer Cross now being fully fit, it was impossible for Ronnie Allen to leave 'Big Cyrille' out for our next game, at home to Middlesborough. Bryan Robson had given us the lead when Cyrille again took centre stage. He received the ball in his own half and just starting running like a charging rhino with Boro players bouncing off him. Once he had sight of goal, he let fly and in it went right in front of the Brummie Road. I went crazy; we had a new hero to fill Astle's boots and finally do the No. 9 shirt justice. He scored again in our 3-0 win at Newcastle the following week, where he was pelted by bananas as well as having to endure endless monkey noises, along with Laurie Cunningham (who also scored). Regis added another in our 3-1 home victory against Blues. The racial abuse that our black players had to endure had become a regular feature of our games. I didn't have a problem with them at all, if they wore a navy blue and white striped shirt I wasn't bothered what colour they were.

I travelled to Coventry and QPR to see us clock up further wins and we thrashed Manchester United 4-0 at The Hawthorns for the second season running. In the League Cup, Graham Taylor's Watford were our visitors and we witnessed the bizarre sight of their chairman, pop star Elton John sitting in the directors' box. With his large hat and trademark glasses, he stood out and was an obvious target for the merciless Brummie Road. 'Elton John and his homosexuals' was chanted throughout.

Our 1-0 victory led to a novelty fourth-round trip to Third Division Bury, although the game was in grave danger of being called off when fog descended as we neared Lancashire. Inside Gigg Lane, the visibility was so bad we couldn't see the far goal. A large Albion following sang their hearts out to Queen's 'We are the Champions' before kick-off. Unfortunately, we played nothing like champions and succumbed to a shock 1-0 defeat. David Cross was back but we really wanted to see Regis leading the line. We got our way when he was introduced as a second-half substitute, but even he couldn't save us this time.

Ronnie Allen quit in January to take over the Saudi Arabian national side for a reported king's ransom. We were fourth in the table but had managed to lose two managers in just eight months. The players were putting a strong case forward for skipper John Wile to take over to keep the momentum, but the board had other ideas and in came Ron Atkinson from Cambridge.

Big Ron's first win came at St Andrew's. He had brought in his previous Cambridge captain, full-back Brendon Batson, who was thrust straight in. Our three black players were getting loads of abuse from the Birmingham City fans and it really seemed to get to Batson, who had a bit of a nightmare debut. Fortunately the two Browns, Tony and Ally, made sure of a 2-1 win. Our black trio became known as 'The Three Degrees' after the female pop group of the time. The singers even appeared on the pitch in Albion shirts before a home game.

Going to Wolves was always 'fun'. There was only one safe way to travel and that was on the train. We would be escorted to Molineux past the infamous subway, to our allocated terrace, which was half of the huge South Bank. Needless to say, missiles would be hurled backwards and forwards throughout the game. In later seasons, a net was put in place from the floor to the roof of the stand. On this particular occasion, John Trewick scored a late equaliser in a 1-1 draw.

After suffering a 4-0 thrashing at Arsenal, we went on a run of five wins on the bounce, beating Bristol City, Leicester, Newcastle, Manchester City and Derby before the wheels came off against Villa (of all the teams) as we lost 3-0 at home in front of 35,000.

We were playing an exciting brand of attacking football, with Regis, Tony Brown and Ally Brown scoring for fun. The final game saw Nottingham Forest secure the League Championship with a 2-2 draw at The Hawthorns. We finished sixth and qualified for Europe.

4

Agony at Highbury, Part I

The Albion team in 1978 was the best I've ever seen. We were already a decent side, but Ron Atkinson added the entertainment factor and I still maintain that this was the best team never to win a major trophy. The team almost picked itself and the names still reel off the tongue: Godden, Batson, Statham, T. Brown, Wile, Robertson, Robson, A. Brown, Regis, Cantello, Johnston (or Cunningham). I can't think of a single weakness in that line-up.

The 1977/78 third-round FA Cup draw paired us with Blackpool at home. Regis was on the score sheet and had now netted on his League, FA Cup, League Cup and reserve debuts for Albion. An easy 4-1 victory saw us through and, in those days, the draw always took place on a Monday lunchtime live on Radio 2. I still remember those words 'Manchester United will play … West Bromwich Albion' I hadn't been to Old Trafford, so this was a must.

Football Special train tickets were booked along with 80p match tickets for the Groundside Scoreboard enclosure. Off we set to the 'Theatre of Dreams' on a cold January morning. The train was rammed, with everyone in good spirits. As we neared Old Trafford Station, we were in full voice and 'We're the barmy West Brom army, la la la la la la' rang out as we disembarked. We were greeted by hundreds of United 'boot boys' threatening us with throat-slitting gestures and informing us we wouldn't be returning home. Nice to see you, too!

Thanks to a police escort, we safely made it to the away enclosure. There was a great atmosphere in the ground and we very nearly won thanks to Willie Johnston's goal. United equalised through Steve Coppell with virtually the last kick of the game. We were locked inside the ground 45 minutes after the final whistle before being escorted back. It was common for away fans to be kept in, but the natives were so restless on this occasion that no risks were taken. Fortunately by the time we had exited the ground, most of the crowd had dispersed, so the pre-match threats didn't come to fruition.

I couldn't concentrate at work over the next few days. All I could think about was the Wednesday night replay. 37,792 crammed in for a titanic Hawthorns struggle which stood 2-2 at full time. The battle between John Wile and Joe Jordan resembled a heavyweight boxing clash as both left the field covered in blood. Into extra-time and Regis grabbed the winner. Cue pandemonium! We had knocked out the holders. Surely nothing could stop us now?

Derby County away were next. Such was the interest that the tie at the Baseball Ground was made all-ticket; a rarity in those days. I managed to get a £1 ticket for the Colombo Pop Side. After a midweek rearrangement, we finally headed off to the East Midlands in confident mood on 22 February and were not to be disappointed. It was a classic which we edged 3-2 thanks to another two from Cyrille and one from Willie. Sadly, what I remember most are the crushes in the away section before the game. A lot of Albion fans must have arrived without tickets and, in an attempt to get them in, the police pushed everyone forward to create room. What they didn't realise was that bad crushing was occurring at the front. It was really frightening and we were kept busy lifting women and children over the fences to the safety of pitch-side. This was eleven years before the Hillsborough disaster, but the same thing could easily have happened that evening in Derby. It still makes me shiver.

We were up against Brian Clough's League leaders Nottingham Forest in the quarter-final and a 36,506 Hawthorns crowd again created a magnificent atmosphere. Goals from Mick Martin and a cracker from Big Cyrille past Peter Shilton in front of the Brummie Road End edged us ever closer to Wembley. Our victory ended Forest's unbeaten run of twenty-two games.

We were hoping for Orient in the semis and to avoid Arsenal. We achieved the second of those objectives when out of the hat came Ipswich and their popular manager, ex-Baggie Bobby Robson. The tie was at Highbury with Albion fans allocated the famous North Bank. I opted for 'lucky' Global for my trip (on condition that it wasn't the double-decker). I spent each evening in the week leading up to the game in Dad's shed, making a full-size replica of the FA Cup out of plywood, painted silver, embossed with 'WBA 1978' and adorned with navy blue and white ribbons.

On an exciting journey down to the capital, every service station seemed jam-packed with confident Baggies. After dispatching United, Derby and Forest, surely Ipswich would be cannon fodder? Heavy traffic in North London denied us a pre-match pint, so it was off the coach (still stuck in traffic) for a brisk walk straight to Highbury. I had no idea where the coach would be after the game and didn't really care. Fortunately, we had an extra 15 minutes as the game wasn't kicking off until 3.15 p.m. due to the other semi-final being played across London, at Stamford Bridge.

Ron Atkinson made a massive mistake by taking the team to Wembley a few days beforehand. Apparently Bobby Robson and Ipswich were also invited, but they declined. Film footage of Ron holding a replica FA Cup and our players in the stadium appeared on *Sam Leitch's Football Preview* on the Saturday lunch-time. This display of over-confidence surely must have wound Ipswich up and effectively provided Robson's team-talk.

I managed to get my plywood Cup through the turnstiles and found a good spot towards the back of the North Bank. As kick-off approached, more and more fans packed in, causing numerous crushes. Just to my right, a large banner was unfurled (actually a scroll used to display the destination at the front of Midland buses) with the message: 'There's only one Arthur Negus' after the elderly personality who presented *Going for a Song* on TV. This ditty was just one of a vast repertoire of mad songs delivered at home games by a group of fans known as The Heads. They also sang about having lardy cakes for breakfast (I kid you not). There was a rival group known as The Duffel Bags. I guess that have barmy fans and those days were no different.

On the Highbury concourse, various Albion fans were doing the 'dying fly' routine made famous by Saturday morning TV show *TISWAS*, it involved lying on your back and waving your arms and legs in the air. On the terraces, regular surges occurred as fans needed to relieve themselves of the lunchtime drinking session. Delightfully, there was a constant flow of urine running past and under my feet.

Nearly 60,000 fans crammed in that day to witness one of the biggest disappointments of my Albion-supporting life. Everything went wrong; Brian Talbot headed Ipswich in front after just eight minutes, splitting John Wile's head open at the same time. The photograph of our skipper with his head bandaged but still covered in blood remains as one of football's iconic images. Every ball he headed would result in more blood as he battled on as a true leader. I can't imagine this scenario ever happening these days, when players are forced to leave the pitch following the slightest sight of blood.

Willie Johnston injured his shoulder and was unable to run, but for some reason he stayed on, although we had Laurie Cunningham on the bench. Mick Mills added a second for the 'Tractor Boys' on 20 minutes and, to make matters worse, Mick Martin was sent off. Wile ripped his bandage off in disgust when he was finally replaced.

Bomber pulled one back after referee Clive Thomas pointed to the spot with ten minutes left. The massed ranks of Baggies urged the ten men on, attempting to suck the ball into the North Bank goal. Sadly it was all in vain as John Wark made it 3-1 on the stroke of full-time and it was all over. I don't think I spoke a word all the way home, or for the next few days for that matter.

Arsenal beat Orient in the other semi-final but were upstaged at Wembley by the underdogs, the late Roger Osborne scoring Ipswich's winner and sending the FA Cup to Suffolk for the first time.

5

Viva Espana!

Through our creditable seventh-place finish in 1976/77 and thanks to Liverpool winning the European Cup, we secured a UEFA Cup place – our first time in European competition since 1968/69.

I desperately wanted to go to the games in Turkey and Portugal, but I couldn't afford the air fares. Instead, I had to make do with switching on the radio to listen to Tony Butler's broadcasts on BRMB. He would tell listeners to get their prayer mats out and shout: 'Hail Atkinson, Hail Addison, Hail Albion'. It seemed to do the trick.

In the opening round, we were drawn against Galatasaray, but, instead of playing in their home city of Istanbul, Albion headed for the Ataturk Stadium in the port of Izmir, some 250 miles away in the south. It was far from straightforward, with no suitable accommodation, and the players had to change en route due to congestion and thugs attacking the coach, rocking it from side to side. Thankfully, class showed and, in front of 38,443 mainly Turkish fans, goals from Bryan Robson, Alistair Brown and Laurie Cunningham gave us a 3-1 win. The same score at The Hawthorns ensured a 6-2 aggregate victory.

Next up were top Portuguese side Sporting Braga, the first leg taking place over there in another sea port. After an initial onslaught by a side containing five full internationals, Albion took control and a second-half double from Cyrille Regis gave us the upper hand. A professional performance in the second leg secured a 1-0 win (3-0 on aggregate) and our European adventure was progressing nicely.

We then drew a plum tie against Valencia, who were considered one of the best club teams in the world at the time and boasted World Cup stars Mario Kempes, who picked up a winner's medal with Argentina in the previous summer's final, and West German midfielder Rainer Bonhoff. It was announced that the Supporters Club were chartering a plane for the away leg that would cost £78 return. I could just about afford it. This offer was on a first-come-first-served basis, so, along with one of my best mates, Tony Jones, I headed straight for The Hawthorns Throstle Club to see Harold Whitehouse and secure our flight and match tickets. We also booked on the coach to Luton Airport.

In 1978, as a seventeen-year-old, I had never been on a plane before. Now, nearly forty years later, I have visited over 120 countries. The day remains as one of the most memorable experiences of my life. Two days before my eighteenth birthday, Tony and I boarded the coach at the Throstle Club with fellow Great Barr Baggies Kevin Pitt, Ken Jones, Paul (Taz) Taylor and Nigel (Bella) Bellmore. Bella followed Albion everywhere, but didn't have any holiday left for this trip, so he said to his boss: 'I won't be in tomorrow as I have a dentist appointment.' He underestimated his football-loving gaffer, who simply replied: 'Get me a programme.'

Everyone was in good voice at Luton Airport with songs such as 'A Spanish Fly Flew in my Eye' and 'Franco was a Puff' added to the usual repertoire. Once aboard on the Dan-Air plane with 119 other Baggies, I didn't get chance for first-flight nerves. The noisier passengers refused to sit down and even attempted a 'Knees up Mother Brown' during take-off. Just before landing a hat was taken round for a collection for the pilot!

It was lovely to step into warm Spanish air. Located on the south-eastern Orange Blossom Coast, Valencia is Spain's third biggest city and known for its arts and sciences. It would have been good to have had a few hours to explore but time was at a premium. A coach ferried us sharply to the stadium, with solid match traffic for the entire route. It looked like we would miss the kick-off, but we were still having loads of fun gesturing at all the model-like local girls and admiring the trees full of oranges. We arrived with a few minutes to spare and just in time to buy a souvenir pennant, before entering the stadium as the fanfare went up for the teams. Timed to perfection!

Our seats were high in the stand and we were surrounded by Valencia fans who offered us wine and the obligatory local oranges. Unfortunately, Tony Brown had picked up a groin injury in the previous game at Bolton, so he sat with the 47,746 that packed the stadium. The Estadio Luis Casanova was built in 1923 and was used as World Cup venue in 1982. It changed its name to Estadio Mestella in 1994.

The game started at a frantic pace with Kempes dictating the play and shots being whipped in from all angles. It wasn't a surprise when Tony Godden failed to gather a corner on 15 minutes and Daniel Felman had a simple task of heading into the empty net. We sat back preparing for a thrashing. Amazingly, we weathered the early storm and started to control the game with Laurie Cunningham playing out of his skin. We began to ooze confidence and, 3 minutes into the second half, Bryan Robson found Ally Brown who, in turn, fed the 'Black Pearl'. Cunningham picked up speed, bursting past Manuel Botubot and Ricardo Arias before firing home. It could have been more as Cyrille missed a couple of gilt-edged chances before Valencia 'keeper Carlos Pereira somehow saved a Len Cantello shot with his head. We finished the game as the better side.

At the final whistle, we stood there bursting with pride as the Valencia supporters applauded Albion's players off the pitch. Cunningham's unbelievable performance went a long way in securing his £900,000 transfer to Real Madrid. The game was shown live on Spanish TV and there's no doubt Laurie alerted the Spanish giants to his undoubted talents. Ron Atkinson once said of our prize possession: 'He could run on snow without leaving footprints.' Anyone who witnessed him gliding past defenders with his socks round his ankles on that memorable night knows exactly what he meant.

With no time for a celebration drink, we headed straight back to the airport. Once we had checked in, we heard that the team were arriving shortly for their charter flight to Birmingham, so we all lined up on the balcony to welcome and congratulate them. In they came to deafening applause and a mass chorus of 'We're proud of you.'

We arrived back at the Throstle Club at 2.00 a.m. I still managed to get to work the next day though, and, on my usual buses to West Bromwich then Great Bridge, everyone was talking about Albion's great performance. I couldn't help but join in, saying: 'It was indeed a great night, I was there.'

The second leg was one of those very special Hawthorn's nights. The freezing Black Country in early December didn't suit Valencia's players and a 4th-minute Bomber penalty followed by his classic volley in the second half put us through to the quarter-final.

The draw paired us with mighty Red Star Belgrade, who had knocked Arsenal out in a previous round. Now I had a dilemma. I had enough money to travel to Yugoslavia (as it was then), but wouldn't have enough for the semi- or the final, if we progressed. I gambled because I had every confidence that we were destined to go all the way, so I forfeited the trip to ensure I didn't miss the next two. However, my customised Union Jack flag (adorned with Albion silk scarf) did travel courtesy of my friend, Andy Withers.

In front of 95,300 fanatical supporters, Red Star won the first leg 1-0. Two people were killed in the stadium prior to kick-off when supporters from the two Belgrade clubs, Red Star and Partizan, clashed on the terraces. No Albion fans were involved.

I was still hopeful that I had made the right decision. Another full house packed The Hawthorns for a second leg that remains one of the 'lows' of my decades following the Albion. Cyrille put us ahead five minutes before half-time to bring the tie level on aggregate. With extra-time looking a certainty, we watched in agony as Milos Sestic scored for the Yugoslavs, pushing the ball past Ally Robertson before putting it past Tony Godden directly in front of the Brummie Road. We were out.

I have always regretted not travelling to Belgrade. If we had got through, I'm sure I would have found the money from somewhere.

Another adventure I really wanted to go on was Albion's ground-breaking 1978 summer trip to China. It was the first time a Western team had travelled behind the 'Bamboo Curtain' and I could have travelled with the team for two weeks for £875. It was a hell of a lot of money then (still is), but I so wish I had taken out a loan for this trip of a lifetime; even if John Trewick thinks I didn't miss much. At the Great Wall of China, he famously stated to a TV crew: 'When you've seen one wall, you've seen them all'.

Brendan Batson was kind enough to give me his fully signed copy of the official tour brochure and captain John Wile handed me a video copy of the documentary that was made of the tour. Items of compensation from a trip that I still regret not going on.

6

So Near, Yet So Far

During the summer of 1978, I once again had the World Cup for my football fix. England had again failed to qualify, so Albion eyes were on Scotland, who included Willie Johnston in their squad as Ally Macleod's 'Tartan Army' headed for Argentina. Sadly, it all ended in tears as Willie was sent home in disgrace for alleged drug abuse. He was subsequently banned from international football and his career in England was effectively over. Despite claiming his innocence, he was labelled as 'Junky' Johnston and, after just three more starting appearances, he was sold to Vancouver Whitecaps for just £100,000. He would later turn out for Birmingham before returning to Scotland with Rangers, Hearts and East Fife.

1978/79

In readiness for the new season, I painted a life-sized picture of Cyrille Regis and the club crest on my bedroom wall. I was convinced this was the season we would win the League.

We certainly hit the ground running, gaining victories in our first three games – against Ipswich, QPR and Bolton. The big match came on 23 September against Liverpool, when Laurie Cunningham put us ahead and it looked like revenge was on the cards until Tony Godden rolled the ball, not noticing Kenny Dalglish lurking. The majority of the 33,000 crowd shouted 'Behind you' but it was too late. The Liverpool striker had equalised. I was gutted and it felt more like a defeat than a draw when the referee blew the final whistle.

We took it out on Chelsea the following Saturday, outclassing them and winning 3-1 in front of only 21,000 at Stamford Bridge. Tony Brown broke Ronnie Allen's League-scoring record with his 209th goal in our 3-1 win at Leeds. Regis was still in lethal form and bagged the other two at Elland Road.

We always appeared to have the 'Indian sign' over Coventry (we would always beat them in any competition) and, when they turned up at The Hawthorns in an all-chocolate brown strip in October, we absolutely tortured them. With the deadly double act of Regis and Cunningham helping themselves to two apiece, we ran amok to the tune of 7-1. Even left back Derek Statham was among the marksmen.

The natives were certainly not happy when we won 3-0 in Wolverhampton just before Christmas. The victory set us up nicely for what was to become a memorable festive period. Unfortunately, I wasn't well, so I didn't travel to Arsenal on Boxing Day to see us record a fantastic 2-1 win. I hadn't recovered four days later and it remains one of my biggest regrets that I wasn't at Old Trafford to witness our famous 5-3 victory. Fortunately the television cameras were there and I have watched this incredible game dozens of times since. The football we played was sublime; two goals from Bomber and one each for Cantello, Cunningham and Regis destroyed Manchester United. Amazingly, it could have been even more had United 'keeper Gary Bailey not pulled off world-class saves from two Cyrille pile-drivers.

I still wasn't 100 per cent, but wasn't going to miss our next home game. Due to the heavy snow, our match against Bristol City was one of few played on New Year's Day. The Hawthorns was white over and partly frozen. Fortunately, 'Big Ron' was prepared and issued the players with AstroTurf boots with tiny rubber studs – ideal for running on a hard, icy surface. The Robins were well beaten 3-1 with our 'passing' football, making it five wins on the trot.

We were all full of confidence as we caught the train to Norwich on 13 January. Most of the country remained knee-deep in snow, but Norfolk was largely unaffected. Compared to our previous five performances, this was not great. Regis got our goal in a 1-1 draw that put us top of the league. We were ecstatic and the chant as we left Carrow Road was: 'and now you're gonna believe us, we're gonna win the League'.

Atkinson splashed out a new British record fee of £516,000 in January for Middlesbrough midfielder David Mills. It was unheard of for Albion to part with this sort of money. Things were certainly looking up. Then the bad weather really kicked in. We didn't play another League game until our table-topping clash at Liverpool three weeks after the Norwich match. For some reason, I wasn't at the game but chaotic scenes were reported by my mates. The gates were locked long before kick-off and around a thousand Albion fans failed to gain entry in a 52,000-strong full house. We were rusty after our enforced lay-off and the Kop were in full voice. In a hostile atmosphere, we lost 2-1 and suffered a hangover in our next game – a 2-1 home defeat to Leeds.

Normal service was resumed at Highfield Road, home of our whipping boys Coventry, new signing David Mills got his first goal in our 3-1 win. This started a fantastic six-game winning run, during which we also accounted for Chelsea, QPR, Derby, Manchester City and Everton. The City game was particularly pleasing as we hammered them 4-0.

There was real disappointment on Easter Monday when we travelled in massive numbers to Bristol City. The long season was taking its toll and the thousands jammed in the open terrace saw our worst performance for a long time as we deservedly lost 1-0. After three draws, we had to play our final six games in just eighteen days, amazingly winning another series of four on the bounce including Man United once more (only 1-0 this time) and a rare success at Villa Park, with John Trewick carving his name into Albion folklore with the winner (any Albion player who scores the winner against Villa, is a legend to me). We had now conceded the title, but this win ensured that we were the top West Midlands' team and we still had the runners-up spot to play for.

We lost 1-0 at Spurs, leaving us needing at least a draw in our last game of the season – at home to Nottingham Forest – to secure second place. With just 9 minutes remaining, Forest's million-pound signing Trevor Francis scored the winning goal, pushing us into third spot behind his new team. Although this was our highest finish since 1954, I was still distraught. A season that had promised so much had ended in despair. Little did I know it, but things were going to get much worse over the next few years.

Our FA Cup adventures had taken us on another train journey to Coventry on a cold January evening after the original game had fallen victim to the weather. It was a cracker with Cunningham and Ally Brown scoring in a 2-2 draw in front of a Highfield Road full house of over 38,000. Coventry must have hated us as we gave them another good spanking in the replay (4-0). Next were Leeds, with whom a 3-3 home draw was hardly what we wanted. However, it gave John Wile the opportunity to renew acquaintances with his old sparring partner Joe Jordan, who was now turning out for the Yorkshiremen. Due to crowd trouble at Elland Road, Leeds were banned from staging home Cup games, so the replay was also at The Hawthorns. After 90 gruelling minutes, with both teams on their last legs, the tie dragged on into extra-time before we somehow mustered a couple of goals to see us through. Yet another unwanted replay after a home draw with Southampton saw us unsurprisingly losing 2-1 at The Dell. The players looked absolutely knackered.

In the League Cup, it was our 'friends' from Leeds again, and, after two 0-0 draws, it went to a second replay at Maine Road, Manchester. Only 8,000 turned up to see us bow out 1-0. We played against Leeds an incredible seven times during the season.

After leaving school, I still played every Sunday for the Red Admiral in the Festival League. We also formed our own team, Great Barr Harriers (GBH), who played in the North Birmingham League; and I was the regular goalkeeper for Withy Athletic and Langdale Sunday League teams.

I had now passed my driving test and purchased my first car; a Mini Traveller off my Uncle Stan for a bargain £100. This gave me another option for away games and also allowed regular trips to Borth in mid-Wales. My mate, Rob Price, had the free use of his aunt's caravan, so we headed there nearly every summer weekend, using the Brynowen club for a shower and other facilities although our caravan was on a different site. We soon got 'friendly' with the local Welsh girls, which gave us the perfect excuse to head out there even through the season if there was a blank weekend. We would often drive home at some unearthly hour on a Sunday morning to get back to play, complete with raging hangovers and, in some cases, still drunk. There were no bans for drink-driving in those days.

It was during one summer in Borth that I played against Chelsea. Borth United were opening their new dressing rooms and the Chelsea team were based just down the road having just played Aberystwyth. Manager John Neal agreed to send a team along for the occasion. Borth's regular 'keeper was on holiday and my Welsh girlfriend's dad knew I played regularly, so I was invited for a trial on the Thursday evening. It went well and I was named in the team for the commemorative game. It was ridiculously one-sided and Borth were 2-0 down after just ten minutes. I then left my line to collect a corner and landed awkwardly, resulting in being stretchered off and taken by ambulance to hospital. I had torn ligaments and spent the next two weeks on crutches. On the plus side, I couldn't work, so stayed in Borth. As all the locals had attended the game, I gained a massive sympathy vote and didn't have to buy a drink for the whole fortnight.

Back at The Hawthorns, in came Gary Owen from Manchester City for £465,000. We then 'broke the bank' by investing £748,000 in City's England winger Peter Barnes, who replaced Laurie Cunningham – who had signed for Real Madrid for a record incoming fee of £995,000. Striker John Deehan was also signed; the first player to join us directly from Aston Villa since 1908.

My only surviving grandparent sadly passed away in the August. My nan had lived with my aunt and uncle in Essex Avenue, Hateley Heath, for as long as I could remember. She had eight children. Unfortunately, one pair of twins died at birth but the other six were brought up through the war years and all turned out to be good Baggie folk.

1979/80

It was not the best of starts to the new season. A home draw with Derby was followed by a midweek defeat at Man United. My car was given a run to Liverpool on 25 August. After the madness there the year before, we bought tickets with the home fans, right next to the Kop. Despite losing 3-1 and having to keep quiet all game, I spent most of the 90 minutes watching Liverpool's fans surging up and down to my right. It was on a larger scale to the atmosphere in the Brummie Road, with a lot more flags and banners and I was well impressed. Peter Barnes scored our goal and he was becoming a 'Marmite' character. You either loved him or hated him. In fairness he had hard acts to follow. Our previous wingers included Chippy Clark, Willie and Laurie. On his day, he could be brilliant but I wasn't a big fan. Whenever he had an England game coming up, he would do as little as possible, passing back immediately when he received the ball. While the rest of the players would leave the pitch covered in mud, Barnes's kit would be immaculate. He opted for this tactic at Villa on 13 October. It was unforgivable and he was rightfully dropped afterwards.

We got spanked good and proper by Nottingham Forest. This was a terrible performance and the team deserved to be booed off. Our next home game couldn't have been more different as goals from Robson, Ally Brown, Gary Owen and a rare strike from Kevin Summerfield slaughtered Manchester City 4-0. We also beat Manchester United again at home, this time 2-0 with goals from Robson and Deehan. Southampton were next up at home and we gave them a 4-0 thumping. Then it was the turn of our old friends Coventry to take their annual punishment. This time it was 4-1, with the Brown 'brothers' sharing the goals equally.

In November, I decided to drive to Leeds for the first time since the riots in 1976, this time deploying our safe tactic of going in a home section of the ground. We opted for the seats and kept quiet throughout our 1-0 defeat.

On the first day of December, I drove to Everton. After parking, I found myself surrounded by little 'scallys' asking me if I had the time. This was their trick to suss you out, but they didn't have to wait for me to reveal my Midlands accent. I just snapped: 'Yes, we're from West Brom. What are you going to do about it?' Off they ran, presumably to report us to the bigger boys round the corner. We held our nerve and made it to Goodison Park intact to see Regis score in our 1-1 draw.

Ron Atkinson loved a friendly, so our regular appearances in testimonials proved ideal for visiting new grounds. One night, we drove to Cambridge for a Trevor Eades testimonial game which we won 2-1 at the homely Abbey Stadium.

I consider Ipswich away on 1 January to be a monumental day in the history of Albion supporters. Due to it being the morning after a party in the Red Admiral, we decided to travel in pyjamas. To my knowledge, this was the first time our fans had worn fancy dress of any description at a game. Ten of us met up on the 'Addy' car park at 8.00 a.m. for the long trip. Apart from the drivers (Tony Jones and myself), everyone was the worse for wear from the night before – or just a couple of hours before, in a couple of cases. The fun we had, pulling my Mini Traveller and Tony's Austin Cambridge in at several little country pubs, completely overshadowed our 4-0 defeat. I believe this laid the foundations for the end-of-season theme parties that became so popular many years later.

I visited Selhurst Park for the first time three weeks later to see a young Remi Moses make his debut in a 2-2 draw with Crystal Palace. He certainly stood out and went on to make the No. 4 shirt his own for the rest of the season.

After easy pickings at Coventry with another 2-0 win, I rounded up the troops for the long drive to Norwich on 22 March. Five of us crammed into my tiny Mini; Tony Jones, Karl Bowker, Dave Loats and Bob Harris, with me driving. We called in at a nice little country pub and the lads relieved the pub garden of several gnomes and the beer towels off the washing line. We were merrily driving through the picturesque countryside near Thetford when I slowed down for a car full of schoolboys. They were looking for a football pitch and suddenly spotted their turn-off as I was overtaking them. Their car hit mine on the side and forced it onto two wheels. We went down a grass bank and ended up in a field 200 yards from the impact. My car floor was split wide open and petrol and mud sprayed everywhere. Amazingly, we all squeezed out unharmed, but the car was a right-off. We looked round and knew it was a lucky escape. If it had happened a few yards further back, we would have ended up in a river. One problem remained. We had to make the garden gnomes disappear before the police arrived. Although the other car had actually hit me, I was charged for overtaking at a crossroads, albeit just a dirt track.

While Tony and Dave hitch-hiked to the game, which ended 1-1, I was too shook-up so I got a lift to Peterborough with Bob and Karl and caught the train home. I made arrangements to get the car towed out of the field and scrapped. Mom ended up with the gnomes.

My next car was a Ford Escort Estate and it was soon given runs to Bristol City and Arsenal before the season finished. At Highbury, we thought we had struck lucky when we found a parking place in the street adjacent to the famous marble halls. It was too good to be true and, when we returned after our 1-1 draw, there was my car behind a locked gate. It cost us a tenner to get the gate opened. Highbury was another rough place to go in those days as away fans were guided to the middle of the Clock End, surrounded by Arsenal fans with little segregation. You daren't go to the toilet.

It had been a distinctly average season and we finished tenth. Unfortunately, we fell at the first hurdle in the UEFA Cup against Carl Zeiss Jena. It wasn't easy to travel to East Germany, so I decided to give it a miss and save money for the latter rounds. If I had known that we wouldn't progress any further in the competition, I would definitely have made the effort to get there. Yet another regret.

In the FA Cup, we were knocked out by West Ham in a replay. In the League Cup, we beat Fulham away in a replay and were effectively given a 'bye' in the third round when we were drawn at home to Coventry, sure enough, we progressed. Our run came to an end at Norwich, who hammered us 3-0, again after a replay.

After learning my trade at Thorne Brothers, I had moved to a company called HBDS (House Building Design Services) in Quinton. The business was set up to carry out urban renewal work, mainly in Handsworth. This was a great job for learning different trades as we would have to 'gut' old houses and fit new windows, doors and skirting boards. We also had to rip out the ornate fireplaces, brick the hole up and plaster over. These 100-year-old fireplaces sold for a fortune a few years later. In 1980, we just threw them in a skip. I wish I'd had the vision to store them somewhere.

Every year, through the Festival Football League, my local, the Red Admiral, received two tickets for the FA Cup Final and 1980 was no exception. As the final was an all-London affair between West Ham and Arsenal, there was no need for the usual raffle so Tony Jones and myself took the tickets. It was a great experience going to an FA Cup final at the old Wembley. We were on the terraces at the Arsenal end. However, when Trevor Brooking scored the winner, it was evident there were many West Ham fans around us. It remains the last time a team outside the top flight lifted the Cup. We also tried in a bit of 'ground-hopping' (a strange obsession for visiting football grounds) during the trip, calling in at Luton on the way and Watford on the return journey.

Rat Trap

I love visiting new grounds, so, in the summer of 1980, I started driving to pre-season games for the first time. I went all the way from Borth to see us lose 4-2 at Reading and then a few days later to Swindon, where we won 3-1.

1980/81

I was now nineteen and eagerly looking forward to the new season. We drove to Stoke for a midweek draw after losing at home to Arsenal in our first game. The old Victoria Ground could get a bit violent and, although I never got in trouble there myself, I saw a few scrapes and heard plenty of tales of ambushes by Potters fans.

Our second trip was a nice summer weekend at the seaside and Brighton's Goldstone Ground. Two car loads of us headed down on the Friday morning, calling in at Reading's Elm Park and Aldershot's Recreation Ground on the way. We stayed in Eastbourne overnight and got into bother with some locals at the end of the pier. Next morning, after a game of football on the beach, we headed into Brighton (or Hove to be precise) and purchased various masks. Again, we were years ahead of our time. When we reached the ground, the police made us remove our masks. They must have thought we were an organised gang. A mass chorus of 'Oh I do like to be beside the seaside, oh I do like to be beside the sea. I do like to walk along the prom, prom, prom where the brass bands play WEST BROM, WEST BROM' was sung as we left the ground celebrating our 2-1 win. Regis and Owen bagged our goals.

After beating Norwich 3-0, we were stuffed 4-0 at Anfield, abruptly bringing to an end our 244-day (eight-month) unbeaten away run. On 1 November, we kept the pyjama tradition going at Ipswich. This time, we hired a minibus and, to our surprise, were not alone in the nightwear department. We had obviously created quite an impression the season before and it was great to see that word had got round. About 100 fans were similarly attired, some in dressing gowns, at the goalless draw. We agreed that Ipswich away would become an annual pyjama party and in fairness, it did, steadily morphing into fancy dress as the seasons passed.

I had stopped travelling by coach as our fans would often be treated like animals; pulled over by police, escorted straight to the ground, then locked inside afterwards before being escorted back to the coach. I would therefore drive to most venues but often avoided the away section at some grounds as a police escort was of no use to us. In fact, it made us obvious targets to the home supporters once we broke away from the escort to get to the car. We would deliberately pay to stand with home fans. This strategy created new adventures. Just after my twentieth birthday, Dave Loats (Skin) and I went on the 'Shelf' at White Hart Lane and stood right in the middle of the main Spurs boys. Perversely, I loved mixing with the 'enemy' and listening to the biased comments and chants. On this occasion, just when we needed to keep quiet, Robson, Barnes and Ally Brown all scored to put us 3-0 up by half-time and we were unable to offer so much as a smile. Tottenham pulled two back but, after our unexpected victory, we were relieved to get back to the car without being sussed out. We waited until we were a couple of miles away from the ground, then pulled over and let out our pent-up emotions.

In December, we arrived at Highfield Road for our usual two points. We had become so used to beating Coventry that our players barely turned up. A dreadful performance gave the Sky Blues a shock 3-0 win. It didn't put me off getting my traditional Boxing Day fix. We set off nice and early on the long drive to Sunderland, where I'd been looking forward to witnessing the famous 'Roker Roar'. Again, we avoided the away section and stood on the side with the home fans. I loved Roker Park, a proper old stadium, with great atmosphere. The goalless draw was the perfect result for hiding visible emotions.

Yet another great day followed against Man United (they must have hated The Hawthorns). Regis, Owen and Barnes scored in a 3-1 win. This was followed a few weeks later by a rare 2-0 victory against Liverpool, with Robson and Regis on target.

In stark contrast to the official HATS (Hawthorns Away Travel Service) we had formed the RATS (Red Admiral Travel Section), taking minibuses to away games. John Skeen, one of the regulars, hired a coach for Southampton in February, our first trip courtesy of 'Skeeny tours'... A great afternoon was had by all and our drunken gang from Great Barr led the singing, with Andy Payne standing on the crush barrier shouting 'Too much too young' at random intervals, prompting Albion fans to deliver their own version of The Specials' moon stomp. The Old Bill soon piled in and, just as we thought that Andy was going to be arrested, the copper said: 'Oi, Ginger, get back on the barrier, use that big mouth of yours and tell your lot that they're going to be locked in at the end'. Goals from Robson and Regis ensured that we gained a point for our troubles.

Brendon Batson must take some responsibility for Villa winning the League that season. First, he scored a very rare goal in our 3-1 home win over their championship rivals Ipswich. Then, in the crunch game at Villa Park, he hit a weak back pass that let in Peter Withe to score a late winner.

Despite 'that lot' winning the title, it had been a good season and the victory against Spurs in our last home game secured fourth spot and a UEFA Cup place. We tore them apart and won 4-2 with goals from Robson, Barnes, Ally Brown and Nicky Cross.

In the FA Cup, we eased past Grimsby 3-0 at The Hawthorns before being drawn at Middlesbrough. I hadn't been to Ayresome Park and loved the Cup, so we decided to make a weekend of it, booking in at my old Hamstead mate Steve Battye's parents' guest house in Bridlington. We arrived in Middlesbrough in good time for a few beers, so we set up base camp, together with around thirty fellow Baggies in a town centre pub. Every now and again, a Boro fan would walk in, have a look round, then disappear. We feared something was being arranged but could do nothing about it except all stick together. We left the pub at 2.30 p.m. and started walking towards the ground. All of a sudden, a mob of around 100 Middlesbrough lads ambushed us. They came running down the street throwing bottles and bricks. We were in a dead end with just a wall behind us, so we had to stand our ground. The police suddenly appeared and all hell broke out. They let the dogs loose on the innocent Albion fans and, when I looked round, my mate Dave Foxall had an Alsatian hanging off his arm. We somehow made it into the ground, but poor Dave spent the afternoon being stitched up in hospital. We complained to the coppers in the ground but they just laughed and launched a barrage of abuse against us. After our 1-0 defeat, the walk back to the car took us past a cemetery; how appropriate. This day was up there with Leeds, 1976, in the roughest away day stakes.

We thankfully all made it that evening to the resort of Bridlington, where the police followed us from pub to pub. We visited as many as possible, with the main conversation being about the attack on us earlier in the day.

In the League Cup, the second round was now a two-legged affair. Leicester were our opponents and the home leg was won 1-0 thanks to a Peter Barnes goal. I took my Ford Escort to Filbert Street and, after Regis had secured our progress, my mates were hanging out of the windows giving the Foxes fans some abuse as we drove away. Unfortunately, we hit a traffic jam, the Leicester fans caught us up and proceeded to rock the car. Our lot fought back with anything they could find. Even the 'Crooklock' was wielded in an attempt to keep them at bay. The traffic started moving and I sped off as quickly as I could, sadly not before a few boots caused considerable damage to my car.

At Everton in round three, we were locked inside Goodison Park for our own safety after our great 2-1 win. Dave Foxall had ended up standing with the Everton fans and we could see him through the gap in the gates among the baying Scousers taunting us outside. After the police had finally cleared the crowd, we were allowed out and Dave joined us as we made our way through Stanley Park to the car. Lots of Everton fans were waiting in the shadows and we were followed, causing us to walk faster and faster, then start running as the Scouse voices behind us sounded louder as they got closer. The car was almost in sight when we came to an abrupt halt – we were stopped in our tracks by a river – shit! We ran along the footpath and fortunately found a bridge, we jumped in the car and sped away as fast as possible. Phew! After drawing at home to Preston in the fourth round, I drove to Deepdale to see their classic old-fashioned stadium for the first time. We drew again and beat them in a second replay. Just as we were starting to dream about Wembley, Man City put us out 2-1 at Maine Road.

8

Hopping Mad in Zurich

We had once again qualified for the UEFA Cup following our fourth-spot finish in 1980/81. I now had a decent job and some savings to allow me to travel to wherever the first-round draw sent us. Out of the hat came Grasshoppers of Zurich, the most famous team in Switzerland, holding the record for the most national championships. The trip was a must.

A group of us from the Red Admiral decided to make a week of it and drive there, camping en route to cut costs. Due to the high risk of hooliganism and the reputation of English fans, Albion announced that tickets would be unavailable to any fans travelling independently and that tickets could only be obtained through booking on the official supporters club coaches. We agreed to chance it as we believed the club statement to be a smokescreen to put fans off travelling independently. We really had no choice as most of our party were skint and planned to visit one of the world's most expensive cities with just £20 in their pockets. To enable us to eat on the trip, we launched a 'Food for Zurich' campaign in the Admiral. The regulars donated various tins of food, so a Calor gas stove was packed in the car.

The week of the match soon arrived and our plan was to drive in two cars to see Albion at Nottingham Forest on 12 September, then head to Dover for the overnight ferry to Zeebrugge. Our travelling party consisted of David Loats (Skin), Michael Silvester (Silve), Tony Jones, John Skeen (Skeeny), Malcolm Llewellyn (Sweat) and Heather Evans (brave girl!), with Andy Payne and myself as drivers. He had a Ford Cortina estate and I drove my Ford Escort.

We agreed to meet at the 'Addy' on the Saturday morning, which is when Andy announced that his car was playing-up. Sweat, our resident mechanic, soon diagnosed that the clutch was on its way out. This was not what we wanted to hear when about to set off across Europe via Nottingham. 'Not to worry,' announced Sweat 'I can fit a new one in a Cortina in a couple of hours.' So off we all went to his house in Friar Park (where I also happened to be lodging at the time). The two hours soon came and went and we were forced to accept that we weren't going to make the Forest game, a great shame as the travelling Albion fans were to be filmed for a television documentary. He eventually managed to do the job but broke the reverse light switch in doing so. We couldn't wait any longer, so we listened to the Forest game on the radio and Andy had to drive with the reversing lights permanently on.

We arrived in Dover in good time and had a Chinese meal washed down with a few beers before boarding. This was the likely cause of a few bouts of sickness among our party. While Andy and myself tried to get some sleep, ready for the long drive next day, the others headed for the bar. Needless to say, they were all a bit the worse for wear when we docked in Belgium. As I drove through Brussels, I was admiring the famous Atom and conducting a one-man sightseeing tour as my passengers, Silve, Skin and Sweat, were extremely drunk and snoring loudly. Silve had purchased a large bottle of Pernod as a present to take home for his mother. I later noticed the bottle, empty on the back seat! He also bought his mom a French baguette which he said he was going to varnish and keep as a memento. He duly ate it in the car.

This was well before SatNav and mobile phones, so all we had were rudimentary maps and the ability to be able to follow each other. We drove through Belgium and ticked off a new country and ground by calling in at Luxembourg's National Stadium before heading for Strasbourg, where Tony wanted to see his French girlfriend. We pitched our tents in a corn field outside the city and had a night out with Claudine and her French mates.

Because the club statement mentioned that no tickets would be on sale within two days of the match, we headed to Zurich on the Monday morning. After a sleepless night under canvas, I found myself day-dreaming at some traffic lights as we entered the city and nearly killed us all as I turned the wrong way and missed an oncoming tram by inches, then drove in the opposite direction down a dual carriageway. Fortunately, we managed to do a 'U' turn and eventually found the Hardturm Stadium, home of Grasshoppers. The stadium was built in 1929 and had been used as a venue in the 1954 World Cup finals. It was closed in 2007 and subsequently demolished, forcing Grasshoppers to share FC Zurich's Letzigrund Stadium. Back in 1981, we just walked in and could have bought as many tickets as we wanted, for a third of the price charged by Albion for the 'official' party. We could now relax and soon found a 'local', The Grasshopper, directly opposite the stadium.

Zurich is the largest city in Switzerland and the wealthiest in Europe. What we hadn't bargained for was the difficulty in finding a camp site. The England national team had played in the country a few months before and the fans had run wild. Sadly, we were tarred with the same brush – all the camp sites we tried refused entry and branded us as hooligans. We ended up pitching our tents in the dark on the side of a railway embankment. This wasn't our best idea as every time a train came past, it nearly blew us away. We also discovered that our temporary 'camp site' was just feet away from a wasp nest. Another sleepless night. In the light of day, we noticed a sign stating '*Camping ist verboten*'.

The next night, we pitched our tents outside a water-pumping station by beautiful Lake Zurich, much to the amusement of the workers clocking in next morning. Fortunately, they took pity on us and let us use their facilities for a wash. The previous evening was eventful to say the least. Skin had thrown a tantrum in the bar and disappeared in a huff. We didn't think much about it until later in the evening, when we realised he didn't know the location of our new 'site.' The lads stayed in the bar and I caught the tram with Silve into the city centre in search of a semi-drunk skinhead. We toured some well dodgy all-night drug dens, asking if anyone had seen a slightly smaller version of Silve (shaved head and Doc Marten boots). We eventually gave up and headed back. Skin somehow turned up the next morning on a 'borrowed' bicycle.

Unfortunately, the nearest bar charged tourist prices, so, having our normal drinking session had proved impossible on our small budget. We actually had clear heads the next day when we headed to The Grasshopper and the lovely city centre. We watched Albion's players training next to the ground and called into the stadium to pose for photographs for the Midlands' media. This was the first time I met my good friend Paul Dubberley (Dubsey), who had arrived from the opposite direction. He was on his way home from a year's globetrotting. While being photographed, we were spotted by Albion's directors, including secretary Tony Rance, who looked horrified when we waved our match tickets at him.

In the city, the locals seemed wary of us. I guess we looked like a troublesome bunch as two of our party were skinheads and some of us were sporting army surplus jackets. We met Ian, who had travelled to Zurich on his motorbike, and ex-Great Barr lad Steve Battye and his Burntwood Baggies. We had our photo taken for the national Swiss newspaper *The Daily Blick*. When we obtained a copy next morning, there we were on the front page, warning of the first hooligans arriving and for shopkeepers to be vigilant. No wonder we were getting suspicious looks. In the city centre, we got talking to a couple of Scousers who basically travelled around Europe to whichever city happened to be hosting an English club in European competition. They then used visiting fans as cover as they set about robbing numerous shops. The police automatically accused the genuine supporters of the crimes while the Liverpool louts disappeared to the next venue. Totally wrong.

On match day, we headed for The Grasshopper and welcomed lots of fellow Baggies off the official coaches. We took great pleasure informing them of the ticket prices we paid. They all agreed not to take any notice of official club statements in future.

The game was a disappointment; (how many times have we said that over the years?) A modest 8,101 crowd saw Grasshoppers' Andre Fimian score the only goal in the 39th minute of a forgettable game. Manager Ronnie Allen, returning to the country where he made his England debut in 1952, said afterwards: 'They were well organised and, although we created a couple of chances, we never really got going in the middle of the park. It wasn't good.' I believe Bryan

Robson had his imminent move to Manchester United on his mind and didn't really perform. This seemed to affect the whole team and we deservedly lost.

A couple of detours were requested on our journey home. Tone was madly in love with Claudine and wanted us to go via Strasbourg again. It was obviously the real thing as he eventually married her and they are still together to this day, residing in Stonnall. Back in Strasbourg, he had managed to sort himself some digs for the night, so we pitched our tents again and arranged to meet him next morning. He turned up to announce that he wasn't coming home and was going to stay in France and look for a job. We thought he was joking and fully expected him to join us, but it soon became clear he was not winding us up. He really was intending to stay put. We drove away slowly, continually looking in the rear mirror in case he changed his mind. We left him behind and headed for our next requested stop to see Skin's sister, Alison, who was sharing a flat near Düsseldorf in West Germany.

As we crossed the German border, Tony's passport was suddenly discovered in Andy's car. We had no idea where he was staying back in Strasbourg, so we made the decision to take it home. It is an offence in France to be caught without cash and ID and you can be imprisoned until you can provide both. We left Tony with neither.

By the time we reached the town of Krefeld, it was dark and we were just in time to meet Alison and her friends. We headed to the designated bar for a well-deserved drink and decided to worry about pitching our tents later. After a skinful of lovely German beer, we were incapable of driving, so put up our tents on the only patch of grass we could find in the town centre. Next morning, we were rudely awoken by two official-looking Germans, who opened our tents and gave us a right mouthful (we didn't understand a word). It all became clear when we ventured out and realised we were on the manicured lawns of Krefeld town hall! The locals were not happy, so we packed away immediately, complete with hangovers, and headed out of town in record time before we were arrested.

We made our ferry back in Zeebrugge in good time and even managed a 'hair of the dog' in a local Belgian bar before heading back to Blighty. Our return journey took us back via Felixstowe and Andy was finally pulled over by the police (for his reversing lights) as we left the British port. He was instructed to remove the fuse to switch the lights off. This rendered the windscreen wipers inoperable, though, so, when it started raining half way up the A12, he had to pull over and put the fuse back in.

Despite the result, we all agreed it had been a brilliant trip. The next morning, I realised I had been left in possession of Tony's passport. I had no idea how to contact him and he was stuck in France whether he liked it or not. I went to his parents' house in Great Barr and informed them that their twenty-year-old son had not travelled home with us and decided to stay 'somewhere in Strasbourg'. As I was faced with a barrage of questions, I made out I was in a hurry, handed them his passport and disappeared.

I finished the week off by taking my usual spot on the terraces at The Hawthorns to see our 0-0 draw with West Ham. Sadly, there were to be no more European trips that season. We lost the return leg 3-1 (4-1 on aggregate) on a miserable night.

9

First Division Mediocrity

In my working life, after a year on urban renewal, I joined Coventry-based Allan H. Williams as a curtain wall/window installer. This was perfect for me as I loved to travel and it allowed me to work on sites all over the UK. One of my first 'out of town' projects was the new Debenhams opposite the castle in Princes Street, Edinburgh. This opened up the new world of Scottish football grounds.

I would try to attend two games every week, catching the train to any destination within reach. I was fortunate to see Willie Johnston play again – for Rangers against Hearts (who he would later join). I always had a soft spot for Rangers and would watch them whenever possible. I saw them lose at the long-demolished Kilbowie, former home of Clydebank, a game I remember for a fight between Rangers' English goalkeeper Nicky Walker and a Rangers supporter behind the goal at the end.

As well as Scotland, I spent a lot of time in London, where I would spend week nights either watching London football clubs in action or going to see a band. I was into punk/new wave music at the time and being based in 'the Smoke' gave me the opportunity to regularly see bands like The Clash, The Jam or The Damned at iconic venues such as Hammersmith Palais and The Lyceum. During my time in London I stayed at a shared flat with four female dancers in Hampstead. I thought all my dreams had come true!

Back home, my pre-match routine would be to meet the lads in the Red Admiral, drive to the ground, park in Forge Lane and have a couple of pints in the Birmingham Road Throstle Club. This club was situated where the East Stand car park is now. It used to be great in there before games, with a big sing-song usually taking place as kick-off approached.

1981/82

In June 1981, Ron Atkinson left us for Manchester United, taking Brian Whitehouse, Mick Brown and George Wright from our backroom with him. It basically ripped the heart out of the club. In came Ronnie Allen for his second spell as manager.

Pre-season, midfielder Steve Mackenzie was signed from Manchester City for £650,000 and he made his debut against his former club in the opening game. Oh, the joys of Maine Road – after running the gauntlet through the notorious Moss Side back alleys, we were put in our usual pen in the Kippax stand, surrounded by hostile locals. David Mills scored from the spot but we lost 2-1.

We also lost our first home game, to Arsenal, before First Division newcomers Swansea came to The Hawthorns. Swansea had won their first two games and were full of confidence. A Regis hat-trick and a goal from Mackenzie sent them packing on the back of a 4-1 defeat.

In October, I travelled to Leeds and this time we were in a caged section on the side. Pre-match, Peter Barnes (now a Leeds player) was on the pitch warming up with his new teammates when Albion fans burst into song: 'Peter, Peter give us a wave'. Thinking it was a sign of our gratitude, he turned around and acknowledged us, only to be met with a thousand 'V' signs! We lost 3-1.

Our next away game was a classic at St Andrew's. Cyrille was on fire and grabbed a brilliant hat-trick in a pulsating 3-3 draw, despite having to once again endure monkey chants throughout.

Bryan Robson and Remi Moses had now inevitably joined Big Ron at Manchester United for £1.5m and £500,000 respectively. In came two Dutchmen, Maarten Jol and Romeo Zondervan. Andy King and Clive Whitehead were also recruited.

We drew at home to Liverpool three days before my twenty-first birthday. Afterwards, I had a party at the Frank Harrison Centre in Bloxwich, organising a coach for the Red Admiral regulars. My cousin's band provided the entertainment and Silve got on the microphone to deliver a punk rendition of 'Happy Birthday.' The night ended with my 'mates' throwing me over a hedge into a bog.

I went in the disabled section for our home game against Wolves, assisting my mate Dave Foxall, who was on crutches. I got a few funny looks when I jumped on to the track when Regis scored the third in our 3-0 victory.

After the previous season's blip, normal service was resumed at Coventry on Boxing Day, goals from Gary Owen and Big Cyrille giving us a 2-0 win at what had just become the first all-seater stadium in the country.

Silve and I drove down to West Ham on 30 January and opted to go in the home end at the notoriously inhospitable Boleyn Ground. Just before kick-off, I decided to go to the hot-dog stand in the corner of the terrace. When I reached the front of the queue, the seller chose me to ask about the team news, saying in a broad Cockney accent: 'Who's in for the Irons today then geezer?' I've never been good at accents, so I just shrugged my shoulders, pretended to be deaf and dumb and walked away. I got some inquisitive looks from nearby fans and never did get a hot dog. We didn't whisper a word to each other throughout our 3-1 defeat and politely applauded when the home side scored.

A midweek testimonial for Spalding United's Paul Kent gave me an excuse to drive to Lincolnshire to see us beat Norwich 3-2 at their tiny Sir Halley Stewart ground. We had only got as far as the outskirts of town afterwards when my car broke down. We were unable to fix it and a local pub kindly provided late night hospitality while my dad came out to rescue us. I had to go all the way back to Spalding next day to get it sorted.

Our lorry driver at work was a Middlesbrough fan and gave me a lift to Ayresome Park, following last season's escapades, I was happy to join him with the Boro fans for out 1-0 defeat. All the way up the M1, Dave the driver was going on about 'the best chip shop in the world' situated on the beach in his home town of Redcar. It sounded like the perfect place for lunch so we diverted to the resort only to find the chip shop closed down and boarded up!

The double was completed over our 'friends' from Staffordshire with another goal from Cyrille and a strike from Derek Monaghan providing us with a pleasing 2-1 win at Molineux. Our incredible sequence of home wins against Manchester United came to an end when Ron Atkinson's new side comfortably defeated us 3-0.

A 2-1 win at Notts County meant that our place in the top division would be safe if we beat Leeds at The Hawthorns on the following Tuesday evening. Leeds also had to win to ensure survival. I was still working in London but wasn't going to miss such an important game, so I caught the train to New Street and a bus to the ground. I must admit to hiding my scarf as the bus was full of Leeds hooligans. Goals from Mackenzie and Regis saved us from relegation, which meant Leeds were almost down. The Yorkshiremen were not happy and long before the final whistle were pulling the fences down at the Smethwick End. Their attempt to invade the pitch was thwarted by the West Midlands police. This wasn't just kids; there were middle-aged blokes wrecking the ground.

The only hope that Leeds had to avoid relegation was if Albion won at Stoke in our final game. After what Leeds had done to our ground, there was no way we were going to help them out. Predictably, Stoke recorded a straightforward 3-0 victory over us and Leeds were doomed, along with Wolves and Middlesbrough. A couple of years later, I was at a Queen concert at Elland Road. In the pub beforehand, there was a ticket from the Stoke v Albion match pinned to the wall. When I asked the gaffer for the significance, he barked 'That was the game that sent us down, the West Brom bastards.'

Back at The Hawthorns, Ronnie Allen moved 'upstairs' in June 1982, taking up the position of General Manager. I was completely underwhelmed with his replacement, the former Villa player and ex-Birmingham captain Ron Wylie. Striker Peter Eastoe joined us from Everton in a deal which resulted in Andy King going to the Toffees.

My parents (front, extreme left) with other members of the Supporters' Club outside White Hart Lane for the Spurs v Albion game in 1951

My mom (standing centre) and my Aunt Barbara and Uncle Tony (far left, standing) with members of the Albion Supporters' Club at Preston North End in 1952

Mom (second from left) and her friends on the terraces at St James' Park, Newcastle after failing to clear the snow off the pitch to get the Gateshead v Albion FA Cup match played in 1952

My older brother Alan aged 9 in 1964, he hardly
wore his Albion strip and it was still in perfect
condition when handed to me a few years later –
I wore it out in a matter of weeks!

With one of my first Albion pennants,
aged 10.

In goal for Hamstead
Junior School 5-a-side
team. Albion Cup winners
1972. Back row: Mr
Dimbylow, John Nash, me,
Paul Hutchinson. Front
row: Craig Sorrill, Chris
Chapman, Paul Tudor. I
still regularly see Chris
and the 2 Pauls. The whole
team were Albion fans.

10

Agony at Highbury, Part II

Four years on from the semi-final despair against Ipswich, we were dreaming of Wembley again, this time in both cup competitions.

In the League Cup, another new ground was visited, Gay Meadow, home of Shrewsbury Town, and we made hard work of it in a 3-3 first-leg draw. They put up another good fight in the second leg, which we edged 2-1.

In the third round, we were drawn at West Ham. A 2-2 draw bringing them back for a replay which was also drawn. We had to return to Upton Park for the second time in three weeks – not so inconvenient for me as I was now working in London. One of the blokes on the building site told me he was a Hammers season-ticket holder and offered to take me to the game and even for a pre-match meal at his house. He lived in Green Street, next to the ground, meaning we didn't have to leave until ten minutes before kick-off. I stood with him and his mates in the famous 'chicken run' – the terrace running along the side of the pitch. Obviously, I had to keep quiet during our 1-0 win, particularly when Regis scored, making it three for him in the three-game sequence. But, once again, I enjoyed the experience of being among home supporters.

A fine 3-1 triumph at Crystal Palace provided us with a 'plum' quarter-final at Aston Villa. I never miss an Albion v Villa game, so boarded the train from London to see Derek Statham score the only goal, directly in front of us at the Witton End in one of my favourite away games. We filed out, gleefully chanting: 'We're going to Wembley, we're going to Wembley, YOU'RE NOT.'

The two-leg semi-final was against Tottenham – the first leg ending 0-0 at The Hawthorns with Maarten Jol and Spurs' Tony Galvin both sent off for fighting. I was now working on a large contract in Bristol, so I caught the National Express coach for the second leg and decided I would go out celebrating and stay overnight in London if we won. Unfortunately, I ended up catching the midnight coach back to Bristol in a sulk following our 1-0 defeat, with Spurs are on their way to Wembley' ringing in my ears. Never mind, we were still in the FA Cup.

The third-round draw paired us with Blackburn at home and we won 3-2 with goals from Mackenzie, Andy King with a penalty and Clive Whitehead. The fourth round provided us with a great away day; Priestfield Stadium, home of Third Division Gillingham. John Skeen organised the travel and a mini-bus from 'Skeeny Tours' set off for Kent. We were in good spirits following our League Cup victory against the old enemy four days earlier and, on arrival in Gillingham, noticed the Match of the Day cameras. Obviously an upset was anticipated. It was a very hard game in the mud, with The Gills probably the better team. As the game headed for a draw and an unwanted replay, cometh the hour cometh the man, Statham lashed in the winner for the second time in five days. It was a terrific day and a couple of off-licence stops were necessary to refuel on the long journey home before we got back in the 'Addy' just in time for last orders.

We were at home to Norwich in round five and a fairly drab game was brought to life thanks to a wonder goal from Cyrille. He collected the ball on the half-way line with his back to goal, turned a couple of defenders and let fly. The ball twisted and turned before ending up in the net. As luck would have it, I was stood in the Smethwick End that day and had a perfect view of what was later adjudged to be the goal of the season.

In the quarter-final, we were at home to our old whipping boys, Coventry City. Work mates Mike Thornhill and Mick Haywood travelled up from Bristol with me for this one. In terrible conditions, Albion overcame the wind, rain and the Sky Blues with a goal from Gary Owen and another Regis special.

The semi-final draw appeared to be kind to us again as we were paired with Second Division QPR and it was back to Highbury. Skeeny carried out his duties and organised a 52-seater for this one. I had kept my plywood FA Cup and changed the year to 1982. Numerous crates of beer and a couple of boxes of champagne were loaded aboard on the Red Admiral car park on 3 April. We had to detour via Spouthouse Lane in Hamstead to get Chris Jones out of bed. We had overbooked and actually had sixty-two people travelling. Some of them requested their money back at Highbury as they had been standing in the gangway for the entire journey and reckoned they had effectively walked to London.

This time, we were allocated the Clock End and the attendance was just short of 50,000. Although our line-up was nowhere near as strong as in 1978, we were still confident. Sadly, we never really got going and it turned out to be a scrappy game. Rangers won thanks to a fluke goal off Clive Allen's knee following a mishit clearance by Ally Robertson. We just stood in silence at the end, struggling to come to terms with our second 1-0 semi-final defeat in seven weeks. Would we ever reach Wembley again? My plywood FA Cup was despatched into a North London garden and the bottles of champagne were smashed in anger.

11

On the Slide

1982/83

Our first game of the season was at Anfield and a routine defeat, this time 2-0 to the eventual champions. Only 11,370 turned up for our first home game and those who stayed away missed a treat as we steamrolled Brighton 5-0 with goals from Jol, Brown (2), Eastoe and Cross. We followed this up with a superb 3-1 victory against Manchester United – Ron Atkinson, Bryan Robson and all – with Martin Bennett, Brown and Eastoe on target.

We made it three wins on the bounce in an amazing game at the old Victoria Ground. Stoke were all over us and we could easily have lost. Miraculously, we scored from each of our efforts on goal, coming away with a flattering 3-0 win thanks to Brown, Eastoe and Regis.

My first visit to Watford wasn't a happy one. We stood on the big open terrace to witness a horrible 3-0 defeat. As unpredictable as ever, our next away day saw us win 3-1 with a Regis hat-trick at Norwich. The following week, Nicky Cross earned himself cult hero status by scoring the winner against Aston Villa.

On 13 November I was at the Swansea home game, where I witnessed one of the funniest things I have ever seen at a match. The game was sponsored by local butcher Walter Belcher and, at half-time, packets of sausages were thrown into the crowd ... big mistake. Most fans in the Brummie Road End had the same idea, so when the Swansea goalkeeper Dai Davies trotted towards us for the second half, he was pelted! Davies dived to the ground, obviously having no idea that the missiles being thrown were harmless. The last thing on his mind would have been sausages. It must have been the first and only time that a kick-off had been delayed due to sausages on the pitch! Throughout the second half, strings of Walter Belcher's finest were still hanging from the goal-net. The entertainment continued on the Smethwick End terraces, where Albion fans staged a massive sausage fight. The match wasn't bad either, a 3-3 draw. Strangely enough, the local butcher has never sponsored another game.

Garry Thompson proved to be a popular signing, joining us from Coventry in the new year. Those among the exodus of players included one-time record signing David Mills, who joined Sheffield Wednesday for only £30,000.

Our form was really inconsistent; a win one week, a loss the next. Then, in February and March, we drew four successive games 0-0. As usual, we relied on our generous friends from Coventry for six points, beating them 2-0 at home and 1-0 away thanks to a goal from orange-haired Micky Perry. Fortunately, we won three of our last four games to add some respectability to our position, finishing eleventh.

There was disappointment in the cups. A home FA Cup win against QPR in the third round was small consolation for the semi-final defeat. We then got knocked out in round four at White Hart Lane with that bloody 'Spurs are on their way to Wembley' song blasting out as we again left the ground in despair.

Our second-round League Cup first leg game was horrific. We lost 6-1 at Nottingham Forest. No wonder only 6,536 turned up for the second leg to see us regain some pride with a 3-1 win. Albion's average home league attendance of 15,260 was the lowest at The Hawthorns since 1914/15.

Club legend John Wile became manager of Peterborough United after 619 appearances for the Baggies over thirteen years.

In the 1983 summer break, it was off for two weeks of madness with my good mate Skin (Dave Loats) in Lloret de Mar. We lived life to the full, attempting to drink our weight in beer during a fortnight of Spanish debauchery. Skin was now working with me after quitting his job at the Great Barr Post House. It's fair to say we had some great days working away in different towns all over the UK, from Glasgow to Brighton.

A memorable weekend with the lads came in Skegness, where a friend smuggled us into a chalet at Butlins. After a night of heavy drinking, Micky Winnitt went out to buy something to cook for breakfast. Nearly an hour had passed and there was no sign of Mick. He eventually returned with a frying pan containing half-cooked bacon and sausages sizzling away. He had gone to the wrong chalet; thought we had gone for a walk and started cooking. Only when he noticed a beach ball and some children's toys did he realise his mistake. I can't imagine what the family must have thought when they returned to a strong smell of cooked food and a missing frying pan!

1983/84

Ken McNaught joined us from Villa during pre-season and lined up against his former club in the opening game. In keeping with tradition, we caught the train from Hamstead to Witton, packing out the Beaufort Arms on the lunchtime. It was a cracker, real end-to-end stuff. Unfortunately, I only saw the first-half 'live.' Because, as the teams trotted out after half-time, Villa goalkeeper Nigel Spink was getting loads of stick from the Albion fans with sarcastic chants. For some unknown reason, the police came wading into us and arrested me. It was sweltering and I had my shirt tied around my waist. I was led round the pitch in front of the Villa fans (some of whom recognised me) before being thrown out at the Holte End. I tried to get back in but to no avail, so ended up watching the game on a monitor in one of the TV broadcasting vans on the Witton End car park. I managed to gain entry again with just a few minutes to go in our 4-3 defeat.

It didn't get any better at Stoke in midweek; another defeat, this time 3-1. Fortunately, things picked up after that, with home wins against Leicester and West Ham. Then it was off to Ipswich again in no-holds-barred fancy dress. There was a Pink Panther, a boxer, pirate, Danger Mouse, a sea monster and many other outfits on display. This time we saw a fantastic game and goals from Romeo Zondervan, Garry Thompson (pen.), Cyrille Regis and Micky Perry gave us a 4-3 victory. On our return, our minibus stopped off in St Neots market square for a few beers. A scarecrow was relieved of its duties in a Suffolk field and relocated on the Gorse Farm island in Great Barr.

We helped ourselves to the usual easy pickings at Coventry in October, with Regis and Perry on target in a routine 2-1 win. I wish we could play the Sky Blues every week!

Wolves were rock bottom and hadn't won a game when they came to The Hawthorns at the end of November. Albion have always been good at ending runs (good or bad) and this was no exception. We were well beaten 3-1 and had to leave the Brummie Road to the sound of the Wanderers fans celebrating as if they had won the League.

After a surprise win at Arsenal in December, Derek Monaghan getting the winner in front of only 22,272, we went on a four-game losing run which included a 3-0 drubbing at Sunderland.

Then, to 14 January 1984, and one of my favourite games ever. Home to Aston Villa on a bleak mid-winter's day, we were in a bad run and 1-0 down. I was standing there, with 15 minutes to go, thinking about the stick I was going to get from the claret and blue contingent of Great Barr, when Garry Thompson and Cyrille Regis suddenly ran riot. First 'Thommo' grabbed an equaliser, then put us 2-1 ahead. We were already going crazy when it got even better, Cyrille racing from the half-way line, leaving the Villa defence trailing in his wake and scoring a wonderful goal. Absolute pandemonium in the Brummie Road. I couldn't believe the turnaround. After feeling totally depressed, I was now jumping around like a maniac. Pure ecstasy!

Sadly, this proved a one-off. In our next home game, we were thumped 5-0 by Nottingham Forest. Something had to change, Ron Wylie had never been a popular manager and he was duly given the bullet.

Enter Johnny Giles – The Messiah returned, this time bringing his 'dream team' with him in the shape of his ex-Leeds teammate Norman Hunter and his brother-in-law Nobby Stiles. His first game back in charge was a home fifth-round FA Cup tie against Second Division Plymouth. The script was written; surely Giles would take us all the way to Wembley? His homecoming added 10,000 to our regular attendance and there was a totally different atmosphere but we lost 1-0. 'Semper te fallant' – they always let you down.

The usual new manager's 'honeymoon' period simply didn't happen. We had to wait until mid-March for Giles's first win, a terrific 1-0 success at Spurs thanks to a Regis goal. Our new midfielders, Steve Hunt and Tony Grealish, made a big difference. We suddenly burst into life and followed up the win at Spurs with a 3-0 against Stoke and a satisfying 2-0 home victory against Man United. Things seemed to be looking up but sadly the new management team could do nothing to prevent our annual mauling at Anfield (3-0).

Wolves were already relegation certainties when we caught the train there for the usual 'warm welcome' on 28 April. Only 13,404 turned up to see a dreadful 0-0 draw. Garry Thompson became our first player to be sent-off in a Black Country derby.

I drove to our last away game, against QPR, to see us on Astro Turf for the first time. Thommo scored in a 1-1 draw. We finished the season off with two home games, beating Luton 3-0 and losing 2-0 to Southampton. Oh well, we could all look forward to next season with Giles in charge from the start. It could have been a lot worse. Wolves finished bottom.

The FA Cup gave me the opportunity to visit another new venue, Rotherham. The entrance to the away end at Millmoor was down an alleyway among a row of scrapyards. A good Albion following witnessed a poor 0-0 draw. Back at our place, there was no messing about and we comfortably beat the Merry Millers 3-0, new signing Tony Morley bagging a brace and Thompson getting the other. We made hard work of it against Scunthorpe in round four, a rare goal from Michael Forsyth seeing us through. Defeat to Plymouth on Giles's return and we were out of the competition.

I didn't travel for the first leg of the League Cup second round at Millwall, but heard lots of stories about our coaches being ambushed, smashed up and, in one instance, turning back and refusing to take our fans to the game. In front of a hostile crowd, we went down 3-0. While working in London I visited the old Den a few weeks later to see Millwall play Middlesbrough. It certainly lived up to its reputation. There was only one way to the away turnstiles. Fortunately, I went with a Millwall fan and stood in the home end.

There were memorable scenes in the home leg, with more than a thousand Millwall fans at The Hawthorns, confident of their side defending their 3-0 lead. In an amazing performance, we beat them 5-1 and their notorious fans weren't happy. I have vivid memories of numerous attempted pitch invasions and their hooligans running on top of the executive boxes in the Rainbow Stand. Before the end, there must have been double the number of police in the ground than at kick-off. It was chaos and, had it not been for the perimeter fences, I fear there could have been hundreds of casualties. 'No one likes us, we don't care,' they chanted. Too true.

Being in London made the next round at Chelsea an easy one for me. Stamford Bridge was another dodgy old place, so I opted to stand with their fans and saw Thommo get the winner.

In round four, we were once again up against our old foe. And, despite a Regis goal, Villa beat us 2-1 in front of 31,114 at The Hawthorns.

I was working away Monday to Friday every week, so each weekend it was generally a case of 'wherever I lay my hat.' After renting bedsits in Sutton Coldfield and Handsworth Wood, I moved in with my good mate Silve. The tenth-floor flat in the Hamstead House tower block was legendary in Great Barr circles; every Friday and Saturday night, after the pubs closed, you never knew who was going to turn up with assorted takeaways. Next morning, Silve would collect all the 'scraps' and fry them for breakfast – a strange mix of curry, fish and chips, kebabs, pizza and Chinese. Lovely! At the end of one of our regular West Bromwich High Street pub crawls (fifteen pubs), in a very drunken state, who should we bump into playing pool in The Marksman? The main man

Cyrille Regis. I'm sure he was really pleased to see us! In those days it was quite common to see players in the local pubs, it created a bond with the fans that is sadly missing in recent years.

We had reformed the Scott Arms football team, assembling some decent players for the Festival Sunday League. Our home pitch was by the golf course in Forge Lane (Sandwell Valley) and we had the perfect pub-team blend of good footballers and maniacs. If nothing else, opposing teams wouldn't be 'mixing it' with us.

1984/85

The new campaign began at QPR, where we always seemed to play at the start or end of a season. We had high hopes after Giles had stamped his mark on the team. Unfortunately, our first game was a disappointing 3-1 defeat, with Mackenzie the only one on target.

Only 14,062 attended our first home game, against Everton, which we won 2-1 thanks to goals from Hunt and Thompson. Another win followed, a 4-0 thrashing of Luton. Maybe Giles was weaving his magic after all?

Sadly, this was not the case. A run of five games without a win followed and, to make matters worse, the legendary Cyrille Regis, who was only twenty-six, was sold to Coventry for a cut-price £300,000. In fairness, he had been struggling for a while and relying heavily on his strike-partner Garry Thompson, who had been doing the 'donkey work' for most of the year. David Cross came back in and was joined by Carl Valentine and Jimmy Nicholl.

A much-needed 4-1 win against Forest featured a classic 'Thommo' hat-trick, Albion's first in the League for three years. We lost another fancy-dress game at Ipswich 2-0 before winning five of our next seven, one of them 'the gift that keeps on giving' in the shape of Coventry City (including Regis). We gave them a good spanking at The Hawthorns, with the 5-2 win based on five different scorers – Statham, Grealish, Thompson, Mackenzie and Valentine.

We started 1984 terribly, having to wait until 16 March for our first win, Nicky Cross and Gary Owen netting in a 2-0 victory over Nottingham Forest. In the poor run beforehand, we had two players sent off in the same match for the first time when Martyn Bennett and Jimmy Nicholl were dismissed in the 0-0 draw at Stoke.

Liverpool helped themselves to their usual three points by putting five past us at home, then Valentine achieved immortality three weeks later by scoring the winner against Villa. The euphoria didn't last. We lost the next two games, which resulted in a crowd of only 7,423 turning up for the 1-0 home win against Sunderland; the lowest Hawthorns attendance for twenty-eight years. The following Saturday we lost 4-1 at eventual champions Everton.

We finished the season well with a 5-1 mauling of West Ham in front of just 8,834, a 2-0 win at Watford and a 2-2 home draw with Arsenal. Twelfth place was considered a disappointment after so much was expected from the new management regime.

In the FA Cup, we embarrassed ourselves by losing 2-1 at lower-division Orient in the third round. The League Cup is usually a good opportunity for new grounds and the second round took us to Wigan Athletic on a grey September evening. In the bizarre former non-League Springfield Park, we were housed on a semi-grass bank which acted as an excuse for a terrace. The football matched the surroundings and we were lucky to come away with a goalless draw before we saw them off 3-1 in the second leg. Second Division Birmingham were our next opponents at St Andrew's, a hard-fought 0-0 draw bringing the tie back to The Hawthorns, where our class showed in a deserved 3-1 win.

Skin and I were working in Harlow come round five and the owner of our digs (a Spurs fan) joined us for our tie at Watford. We drove back to Essex embarrassed after the Hornets stung us 4-1.

12

Decline and Relegation

I had now purchased my first house; a semi-detached in Jill Avenue on the Pear Tree estate in Great Barr. It cost me £24,000 from an ex-girlfriend's parents. They were emigrating and left the house fully furnished, even leaving food in the kitchen. Young Gary Robson, already an Albion first-teamer, lived opposite and became a good friend who often sorted away match tickets for me. I once took him to open the newly-formed Gloucester Branch of the Albion Supporters Club as a favour for my good mate, John Bishop. On the way back, we were pulled over on the M5. I had sunk a couple of pints of Guinness and hadn't eaten, so was somewhat relieved to pass the breathalyser.

I had something to savour with my Sunday League team. After a tense finish to the season, Scott Arms FC pipped Small Heath Alliance (a team of Blues fans) to the title. We held a Champions' Ball at The King's to celebrate with everyone from the 'Scotts'. We also had a great night at the Tower Ballroom in Edgbaston when collecting our trophy. Some time back, when hiring a minibus to Ipswich, I had managed to read our captain Godfrey Maclean's driving licence, noting his middle name was Ivanhoe. I kept this quiet until the time came for him to go on stage and collect the trophy, then as he walked towards the front, we all started singing 'Ivanhoe, Ivanhoe, Ivanhoe.' He took the microphone and just said: 'Bastards!' During a very drunken evening, we somehow managed to break our shiny new trophy.

1985/86

I treated myself to a day out at Peterborough pre-season to tick off London Road and see what I thought could be a promising strike partnership; new signing Garth Crooks and Garry Thompson. They certainly looked good together in our easy 2-0 win. Obviously, Johnny Giles didn't see the same promise. Days later, Thommo moved to Sheffield Wednesday. Why? I have never understood Giles's thinking behind this, he was a class striker. In came Imre Varadi to replace him and Mickey Thomas arrived from Chelsea.

We kicked off our first division campaign with a 1-1 home draw against newcomers Oxford, 'Ollie' Varadi scoring a debut goal. This was as good as it got until October. We lost our next *nine* games, including 5-1 hammerings at Watford and Man United, and 3-0 thrashings against Chelsea, Villa and Coventry. Yes, even bloody Coventry. Things were getting desperate and only 7,720 turned up for our home defeat to Ipswich. It wasn't just Albion who were suffering. Football in general was in the doldrums and Leicester attracted a meagre 7,237 crowd to see our 2-2 draw there, Crooks bagging our goals. I was still there and always will be. I believe that in life you can change your wife, but you can *never* change your football team. You have to stick by them through thick and thin.

It all proved too much for Giles, who walked out for the second time. The reluctant Nobby Stiles took over on a temporary basis and had a good start. On 19 October, we finally secured our first win, 2-1 against Birmingham in a basement clash at The Hawthorns. Varadi and Carl Valentine hit our goals.

Normal service was soon restored and we went on to lose our next four League games, conceding four at Liverpool and West Ham. We played our first Hawthorns Sunday game in December, notching only our second victory of the season, 3-1 against Watford – a game featuring our new signing from Newcastle, George 'Rambo' Reilly.

There was a rare glimmer of hope at Villa over Christmas when Steve Hunt scored for us in a decent 1-1 draw, played out in front of a depressingly low derby crowd of 18,796. We certainly made our presence felt, packing out the Witton End terrace and seats.

An even lower attendance of 11,514 turned up at St Andrew's to see us complete a double over Blues, with Martyn Bennett grabbing the winner.

Just when I thought things couldn't get any worse, they did. Enter Ron Saunders. The dour former Villa and Blues boss was appointed manager on Valentine's Day. How romantic. He immediately delved into the transfer market, bringing in goalkeeper Stuart Naylor from Lincoln, followed by Craig Madden from Bury.

Saunders made an immediate impression – we lost 3-0 at Man United, followed by a 5-0 reverse at Spurs, his only win coming in a 1-0 over Southampton (only our fourth victory of the season). He brought in centre half Paul Dyson and gave local lad Carlton Palmer a run. Young David Burrows also made his debut.

We had reached rock bottom and the farcical sight of Nobby Stiles having to drive a minibus containing the first team to Luton on April Fool's Day made us a laughing stock. So much so that just 6,201 attended our penultimate home game, against Sheffield Wednesday (1-1). A massive West Ham following descended on The Hawthorns for our final game to see their team win 3-2 and clinch third spot in the League. Deservedly, we had finished bottom and were relegated with Birmingham and Ipswich.

This was Albion's worst ever League season. Our record included fewest wins (four), most defeats (twenty-six), fewest points (twenty-four) and just twenty-one home goals. Bottom from the third game onwards, in the end we were eighteen points from safety, having used a total of thirty-three players.

In the FA Cup, we were drawn at Sheffield Wednesday. There was snow all round when we set off, safe in the knowledge that Hillsborough had under-soil heating. Naively, we listened to cassette tapes on the journey, so didn't hear the news. As we drove into Owlerton, we commented on how quiet the roads were and there seemed to be an unusual number of parking places available. All was revealed when we saw the 'Game Off' signs on the stadium gates. Although the pitch was okay, the terraces were deemed unsafe.

We went to the nearest pub and Steve Fisher called his mom to get her to look on Teletext to see what games were still on. We ended up at The Shay, home of Halifax, to see their Fourth Division game against Crewe. At least we got to visit a new ground. When the Cup-tie got played, we drew 2-2 before losing the replay 2-1.

In the League Cup we beat Port Vale 1-0 in the second round, first leg, Gerry Armstrong scoring, before travelling to Vale Park, the so called 'Wembley of the North' (it was initially planned to be an 80,000-capacity stadium). Varadi got a brace in a 2-2 draw.

We met Coventry yet again in round three and, after drawing 0-0 at Highfield Road, they were obviously feeling sorry for us, allowing Albion to win 4-3 at The Hawthorns. Out of the hat next came Aston Villa and a battling 2-2 draw in Witton brought them back to God's country. Sadly, Steve Hunt's goal wasn't enough and we exited 2-1 on the night.

Later in the year, I got engaged to Elaine Whitehouse, a student nurse I'd met at a mutual friend's twenty-first. She was from Charlemont in West Bromwich and had two Albion-supporting brothers, twin Neil and the older Paul. Her dad and uncles were also good Baggie people. Her late grandad Edward Lane had actually been on Albion's books in the 1930s. Our engagement party was at The Kings in Hamstead (formerly the Golden Throstle Club). Half of Great Barr attended, including my good mates Dave Foxall and Chris O'Nyan who arrived dressed as Batman and Robin.

1986/87

Our two summer signings, Stewart Evans and Bobby Williamson were nothing to get excited about. Lots of players were released as Saunders set out to reduce the wage bill. I still travelled to Hull for our Division Two opener – a very dull game that we managed to lose 2-0. Not the best of starts. We did, however, win our first two home games, beating Sheffield United and Huddersfield 1-0 with goals from Evans and Bennett respectively. The attendance at both struggled to 9,000.

Two away draws followed and in our next home game, against Ipswich, we saw a young striker make his debut, looking good and scoring twice. His name: Steve Bull. We still lost 4-3, with John Deehan becoming the first former Albion player to return to The Hawthorns with a visiting club and score a hat-trick. Bull made two more appearances before being sold to Wolves for just £65,000. Saunders famously said he had a poor first touch. I wonder what happened to him?

Despite this blip, our early-season home form was quite good. We won seven out of our first ten, including 3-0 against Leeds. We also pulled off an amazing 3-0 victory at Sunderland, Martin Dickinson, Bobby Williamson and Garth Crooks scoring our goals. On a long drive down to Plymouth, Kenny Hazel joined our gallant car load. After our 1-0 defeat we got back to the car and there was no sign of Kenny, we gave it 30 minutes and he still hadn't turned up. No mobile phones back then so we gave it an hour before we set off back to the Midlands, leaving him behind. Apparently he had got drunk and completely forgot where we had parked. His brother picked him up the next day.

With Valley Parade closed following the 1985 fire, our game at Bradford City took place on a Friday at Odsal rugby stadium. On a ridiculously windy evening, we deservedly won 3-1 with new signing Robert Hopkins getting our third.

Darren Bradley, a future skipper, made his debut in January and, after a terrible run of one win in fifteen (4-1 win against Stoke), we signed Don Goodman from Bradford for £50,000. He managed two goals before the end of the season, one against his former club in our last home game. Steve Lynex, a West Bromwich lad, also came into the team.

There were very few highlights in the second half of the season and winning at Birmingham with a Reilly goal was as good as it got. From a personal point of view, I was happy to get to a few new grounds, including Plymouth, Huddersfield (Leeds Road) and Grimsby. I always enjoyed going to Blundell Park (actually in Cleethorpes) as you could always guarantee a good fish and chips lunch. Our performance there in March led to chants of 'Saunders out' for the first time. We played in the Full Members Cup for the first time in October and 957 hardy souls witnessed our defeat at Millwall, John Smith making his only appearance for us in this game.

In the FA Cup, we were drawn at First Division Swansea. I hadn't seen us at Vetch Field before, so Silve, Proto and myself headed off fully expecting to see us lose. We called in at one of my mom's old pen friends for lunch and her son was ribbing us by saying Swansea were going to win. To his surprise, we agreed. A 3-2 defeat followed.

In the League Cup second round, a 4-1 defeat at Derby, with Bull on target, made the second leg a non-event and we lost 5-1 on aggregate.

For the first time since 1910, Albion's average home League attendance dropped below 10,000 (to 9,280) as we finished a disappointing fifteenth.

The summer of 1987 was eventful for me. I married Elaine on 23 May at All Saints in West Bromwich, the same church where my parents were married thirty-six years earlier. Dave Loats (Skin) was my best man and the reception was at GKN Social Club in Bearwood. We couldn't afford a proper honeymoon, but managed a few days in a caravan at Porthmadog.

I had a joint stag night with Andy Sullivan and Volker Doefer, who were marrying the Loats sisters in a joint wedding the week before. Stag nights were simpler in those days; just a load of beer and a 'strippogram' in the Red Admiral.

1987/88

Oldham Athletic came to The Hawthorns for our first League game. Tony Morley was back, making his second debut in a desperate 0-0 draw. It got worse. We lost our next three games to leave us rock bottom.

Enough was enough and on 1 September, Saunders was fired. In came Ron Atkinson for his second spell, bringing with him his former assistant Colin Addison. We had high expectations, although a fair few fans hadn't forgiven Big Ron for ripping the guts out of the club when he left for Manchester United. This was reflected in the attendance for his first game back to see us beat Shrewsbury 2-1.

Let's compare the Albion line-up from Atkinson's previous home game with us in 1981 to the team he now inherited:

1981: Godden, Batson, Statham, Moses, Wile, Robertson, Robson, A. Brown, Regis, Owen, Barnes. Attendance: 17,218

1987: Naylor, Palmer, Cowdrill, Steggles, Dickinson, Kelly, G. Robson, Goodman, Williamson, Singleton, Morley. Attendance: 8,560

Not one survivor from our excellent team of just six years earlier and losing more than 50 per cent of our support. How could we possibly have sunk this low so quickly?

Atkinson must have realised the task he had taken on when Crystal Palace beat us 4-1 just three days later. As a quick fix, he brought in old warhorse Andy Gray on loan from Villa. He had an immediate effect by scoring two in our 3-3 draw at Plymouth, Palmer getting the other and George Reilly missing a re-taken penalty. Villa had now also joined us in Division Two and, amazingly, Gray was allowed to play against his 'parent' club in the derby at The Hawthorns. It didn't help us. We lost 2-0.

We did win three out of our next four to haul ourselves out of the bottom three, Bournemouth (3-0), Birmingham (3-1) and Reading (2-1 at Elm Park) being overcome. This latter day out was very pleasant, my good mate Chris Edwards travelling with me to an away game for the first time. Williamson and Gray bagged our goals.

Morley helped himself to a hat-trick in our 3-2 win against Huddersfield, which was followed by a 4-0 thrashing of Sheffield United. We had to wait eleven games before another win came along, 1-0 at home to Plymouth. During that depressing run, I had driven up to Barnsley for the first time, only to see another defeat (3-1).

Brian Talbot was signed to add much-needed experience to the team and centre-half Stacey North joined from Luton.

A pleasant afternoon in Shrewsbury was made even better when a Colin Anderson goal gave us a 1-0 win. Self-confessed 'Blue Nose' Robert Hopkins then scored our winner at St Andrew's against the team he supported. It gave us valuable breathing space. We didn't win any of our last six games and avoided relegation by one point. Twentieth in Division Two was our lowest ever League position.

It was the FA Cup that provided me with a new ground this time, Wimbledon. I went on the coach and we parked on the greyhound stadium just down the road which seemed to be a much better stadium than Plough Lane. In fairness, the 'Wombles' had been a non-League side just eleven years earlier, being elected to the League in 1977. Their rise had been meteoric and they were now sitting comfortably in the First Division. We were awful there and had no answer to the 'Crazy Gang's' route one football. We were well beaten 4-1 and I never visited Plough Lane again.

The League Cup paired us with Walsall and we managed to go out at the first hurdle in this competition, too. The Saddlers beat us 3-2 at The Hawthorns and held on 0-0 at their old Fellows Park ground to progress.

I was asked to be best man at Skin's wedding in Tynemouth, near Whitley Bay in Geordieland. He was marrying Lisa, who he'd met during the lads' holiday in Magaluf. My duties included organising the stag night. Nobody went away for the weekend in those days, so it was just a case of taking him for a pint, or sixteen. Yes, it was the West Bromwich High Street crawl, which consisted of: The Lewisham, Olde Wine Shoppe, Waggon and Horses, Prince of Wales, Fox and Dogs, Hornpipe, Great Western, Star and Garter, Sandwell, Anchor, New Hop Pole, Oddfellows Arms, Old Hop Pole, Wheatsheaf and The Marksman. We met at the Scotts for a quick pint beforehand, before around twenty of us headed into town for a further fifteen.

13

From Beachwear to the Arctic Circle

Pre-season in 1988, Albion announced they would be playing at Dumbarton in a re-staging of the 1888 game billed as the 'World Club Championship.' The original game had taken place at Hampden Park against a team called Renton (from Dumbarton). It pitched the Scottish Cup winners against the FA Cup winners and we let our country down by losing 4-1 in front of a crowd of 6,000 in the huge national stadium.

This time around, it provided a great opportunity to visit a new Scottish venue and do some ground-hopping en route. I cleared out the works van and arranged to pick everyone up at the ridiculously early hour of 3.00 a.m. on 6 August. Ten of us crammed in and I volunteered to drive. Fortunately, I had Neil Lewis in the front and his memories of games from the past made the journey fly by. I woke everyone up on the car park of Palmerston Park, home of Scottish team Queen of the South, at 6.00 a.m. Not surprisingly, it was locked at such an hour, but I was desperate to get a couple of photographs. As luck would have it, I had kept the ladders in the van, so I propped them up against the wall and gained a perfect view of the ground. Next stop was the port of Stranraer, a town closer to Belfast than Glasgow. Their Stair Park ground is in a public park, so we just walked in.

From Stranraer we headed up the coast to Ayr United's Somerset Park, onto St Mirren in Paisley and then Partick Thistle as we drove through Glasgow. We finally reached Dumbarton in time for a few beers in a pub near the ground, the delightfully named 'Boghead Park'. Dumbarton are the fourth oldest club in Scotland and their ground was the oldest in continuous use at the time of its closure in 2000.

Advertised as 'The Centenary Challenge Match of the World Club Championship', the match itself didn't exactly catch the public's imagination. Only 745 turned up with at least half the crowd made up of Albion fans.

Our performance was desperate and, at 1-1, we would have settled for a draw to share the trophy. Dumbarton couldn't believe how bad we were, so, just for a laugh, they sent on their middle-aged, balding physiotherapist for the last 15 minutes. Just when we thought it could not get any more embarrassing, he hit a screamer from 30 yards that flew past Stuart Naylor for the winner.

Before the game, a group of Albion fans were chatting to Dumbarton keeper Hughie Stevenson. They told him which way Brian Talbot placed his penalties. Lo and behold, we were awarded a penalty and Stevenson dived the way he had been advised – and duly saved Talbot's kick. He was chaired off at the end and gave the said fans the thumbs-up.

As our players trundled off, I shouted to Paul Dyson: 'That was awful Dyson.' He walked across to me, looked me directly in the face and just said: 'What was?' I was so tempted to punch him!

I really wanted to be able to brag that we were 'Champions of the World'. Instead, we had to watch Dumbarton deservedly collect the trophy, which I presume they will retain for another hundred years.

On the long journey home, we called in at Carlisle for a drink in the Brunton Park social club before finding a pub in Cumbria, where I left the lads to carry on drinking while I tried to get some sleep in the van. We finally got back to Great Barr at 1.00 a.m., some 22 hours after setting off.

1988/89

A pleasant Sunday morning drive to the outskirts of Milton Keynes pre-season for a 9-1 win at Wolverton Town and their delightful old ground. The club sadly folded in 1992.

My nephew Stuart was now a regular attendee of home and away games. My brother Alan would drop him off in Great Barr and I returned him to Hednesford afterwards. A trip to Leicester to start with and new signing John Paskin, a South African, was on target in our 1-1 draw. Another new face was former Arsenal defender Chris Whyte, who immediately added some strength to our defence.

We played Walsall on 17 September for the first time ever in a League match, drawing 0-0. Ron Atkinson walked out on us for the second time, this time taking Colin Addison with him to Atletico Madrid.

Our captain Brian Talbot appeared the obvious replacement and boosted his credentials when he masterminded our excellent 4-1 win at Birmingham. Hopkins (2), Gary Robson and Stewart Phillips shared our goals. It very nearly turned nasty during our celebratory drinks in The Spotted Dog in Digbeth afterwards, some Blues fans didn't take too kindly to our joyous behaviour.

This triggered a run of five wins on the bounce, including a great 1-0 win against Manchester City, a loan signing John Durnin scoring an excellent winner. Talbot was predictably appointed on 2 November, and ended this sequence of Albion managers: Don, Johnny, Ronnie, Ron, Ronnie, Ron, Johnny, Nobby, Ron and Ron. You couldn't make it up!

Don Goodman was benefitting from Stuart Pearson's specialist coaching and we started scoring lots of goals. Our 5-3 win against Crystal Palace included a Goodman hat-trick; he grabbed both against Hull in a 2-0 victory and another two in the 6-0 rout of Stoke, when Paskin (2) and Gary Robson (2) were also on target and a certain Tony Ford (later to become a Baggie) was sent off on the Potters' miserable Sunday afternoon.

Nephew Stuart and I re-visited Oldham on Boxing Day for the first time since that memorable day in 1976. Gary Robson sorted us for tickets and he also scored, along with Hopkins and Goodman, in a 3-1 win. We went top briefly following after our 1-1 draw at Chelsea on New Year's Eve and played like champions two days later in our 4-0 demolition of Shrewsbury. Goals came from Arthur Albiston, Goodman, Robson and an own goal from Shrewsbury's David Moyes (later to become Everton and Manchester United manager).

That turned out to be our last win for eight games. However, I managed to visit a new ground during this poor run, Valley Parade, to see us lose 2-0 to Bradford. We reignited our promotion push through a great 2-1 win over Leeds, with Goodman putting away two crackers.

On 11 March, on one of our regular trips to Oxford, we were drinking in our usual Headington pub The Bell. I had driven there in my Ford Capri, my pride and joy, and parked right outside. During a pleasant couple of beers, I received a tap on the shoulder to inform me someone had driven into my car. I ran outside to see this oik looking at his bumper touching my car. I confronted him and he said, 'What's the problem? I'm from London and this sort of thing happens all the time.' I couldn't help it. I said, 'Well, I'm from West Bromwich and *this* sort of thing happens all the time' and punched him in the face. He hit the ground and his girlfriend became hysterical, threatening to call the police. I had to leave pretty sharpish to avoid arrest.

There was a full house in April to see our first League meeting with Walsall at Fellows Park. It was strange to see young Saddlers' centre-back Dean Smith marking Goodman. I know Dean well as we used to live on the same estate. He was just starting out and I've followed his career as he has gone on to be Walsall's captain, play for Hereford, Orient, Sheffield Wednesday and Port Vale before moving into management with Walsall and more recently Brentford. He did a good job on this occasion, keeping our strike force at bay in another 0-0 draw, but Walsall still finished bottom.

Beachwear at Hull

We had a great day in Hull at our last game. I was now writing regularly for Albion fanzine *Fingerpost* (later to become *Grorty Dick*) and we put the word out to turn the day into a beachwear party. In our own minibus everyone made an effort, turning up in Hawaiian shirts, Bermuda shorts and flip-flops. We even had lilos, beach balls and buckets and spades.

Our stop-offs, including a quick visit to North Ferriby United, caused amusement for unsuspecting locals. When we arrived at Boothferry Park, it was obvious we were not alone; most of Albion's thousand or so fans were similarly dressed. Some even had surfboards. There was also 'The Cornflake Crew', who would take boxes of cereal to away games and throw the contents in the air as the teams came out. On this occasion, the police wouldn't allow cereal in the ground and we were faced with the surreal sight of loads of full cornflake boxes piled up outside the turnstiles.

The game passed us by as we partied on the terraces. Kevin Bartlett scored our winner and we stayed in at the end, demanding an appearance from the players. A bemused Brian Talbot finally led them out of the dressing room and across the pitch. Colin West threw his boots into the crowd as the rest looked on, totally baffled.

Despite lots of end-of-season parties since, this remains my favourite. Nothing at stake, a lovely warm day and sheer lunacy. Brilliant.

On the way home, we turned off the M1 just as it joined the A38 and stumbled upon a little gem of a pub, the Hunter's Arms in Kilburn, Derbyshire. We all piled in and the locals were wary to start with, but we soon won them over and stayed until closing time. We had a fantastic evening, making songs up about all the regulars and they loved it. There was Hippy Man, Little Hippy, Horace, Nigel Clough (a lookalike) and Billy Lloyd on the mouth organ. Our travelling party on that first Hunter's Arms visit included John Bishop, Andy Miller, Dubsey, Chris Edwards, Martin Davies (Davel) and his brother Ian. We said our goodbyes and promised to return. We had won only two of our last nine League games and finished a disappointing ninth.

It was the FA Cup that derailed our season. We should have beaten Everton in the third round in a Hawthorns thriller, the impressive Colin 'Zico' Anderson scoring in a 1-1 draw. Unfortunately, he played too well and Everton's defenders made sure he wouldn't be playing in the replay. He was stretchered off in front a crowd of 31,186. Sadly, without 'Zico', we lost 1-0 and never really recovered.

We had a shocker in the League Cup, losing 3-0 at home to Peterborough in front of only 4,264. We nearly turned it round in the second leg, winning 2-0 at London Road.

Albion's Irish tour of Scandinavia

When Albion announced they were to tour Scandinavia pre-season, it sounded like an exciting trip. I had never been to any of those countries, so when games were announced in Finland and Sweden, the maps were out and we soon rounded up a car-full. The famous five were Tony Jones, Neil Whitehouse, Paul Dubberley (Dubsey), Michael Silvester (Silve) and myself. Flights were booked and car hire arranged. The plan was to fly into Gothenburg, collect a car, drive up through Sweden into Finland to Albion's first game against Kemin Palloseura (KePS), then on to the second game, also in Finland, against Rovaniemen Palloseura (RoPS). Then we would travel into the Arctic Circle before driving back into Sweden for the game against Kiruna FF, down the coast through Norway before flying home from Oslo.

We were all eagerly looking forward to our road trip until, in typical Albion fashion, things took a turn for the worse. I was working in London and, when I called my wife from a phone box, she said, 'I think I should read this out to you from the back of the *Express & Star*.' The article read: 'Albion's games in Finland have been cancelled. Instead, Brian Talbot's men will be going to Ireland.' What?

I contacted the travel company, who wouldn't grant a refund for the 'Apex' flight on the grounds of a football club changing their mind. So, after a few more calls, we decided to go ahead with the trip. Dubsey issued us with 'West Bromwich Albion – Irish tour of Scandinavia 1989' t-shirts. We agreed to adopt a rotating driver's policy and drive through a couple of the nights. Our first stop was the largest stadium in Sweden, the 54,000-capacity Nya Ullevi, home of IFK Göteborg. After a quick photo shoot, we headed north on the long straight roads, calling at Lulea football club, where we had to get a puncture repaired.

After driving around the clock, we crossed into Finland and soon entered the country's sparsely populated northernmost region. The first person we saw was a man dressed as Father Christmas, stood at the roadside ringing a bell, calling us into 'Santa's Village'. As we were in Lapland, we expected to encounter lots of Santas but he was the only one. Maybe he was the real thing!

At one stage, we abandoned the car in the middle of the road after spotting an elk. We left the doors wide open and chased the poor animal just to get some photos.

We headed for the town of Kemi, where we should have been playing our first game. We turned up at the Sauvosaaren Ureilupuisto Stadium, entered the offices and, just for a laugh, pretended we thought the game was still on. We asked for five tickets for 'tonight's game'. The looks on the faces of the staff were a picture and they seemed frightened of us as they tried to explain. They pleaded with us to not cause trouble!

We tried to locate a bar in the town for a well-earned drink. The only sign of life was a tea-dance in some sort of community centre. It had a bar, so we paid and mingled with the pensioners. We drew straws to see which of us should dance with an old Finnish lady. Tony and myself drew the short straws and were soon on the floor, being taught some strange Finnish jig. Before leaving the quaint little town, I sent a postcard to Brian Talbot, saying: 'Wish you were here'.

It was a short drive further north to Rovaniemi, a city just south of the Arctic Circle. We stopped off at RoPS' ground, where the 2,800-capacity Kestusketta Stadium was pretty much deserted. Ex-Albion captain Graham Williams had once managed there.

As we passed the sign announcing we were now in the Arctic Circle, the sun was shining, so we stopped for a photo – in our shorts and t-shirts. We agreed a proper bed was called for as the previous night had been spent in the car, so we booked in at a log-cabin camp site by a massive lake. It was ideal. We spent a lovely summer's evening drinking very expensive beers sat outside a bar. It was nearly midnight and still broad daylight. We asked the waitress: 'When does it get dark?' Expecting her to say 'in another hour or so', she actually replied, 'Not until September.' This was the land of the midnight sun and Silve celebrated by stripping off and jumping into the lake.

Next morning, after raw herrings for breakfast, we drove west and back into Sweden. Our next port of call should have been the game against Kiruna. Once we found the small stadium, it became obvious why the game had been cancelled – the pitch had been dug up and was half-way through being replaced with AstroTurf. Another postcard was despatched to Brian Talbot.

We headed south and crossed into Norway. The roads there were completely different from the straight carriageways in Sweden. They were very winding, weaving their way around the fjords; it seemed take ages to drive even short distances. We pulled over just south of Narvik and booked into a wooden lodge for the night. Conveniently, there was a bar next door so we were soon knocking back a few beers. To our horror, it worked out at £5 a pint – and this was 1989. We agreed to have a maximum of five, just buying one round each. We got talking to one of the locals who spoke good English; the funny thing was that he had been taught by his English uncle, who originated from Bilston. Listening to his bizarre Norwegian/Black Country accent kept us amused.

Next morning, we came to an estuary at which we had to wait to board a ferry. We continued driving all day and our plan was to continue through the night. Our theory was that as soon as the driver was tired, one of us would always be okay to take over. We failed miserably, next morning the car was parked and everyone was fast asleep.

We travelled past a town called Hell and eventually made the outskirts of Oslo. We called in at the Arsenal Stadium, home to Lillestrøm FC, situated in an area east of the capital called Skedsmo. Next stop was Norway's best-known sports venue, the Bislett Stadion. More than fifty track and field world records have been set there. Unfortunately, this lovely old stadium was demolished in 2004 and rebuilt the following year. I'm glad we visited when we did.

We had a few hours to kill before our flight, so we headed to the city for a stroll in the sun. While looking for a parking place, we drove past a group of people outside a hotel. I commented that one of them looked like Pele.

We had a great afternoon soaking up the atmosphere in the beautiful city of Oslo, then after checking in at the airport, I noticed the front page of a local newspaper and there on the front was Pele. Yes, it really had been him. I really wish that we had pulled over and met the greatest footballer the world has ever seen.

It had been a great trip, even without the Albion. In fact, we had got our timings horribly wrong due to Norway's winding roads. We had covered 2,120 miles in just four days and if Albion had played against Kiruna at the time advised, we would have missed our flight by 13 hours!

1989/90

Back home, I did manage to get to one pre-season game, at Newcastle Town in the Potteries, to see our 8-0 demolition job. The new season was looking promising but started with a nightmare 3-0 home defeat against Sheffield United. I distinctly remember the luminous yellow shirts on their players and fans. Former Shrewsbury midfielder Bernard McNally and full back Steve Parkin made their debuts. We had to wait five games for our first victory, 3-1 at Leicester. Another six points were added in tremendous wins at West Ham and Watford, then, typical Albion, we collapsed at home to Wolves with our nemesis Steve Bull coming back to haunt us. This affected our form for the next few games and we were hammered 5-1 at home to Newcastle.

We became incredibly inconsistent. After going four games without a win, we destroyed Barnsley 7-0 at The Hawthorns. Sadly, only 9,317 were there to see a Don Goodman hat-trick, a Kevin Bartlett double, and goals from Tony Ford and Bernard McNally. In this game, Martyn Bennett made his 218th and last appearance in an Albion career spanning thirteen years before moving to Worcester City.

After each home game, I looked forward to the Sports Argus being delivered to the local newsagent. I would always be eagerly waiting, with several other fans, for the 'pink' to be dropped off, so I could digest all the other results and read all about the Baggies.

After beating Leeds 2-1, we prepared for a minibus trip to Sheffield United on 2 December. We had promised to spend the evening with our friends at The Hunters Arms, so, in tribute to Billy Lloyd, we stipulated that everyone had to wear a flat cap and carry a mouth organ. After a couple of pub stops, we arrived at Bramall Lane and paid an old dear to let us park on her drive. The South Yorkshire constabulary weren't impressed with our 'theme'. Once in the ground, we started playing the organs and immediately became a target for the police. Foolishly, we decided to play a tune resembling a police car siren. This really antagonised them and they just came wading into us. 'Little' Steve got arrested. Despite our appeals, he was carted off and we were warned we would be joining him if we said any more. What should have been a fun afternoon was completely ruined by the Old Bill. Oh, and the Albion lost 3-1.

The police watched us all the way back to our minibus and our first stop was the station to collect Little Steve. Then it was off to Kilburn, acquiring a Christmas tree to take as a present on the way. Our hosts had organised food for us and the regulars were out in force to welcome us back. Another great evening was had and Billy Lloyd loved our tribute. We hid the mouth organs until he started to play, then we all pulled them out, put our flat caps on and joined in.

We had to wait until the new year for our next success, a 3-0 win against Brighton, with West, Robson and Bartlett on target. We made our regular trip to Oxford on 10 February to witness Craig Shakespeare scoring a debut winner after signing for £275,000 from Sheffield Wednesday. With the impending FA Cup game against Aston Villa, I had a load of t-shirts printed with the slogan 'Claret and blue makes me spew'. Needless to say, I sold out in the pub and on the Manor Ground terraces before the game.

Gary Bannister joined us from Coventry to boost our strike force, but it took him nine games to break his duck – in a terrific win against Brighton at the Goldstone Ground. In the meantime, local boy and Albion fan Gary Hackett managed a couple of goals in wins against Watford and Hull.

I went to Walsall to see us play in Paul Hart's testimonial, mainly to say goodbye to a good traditional ground. It was the last game played at Fellows Park and ended 1-1. I'm not a big fan of the new B&Q-type of modern stadium. Give me the old mis-matched stands and windswept terraces any day.

Beachwear at Barnsley

After the success at Hull the year before, the 'Beachwear at Barnsley' campaign gathered momentum in the build-up to our last away game. We had now started to drink in the Woodman pub before home games and soon assembled 'The Woodman Beach Crew' to fill a large minibus. We stopped off at our regular haunt, The Travellers Rest, and the landlord kindly laid on some food for us.

It was an important game, as we were hovering dangerously close to the relegation trap-door. Albion fans packed the vast terraces at the away end, with the majority observing the dress code. There were also hundreds of inflatables, including a couple of blow-up dolls, to welcome the team on to the pitch. Following an entertaining 2-2 draw, Albion scraped clear and we again celebrated with the players at the end.

We had pre-arranged yet another evening at the Hunters. This time they had organised a barbecue and a few locals joined in with the beachwear theme. In fact, we had picked up 'Nigel Clough' earlier in the day and taken him to Barnsley. He had a great day. This time we had legendary Welsh Baggie Colin Wood with us. He took centre stage during the evening, 'playing' the bagpipes on an upturned bar stool.

In the FA Cup, we beat Division One teams in the third and fourth rounds. A good performance saw off Wimbledon 2-0 and Charlton Athletic 1-0 in atrocious Hawthorns conditions. Tony Ford's shot hit a puddle in the six-yard box and squirmed over the line. Then, along came the bloody Villa and spoiled our party with a 2-0 win here in the fifth round.

I was now a contracts manager for Allan H. Williams, looking after large façade developments all over the country. During the latter half of 1989, I was managing the CBX contract in Milton Keynes. As Albion had lost the home leg of their second round League Cup tie against Bradford 3-1, the return appeared to be a non-event. Nevertheless, two of our installers, Silve and Neil Ingram, joined me on the journey to Valley Parade. We left Milton Keynes at 4.00 p.m. and made it in plenty of time. Amazingly, we led 3-1 on the night to take the game into extra-time. Our brilliantly named striker John Thomas (Nobby to his mates!) had the best game of his Albion career and hit a hat-trick to add to goals by Brian Talbot and Chris Whyte to win it 5-3. That made it 6-6 on aggregate and we went through on the away goals rule. We knew it was going to be a late night but extra-time meant we got back to Milton Keynes around 1.30 a.m. Not that we were bothered. We were singing: 'Oh Johnny T., from Wednesbury, oh Johnny T. from Wednesbury. He's got a stall on the market, oh Johnny T. from Wednesbury' to the tune of 'When the Saints go marching in' for the whole of the return journey. A classic Albion song if ever there was one. Thomas *did* once have a market stall there, apparently.

We were sent to Newcastle in round four and, after the Bradford success, we had to go. St James' Park was a new ground for me and another one of our installers, Jeff Holmes (a Geordie), joined us this time. After a good run up the M1 and A1 and a couple of city-centre beers, Newcastle exploded the myth that they always fill their ground. Only 22,638 turned up to see the mighty Albion. Chrissy White added to his goal in the previous round and we hung on for a well-deserved victory. Another long journey back to Milton Keynes, but the win certainly helped the time go by.

In round five, we were again drawn against a team from up the M1. The journey had to be done again, so another full car set off from MK. Unfortunately, First Division Derby stopped our run by beating us 2-0 at the Baseball Ground.

Over the season, Talbot used four different goalkeepers – Paul Bradshaw, Andy Marriott, Stuart Naylor and Gavin Ward. Striker Don Goodman became the first Albion player since Tony Brown in 1970/71 to top twenty League goals in a season.

14

Through the Barricades

After missing out on Albion's Irish tour the previous year, I just knew I had to go when a return visit was announced in 1990. For a start, I had never been to Ireland, so it provided the perfect opportunity to visit a new country. There was also a twist. Three of the matches were to take place over the border in Northern Ireland. I missed the first two games; a 0-0 draw with Glentoran and a 4-0 victory against Ards. Newry Town on 9 August was to be my first match.

We decided it was wise to leave my car at Holyhead and hire one with Irish number plates once we disembarked in Dun Loaghaire. Joining me on the trip were Elaine, her twin brother Neil Whitehouse, Silve and Neil Grainger.

We managed a few beers in Holyhead before boarding the ferry to the Republic. Once our hire car was collected, we headed north towards the border. The 'troubles' were still simmering at the time and Newry was commonly known as 'bandit country', so we thought it better to book a hotel just south of the border in Dundalk.

Once accommodation was sorted, we drove the short distance to the border. In stark contrast to the south, the atmosphere was fairly intimidating. We were questioned at the check point by armed police, who were utterly confused when we explained we were heading to Newry for a football friendly. We had to manoeuvre the car round a burned-out bus that was lying on its side, almost completely blocking the road. Helicopters hovered above us and police lined the road. Welcome to Northern Ireland!

We soon located The Showgrounds, home of Newry Town. It was grim with barbed wire preventing any access, so we ventured into the town and had an obligatory Guinness or two in a bar before kick-off. Once entering the ramshackle ground, we were faced with an armoured patrol vehicle inside the turnstiles and police wearing bullet-proof vests, carrying rifles and patrolling the pitch. There was a tiny clubhouse behind the one goal and the Newry fans couldn't have been more welcoming. Legendary Albion fan the late Richie Brentnall, was already perched at the bar, enjoying the hospitality. By kick-off, we were feeling guilty about booking digs south of the border as the Newry supporters wanted us to stay on and join them for a proper night out.

A meagre crowd of 1,650, with just a couple of dozen from England, assembled to see the in-form Gary Bannister (2) and Don Goodman find the net in our 3-1 victory. (Newry would change their name from Town to City in 2013.)

We wished our new friends all the best for the season and headed back towards the border. We were running out of valuable drinking time, so parked up at the hotel in Dundalk and dashed across the road to the nearest pub. It was now 10.45 p.m., so we thought it best to double up the round of Guinness. We needn't have worried. On asking the landlady what time the pub closed, she replied 'Oh, we lock the doors at 11.00 p.m. ... but we lock you inside, not out.' Again, the locals were unbelievably friendly and we finally left around 3.00 a.m.

Next morning, we headed to Dublin ready for the game against Shelbourne. Ireland is a lovely country and it was a pleasant drive down with stops at Dundalk FC, Drogheda United and Bohemians. We also paused to visit the monument erected to commemorate the introduction of the potato to Ireland by Sir Walter Raleigh.

We stayed overnight in a small Dublin suburb, which just happened to have eight pubs dotted along the high street. It was an obvious challenge and the Guinness was soon flowing as we worked our way along. The Irish hospitality was again evident and, in one establishment near the end of the crawl, we said goodbye to the regulars and left. On walking down the street, we spotted another pub to our left, entered the lounge and ordered a round. We glanced across the bar to see the locals we had just said goodbye to. We had re-entered the same pub, albeit in a different room! I blame the Guinness.

Match day, and nursing yet another hangover, we headed into the Irish capital to meet up with the other half of our travelling party – those who had just come over for the Shelbourne game. We found our pre-arranged meeting point and already well into the Guinness were Bill Ahearne, Andy Miller, Chris Edwards and Paul Dubberley, all good friends who I still attend games with. It was obviously going to get messy, so the car was abandoned and the session commenced, rudely interrupted by the match! A crowd of 3,065 with a sprinkling of noisy, drunken Baggies assembled at Tolka Park, a decent ground shared between various Dublin-based clubs. Don Goodman scored again and also missed two sitters while Padraig Dully responded for Shelbourne in this bore draw. On leaving the ground, Andy Miller was interviewed for the local newspaper. His 'I've just bought a season ticket to watch that rubbish' comment made the back page in the next morning's match report.

The game was soon forgotten as we headed for Bill's Uncle Dave's social club, where a good sing-song rounded off a memorable few days.

15

Down, Down with Barmy Bobby

In the summer of 1990, my holiday was spent in Acapulco. This is where I met Steve Conabeer and his then-fiancée Sharon. The Italian World Cup was on, so our conversation by the pool soon turned to England's chances. He explained that he was from Exeter and, when I asked him who he supported, I was pleased that he replied, 'Exeter of course.' If he had been a Man United fan, I don't believe our friendship would have lasted beyond the holiday. As it turned out, we are still good mates, have travelled the world together and he was best man at my marriage to Ruth in 2005.

Back to Acapulco, where we agreed to watch England's games together in a local bar. We also realised we shared a love of football grounds – and a desire to visit the famous Aztec Stadium in Mexico City. After a discussion with the girls, we agreed to fly into the capital and see the Estadio Azteca. A couple of days later, we left them water-skiing and touched down before catching an underground train and public bus, eventually locating the suburb of Santa Ursula and the magnificent 104,000-capacity arena, the venue for the 1970 World Cup final. The security guard kindly allowed us in and I couldn't help but conjure up images of that brilliant Brazil team; Pele, Jarzinho, Tostao, Rivelino and Carlos Alberto. It was now the home ground of Club America and had staged the 1986 World Cup final plus the famous England v Argentina and Maradona's famous 'hand of God' quarter-final.

We even managed to visit a second impressive stadium, the 68,000-capacity Estadio Universidad Nacional Autonoma de Mexico. This was also used for the 1968 Olympics and in the 1986 World Cup. It is the home of Pumas Dorados as well as Club Universidad.

As a base for our West Bromwich-based draughtsman, my company had rented a couple of Rainbow Stand executive boxes as drawing offices during the week. As I was the token Albion fan at the Coventry-based firm, I was given EIGHT executive box tickets for every home game. All we had to do was move the drawing boards and put them back at the end. I was the most popular bloke in the Woodman pub.

1990/91

I don't know what possessed me but I travelled down to Swansea in midweek for a pre-season friendly. Only a handful of Baggies were present in the away end at the old Vetch Field so Swansea didn't open the food hut. At half-time, following negotiations with the police, we were allowed out of the ground to a fish and chip shop a couple of streets away. This unexpected meal was the highlight of the game as we sat on the terraces tucking-in, watching Albion get a 5-0 thrashing with Don Goodman getting sent off. With ten minutes to go, we had had enough and with the gates firmly locked and no stewards on duty we walked around the edge of the pitch giving manager Brian Talbot some abuse as we passed the dug-outs.

The new season began with a drive to the coast to see Gary Strodder make his debut in a 1-1 draw with Portsmouth. Our next trip, to Oxford, secured three points, with Colin West (2) and Gary Bannister scoring in front of a huge Baggies following at the old Manor Ground.

Albion were paired with Bristol City in the League Cup, we got knocked out at Ashton Gate, losing 1-0 on the night after extra-time following a 2-2 Hawthorns draw. I managed to catch up with Steve and Sharon again early in the season. They joined me for the midweek game at Plymouth on 2 October. I was embarrassed by our pathetic performance. We just went through the motions in a 2-0 defeat that I most remember for the fact we played in red and black hoops.

We were winning around one game in five and were soon hovering around the relegation zone, with the unthinkable possibility of dropping to the Third Division. Brian Talbot's last throw of the dice was to recruit old warhorse Graham Roberts from Spurs. We actually won on his debut, 2-0 at home to Blackburn. Sadly, it was a false dawn and it was another six games before we won again. Roberts did put away a couple of penalties in this run.

I had managed to get four tickets for the New Year's Day 'Old Firm' game between Rangers and Celtic at Ibrox, so Dave Foxall, Tony Jones, Michael Silvester (Silve) and I set off for Glasgow nice and early. Once parked up, we got comfortable in a pub to enjoy a few beers. For obvious reasons, we kept our heads down, particularly as it filled up, then it was Silve's round and suddenly a loud voice with a broad Brummie accent boomed across the packed room: 'Oi Tone, do you want ice in your whisky?' Talk about remaining inconspicuous – you could have heard a pin drop! Fortunately, it was a Rangers pub and they have quite a large English following. I dread to think what would have happened if we had been in a Celtic pub.

I was fascinated to see posters of a young Prince William on sale outside the ground. A Rangers fan explained that, when he grows up, he will become King Billy and a reincarnation of William of Orange. I don't believe football and politics/religion should ever mix, but try telling that to those fans.

We took our place on the terrace that runs along the front of the classic old Archibald Leitch designed stand. It had been twenty years since the Ibrox disaster and, before kick-off, a minute's silence was held to remember the sixty-five people who died. Throughout it, the Celtic fans whistled and booed. Rangers supporters' remained silent until the minute was up, then charged towards the Celtic fans along the terrace. We were nearly knocked over in the stampede.

The whole afternoon was fascinating; observing the complete contrast between the two sets of fans as Rangers won 2-0; another tick on my bucket list.

Woking

5 January 1991 is a day etched in Albion folklore for all the wrong reasons. We played non-league Woking in the FA Cup third round and 14,518 turned up to see an accident that was waiting to happen. We had won only once in nine games, and were without long-term injury victim Don Goodman. The late Mel Rees made his debut in our goal.

Colin West nodded us in front in the first half and I breathed a sigh of relief. However, within 20 minutes of the restart, the Isthmian League side had not only equalised but taken the lead. We were stunned. The first chants of 'Talbot out' were heard, then things got even worse. Ten minutes from time, the never-to-be-forgotten Tim Buzaglo completed his hat-trick. Woking's travelling thousands went crazy on the Smethwick terraces while the odd Albion fan would run on to the pitch in mini-protest. Incredibly, Woking scored again and everything changed. Darren Bradley's injury-time consolation was greeted with boos. We had lost 4-2 to a team of part-timers.

I've never witnessed such a strange sight at a match. Woking's players were rightly celebrating with their supporters in the Smethwick End, when Brummie Road emptied and Albion fans stormed on the pitch and headed for the far end. The Woking contingent must have feared the worst. Instead, our fans applauded them, then lifted Buzaglo and chaired him round the pitch. It was our way of protesting about the demise of our once great club.

My anger was immense, but, for some reason, I stood there, proud of the way our fans had reacted. Would the same thing have happened at Molineux or Villa Park? I very much doubt it. After applauding Woking off the pitch and their fans out of the ground, it was round to the directors' entrance to vent our spleen. 'Talbot out, Talbot out' we chanted.

Two days later, he was sacked, with Stuart Pearson installed as caretaker. 'Pancho' immediately introduced more attack-minded football and we notched up some successes, including an excellent 3-0 win at Blackburn. I always enjoyed visiting Ewood Park, especially the friendly Fernhurst pub just down the road and a good meat pie with gravy in the covered away end.

All sorts of rumours circulated about who our next manager would be. One name kept cropping up, ex-Albion forward Bobby Gould, and he was certainly one we didn't want. His teams played horrible route-one football and he had never been very popular here as a player. Just to make sure the board were not considering such an appointment, we sang 'We don't want you, Bobby Gould' at the next few games. So what did chairman John Silk and his buffoons do? They appointed him!

After a honeymoon period 0-0 home draw to West Ham, Gould soon got the gist of things and presided over six straight defeats, in which we scored only twice. I was one of the sad masochists at Brighton on a Wednesday night in March to see our shambles of a team lose 2-0. Our forward line consisted of Les Palmer and Adrian Foster.

Early in his spell, Gould was guest of the now thriving Gloucester branch of Albion fans. I enjoyed the company of John Bishop, Dave Leary and the rest of the gang at the Cheese Rollers pub so I ventured down. I must admit Gouldy came across very well and almost won me over.

On transfer deadline day, he signed three players. His record for discovering talent from the lower divisions was admirable so I was prepared to be impressed. We headed down to Selhurst Park, where homeless Charlton were lodging, to see Paul Williams, Winston White and Kwame Ampadu make their debuts. They made no difference whatsoever. We clocked up another defeat, this time 2-0.

Albion's next result came as a bit of a shock. We somehow beat Swindon 2-0, thanks to a Roberts penalty and a rare strike from full back Steve Parkin. Five days later, I caught the train to Wolverhampton, hoping for a second successive win. Molineux seemed very strange. The 'Tatters' had built the massive John Ireland Stand and moved the pitch across to suit. The Waterloo Road and North Bank stands were deemed unsafe and therefore closed, leaving just the South Bank terrace as the only other open area of the ground. True to form, we were pelted with the usual missiles throughout the 2-2 draw, there were more fun and games as we walked back to the station.

We thought we had secured Second Division safety in our six-pointer at home to Leicester when Goodman scored our winner in the 93rd minute. There were just five games to go. Surely we would be okay? Half-decent draws followed at Barnsley and Watford, then a crazy game at home to Port Vale. Paul Williams and Don Goodman both missed penalties and we also had a perfectly good goal disallowed. Another 1-1 draw. John Silk, under growing pressure from fans, famously stated: 'I didn't miss the penalties against Port Vale.'

It was certainly 'squeaky bum' time. Our last home game was against Newcastle and their new manager Ossie Ardiles. A young Andy Hunt faced us and a very nervy Albion performance at least salvaged a much-needed point.

Togas at Rovers

It had gone down to the wire. We had to win away at Bristol Rovers to stay up; any other result and we would be relying on Leicester losing at home to Oxford. Rovers were temporarily playing at Twerton Park in the Roman city of Bath; a great excuse for an end-of-season party. I must admit to coming up with the 'Togas at Rovers' theme. I know some fans have since said they hated the idea but the majority jumped on board and things could have been oh so different if we had won (Portsmouth 1994 for instance).

We hired our own coach and although the 1,200 tickets were like gold dust, all fifty of us obtained one. Everyone on board had to wear togas or variations on the Roman theme, such as a gladiator outfits. After a nice early start, picking up Colin Wood and John Bishop at various junctions on the M5, we arrived in Bath at 11.00 a.m. for essential liquid refreshments. As we walked from pub to pub, we attracted interest from droves of tourists and we had to stop to pose for photographs every few yards.

We walked the mile or so to Twerton Park and then Dubsey announced he had lost his moneybelt, which included his match ticket. One of our contingent said he had seen a 'moneybelt looking thing' in the central reservation back towards the city centre. Dubsey hotfooted it back and, incredibly, discovered it was still there.

Outside the ramshackle non-League ground, we bumped into Jeff Astle in the car park. The King was now a supporter and had obtained a ticket to stand with the rest of us. He happily posed for photographs while we shouted: 'All hail The King.'

Inside the fenced-in away enclosure, it became obvious there were Albion fans all round the ground, making up a large portion of the crowd of 7,596. Fights broke out all over the place and small groups of Baggies kept spilling on to the pitch and making their way to the away end. A temporary seated stand had been erected to our right and we could see hundreds of Albion fans on the grass bank partially overlooking the ground and even on the roof of one of the stands.

When the team was announced, we were horrified. Gould opted to play the useless Paul Williams up front with West, leaving leading scorer Bannister on the bench. Young striker Foster also started – in midfield. It was as though he was torturing us on purpose. He even threw in another youngster, Darren Rogers, at the back.

We thought the Roman gods were on our side when Rovers' star man, Carl Saunders, was sent off after just three minutes. However, Rovers' players and fans seemed more determined than ever following the dismissal. News filtered through that Leicester were beating Oxford, so we had to win.

We missed chance after chance and then, with 18 minutes remaining, our world fell apart when Rovers went ahead. Bannister was sent on for a frantic last few minutes and Ampadu's shot somehow found its way into the net, but it was too little, too late. The referee blew for full time and we waited for the Leicester result. There was brief elation when news came through that Oxford had scored, but it was disallowed and we were down. We just stood there, totally dumbfounded. A pile of togas resembled a funeral pyre and the air was filled with venom. Two of our party, Dubsey and Kevin Secker, headed for the dressing room. Much to their surprise, the door was open and they were suddenly faced with the players. Gould quickly showed them the door, saying: 'Get out lads, you know how the team must feel.' What a cheek. How the team must feel? What about how we felt? Dubsey and Secker were lost for words and, in a state of shock, left them to it.

Our coach was eerily quiet on the journey back as reality sunk in. We stopped at The Greyhound near Gloucester to drown our sorrows. We bumped into a bus load of Stoke fans. 'Welcome to the Third Division,' they said. Indeed.

16

Questioning My Own Sanity

Strangely, I was eagerly anticipating the new away trips, numerous different pubs to visit and fresh acquaintances to be made. For me, this is what football is all about. Not just the 90 minutes, which are often forgettable, but the whole occasion. I travel with a great bunch of mates who only usually get together on match days. We have some super days out, win, lose or draw.

1991/92

When the fixtures came out, I was really pleased we were playing Exeter at home in our first game; a great excuse to see our good friends Sharon and Steve again, both staunch Grecians.

Before that, I went to see some pre-season action, first at a ridiculously overcrowded Round Oak ground for our game against Dudley Town, then 3,000 Baggies took over The Grove, home of Halesowen Town.

A group of us had decided to get season tickets in the Rainbow Stand paddock, providing us with the option to sit on the upper deck during bad weather. Noone ever checked our tickets and there were always plenty of empty seats.

On a lovely, warm summer's day, Sharon and Steve came to stay and we headed off to The Hawthorns early for drinks in the Woodman beer garden. A crowd of 12,892 turned up for our first ever Division Three fixture, including a fair few from Devon. 'You're not famous, you're not famous, you're not famous anymore' was the chant that they teased us with before kick-off. It was certainly a reality check.

Goalkeeper Alan Miller made his debut following his loan move from Arsenal and, at half-time, we were 2-1 up, thanks to two penalties coolly put away by Craig Shakespeare. We ran out clear 6-3 winners. Maybe this division wasn't so bad after all?

Our first game on the road was against Darlington at Feethams, a ground actually owned by the local cricket club. The natives were not welcoming in the town centre pubs and, although our group were fine, we heard numerous stories of fights involving bricks and bottles. We had to walk round the cricket pitch boundary to enter the ground and it became evident that the packed-out away section was the only part of the ground with a fence.

This was the first time Albion wore red and yellow stripes. I thought we looked ridiculous, just like watching Melchester Rovers except we didn't have Roy Race to score a hat-trick every week. Barmy Bobby Gould claimed the credit for this, publicly stating: 'Red is a dominant and intimidatory colour.' Yeah, whatever Bobby. Young Gary Piggott, a signing from Dudley, made his debut and a late winner from Don Goodman gave us the three points. Not a bad start.

The next home game, against Wigan, was drawn. Our 0-0 at Fulham was a gutless display that consisted of us hoofing the ball down the pitch. As the players headed for the dressing room in Fulham's famous cottage, Albion fans let rip with the chant 'We want football', directed at Gould. He looked shell-shocked and, trying to deflect blame, ordered his players over to thank us. It backfired. The abuse continued. The tide was turning.

Two thousand of us still travelled to Bolton the following Saturday to share the away end at Burnden Park with a new supermarket that had been constructed on half of the terrace. Our forward line of Piggott and Foster never stood a chance and we were deservedly beaten 3-0. To make matters worse, we were held on the car park for over half an hour after the game. Little did we know that, while we were sitting there, Gould had invited the press into the dressing room and had again deflected the blame elsewhere. Crazy.

We briefly kicked into life. We won our next four games and even our poor excuse for a centre forward, Paul Williams, helped himself to some goals, scoring the winner against his old club Stockport, then another in the 4-0 hammering of Peterborough. Gary Robson (2) and 5-foot 3-inch local lad Stewart Bowen, also netted against Posh.

Exeter were at Birmingham on 18 September, so I took Sharon and Steve to St Andrew's to experience the joys of the Tilton Road End. It seemed weird standing on those terraces, not watching the Albion. I was really pleased for Steve when Exeter secured a deserved point in a 1-1 draw.

A novelty game next – a trip to Macclesfield Town's tiny Moss Rose ground, the temporary home of Chester. Three thousand Baggies made the short trip up the M6. The match wasn't all-ticket and, as more and more Albion fans piled in, police had to usher the 800 or so home supporters to one part of the ground; the other stands being packed out by noisy Midlands folk. Darryl Burgess bagged the winning goal near the end, much to our relief. It took us an hour to drive the short distance back to the motorway, such was the traffic. As we tuned into our car radios, horns suddenly started beeping ... we were top of the League. How did that happen?

A home win over Hull cemented our place at the top, then came another new venue, Brentford, and a great excuse for a day in London on the train with our regular gang Dubsey, Andy Miller, Richie Brentnall and Bill Ahearn. Following a particularly heavy lunchtime session, we stumbled into Griffin Park (incidentally, the only ground with a pub on every corner) to see us win 2-1 with a goal from Goodman and an Ampadu winner. We went bonkers in the packed away end as the players celebrated in front of us.

We ended up in The Dolphin pub in Kings Cross afterwards, with the aim of catching the midnight train from Euston. We ordered a round and reflected on the game as Richie fell asleep. We had noticed some rather nasty-looking Leeds supporters and heard them bragging about their escapades at Chelsea that afternoon. We agreed to keep our heads down for a quiet drink before moving on. Then, all of a sudden Richie awoke, letting out a very loud cry of 'The West Brom'. Nice one, Richie! The Leeds neanderthals stormed over and let us know that they weren't particularly keen on our club. One of their main boys grabbed me and said he wanted to take me outside 'for 1982' (the year we sent them down). I politely declined and Dubsey attempted to defuse a potential nasty situation. We drank up and thankfully escaped unharmed.

As Richie worked for British Rail, he got us all in first class on the way back. The carriage was empty, so we spread ourselves out and fell asleep. Due to engineering works, the train made an unscheduled stop in Nuneaton. Andy awoke and, thinking we were in New Street, disembarked. In his still drunken state, he wandered round the streets of Nuneaton, thinking he was in Birmingham, until he got completely lost. He flagged down a taxi and asked: 'Could you take me back to the railway station, please. And where am I?' When we arrived in New Street, we couldn't work out why he wasn't on the train. Little did we know he was bedding down for the night in the ladies' toilets at Nuneaton Station.

Another intriguing away game presented itself midweek at Hartlepool. I was still working in Milton Keynes and none of the lads were interested in joining me this time. It was Bonfire Night and freezing, but I took my place on the away terrace behind the goal with 475 determined Baggies. To my right, the old stand had been demolished and it was just flat waste ground with Portakabins for dressing rooms. This allowed the ice-cold wind to whip in from the sea. The football was atrocious with 0-0 written all over it, then it started to rain, sleet and snow.

This was the first time, in all my years of watching Albion, that I questioned my own sanity. I stood there, soaked through to the skin and shivering, looking at Bobby Gould on the touchline and knowing I faced a four-hour drive back, on my own, to Milton Keynes. I remember asking myself: 'What the f**k am I doing here?'

On 4 December, it was announced that our prize asset Don Goodman had been sold to Sunderland for £900,000. Now where were our goals going to come from? On the same day, we were at Lincoln City in the Autoglass Trophy; yet another 'novelty' game and a new ground for me and presumably the 350 other desperate souls who headed to Sincil Bank. The talking point was the Goodman transfer. However, our pre-match pub had a sign advertising 'topless barmaid tonight'. Now there was a temptation we couldn't refuse. Our hopes of a young Swedish model were soon dashed as the old dear behind the bar whipped her top off and let loose her ample torpedo-like breasts. It was surreal and actually put me off my beer. For the record, we won 2-1.

On Boxing Day, we headed north to the joys of Springfield Park, Wigan. It was a noon kick-off and 2,500 Albion fans were housed on the semi-grass bank behind the goal. The toilets had long since given up the ghost and, at half-time, I witnessed the sight of a flowing stream of urine pouring out of the entrance. Shakespeare got the winner from the penalty spot.

Two days later came our first trip to Exeter and a chance to catch up with my mate, Steve. Our minibus headed for the pre-arranged drinking den, The Victoria Inn, and a good time was had by all as Baggies and Grecians drank together; everyone was in the Christmas spirit. I sat in the main stand with Steve and loved how smokers in the crowd were allowed to go on to the running track by the pitch at half-time to avoiding burning down the wooden stand. 'Shakey' put another penalty away to give us the lead, then we witnessed the bizarre sight of our Chelsea loanee, Frank Sinclair, being adjudged to have headbutted the referee. Sinclair didn't agree and refused to leave the pitch. Suddenly, Welsh Baggie Colin Wood, who for some reason was sat next to the dug-outs, ran to the centre circle, put his arm around our classy defender and calmly walked him off. Colin then retook his place in the stand and neither the police nor stewards said a word to him.

Exeter equalised from the spot with two minutes remaining. Honours were even but the point took us back top. We returned to the 'Vic' for good banter with the locals, including pitch-invader Colin on the bar stool bagpipes. When discussing the delights of St James' Park (the Devon version) and the home terrace, the 'Big Bank,' Andy Miller commented: 'Big Bank? Barclays in West Bromwich is bigger.'

We didn't stay top for long. On New Year's Day, despite yet another Shakespeare penalty, we lost 3-2 at home to Fulham. Then it was back to Devon, this time to another new venue, Plainmoor, home of Torquay. I opted for a seat in the stand, which proved a bad move. The one goalmouth was obscured by a dirty Perspex screen and a pillar. 'Silk Out' banners were again evident and our chairman was targeted with hostile chants from the six steps that made up the uncovered away end.

It was a terrible display and Justin Fashanu put us out of our misery near the end. He had been targeted by anti-gay taunts throughout and it was with some predictability that he scored the winner. He sadly committed suicide seven years later.

After slumping 3-2 at home to Swansea, around 500 fans invaded the pitch, chanting 'Where's the money gone?' and 'Sack the board.' It was heading towards 6.00 p.m. and the fans were still on the Brummie Road terraces, demanding answers. Then Barmy Bobby appeared and attempted to address the madding crowd.

A few days later, Gould played his 'get out of jail' card. Bob Taylor joined us from Bristol City for £300,000. 'SuperBob' didn't take long to make an impression, scoring our second goal on his debut in a 2-0 home win against Brentford and a week later bagging two in an excellent 3-0 win at Birmingham. We had to keep a low profile again in the Spotted Dog afterwards, but at least we had a new hero.

A 4,500-strong Albion army besieged Stoke the week after and our minibus was pulled over as we turned off the M6. We had planned to have a drink in Hanley but the police were having none of it. It was only midday and they wanted to hold us in a lay-by until kick-off approached. We argued profusely and in the end I said: 'We'll go back home then.' The chief superintendent looked confused and didn't have a reply. In the end, they bowed to our wishes and escorted us back on to the M6 south-bound. We came off at the next junction and approached Stoke the back way, finally finding a welcoming pub in Stone. At the Victoria Ground, we were squeezed into fenced pens and the Potters bullied their way to a 1-0 victory.

After our 2-1 defeat at Bournemouth, Bobby Bloody Gould played another master stroke. As disgruntled Baggies made their way out of the ground, their comments could be overheard in the away dressing room. Our manager then invited 'big' Mick Coldicott in to share his thoughts with the players. Mick didn't hold back and told them exactly what the feeling was among supporters. This was just the latest example of Gould trying to apportion blame to others.

We won only two of our next twelve games. Any belief had well and truly gone. After our dismal home defeat to mighty Hartlepool, our popular coach Stuart Pearson was suspended and subsequently sacked. Chants of 'Stuart Pearson's blue and white army' were aired in protest before and during our 1-1 draw at Bury.

The atmosphere at home games had become hostile, with anti-board and anti-Gould chants throughout. This prompted director Trevor Summers to publicly state: 'Albion would be better off playing behind closed doors than in front of our own fans.' We just weren't prepared to put up with this garbage any more.

We were in minibus mode again for our journey to Huddersfield on 28 March. Leaflets had been given out by the Albion fanzines appealing for unity. But, after 90 minutes of standing on the cold Leeds Road terraces watching another truly awful performance and a 3-0 defeat, we had had enough. Along with lots of other Baggies, our full minibus crew headed for the players' entrance. When the team emerged, they received a certain amount of abuse but nothing compared with that reserved for Bobby Gould. He was slaughtered and, if it wasn't for the police, things could have turned really nasty.

A sucker for punishment, I still went to Stockport the following Tuesday. Gould's latest 'motivational' stunt resulted in him driving the players in a minibus to Edgeley Park. We surrendered to another 3-0 defeat and I just lost it. With the game still in play, I climbed over the wall and walked round the pitch towards the dug-out. Silve was on crutches at the time, but still hobbled along with me. I just marched straight past the stewards and found myself face to face with Mr Gould. I was enraged and let fly: 'This is my club and you're destroying it. We are the mighty West Bromwich Albion and here we are losing to Stockport County ... Stockport County for fu**s sake.' I went on: 'Please resign now and give us a chance of promotion.' Gould just looked at me in disbelief and told me to move out of the way. I was then led away by some surprisingly sympathetic stewards. Both Gould and Silk had police escorts after the match.

Coffin for Gould?

There was no turning back now; he simply had to go. Three draws and a defeat at Hull didn't help his cause. We signed off at The Hawthorns with a 3-1 win against Preston, but it didn't really matter. The match provided just another excuse to hurl abuse at him and the board.

The finale was labelled 'Barmy Bobby's Beachwear Party' and 5,000 Baggies headed to Shrewsbury with just one aim, to get rid of the manager. We had been informed that all the pubs in the town would be closed, so our minibus headed off the beaten track and found a welcoming little boozer. Walking to the ground, there was not a Shrews fan to be seen, just Albion fans everywhere. Three sides of the tiny Gay Meadow were packed with beachwear-clad fans. There were thousands of balloons, beach balls, various inflatables ... and a coffin. Just before kick-off, a home-made casket with the words 'RIP Gould' unscripted, was carried along the touchline.

There was surely going to be no stay of execution, yet he still did the unexpected. Before the game, he went on a town centre walkabout with the team in tow. Then, during the warm-up, the players came out wearing beachwear, complete with caps and sun glasses.

The match was a non-event, played out like a friendly with goals from Gary Strodder, Shakespeare and Taylor giving us a meaningless 3-1 victory. With a few minutes remaining, the party atmosphere turned sour. Hundreds of Albion fans invaded the pitch and the players ran for cover. Some so-called fans snapped the crossbar, leaving the referee no option other than to abandon the game. The protests up to that point had been good-natured, but this overstepped the mark.

Our final position was seventh, just missing out on the play-offs. In the FA Cup, we feared another 'Woking' when we were drawn at home to Marlow. Fortunately, history wasn't repeated and we strolled to a 6-0 win. The next round saw us lose at Orient in front of a live television audience. Our League Cup run ended in the first round against Swindon over two legs.

Two days after the Shrewsbury game, Gould was gone. Chairman Silk also resigned, handing over the reins to local businessman Trevor 'The Shed' Summers. We had got our way. We had never wanted Bobby Gould and we weren't going to bow down until he was out of our club. Job done.

17

Ossie's Going to Wembley

So Barmy Bobby was gone. Enter 1978 World Cup winner Ossie Ardiles and I could enjoy the summer of 1992.

At work, AHW had been taken over by Tarmac and merged with Techtonic to form Briggs Amasco Curtainwall. We were relocated to Halfords Lane; very convenient and ideal for parking at matches.

1992/93

Ardiles and his assistant Keith Burkinshaw did some wheeling and dealing before the season. Colin West and Graham Roberts were just two parts of the mass exodus. In came Ian Hamilton from Scunthorpe, Steve Lillwall from Kidderminster, Tony Lange from Wolves and veteran striker Simon Garner from Blackburn.

There was a good feeling. We even had a crazy new kit, with stripes in a barcode design and a return to the popular green and yellow away strip. Our first pre-season friendly saw 2,000 fans descend on Evesham to welcome Ossie. We created a new record attendance at their Crown Meadow ground (sadly sold in 2006). It was a lovely sunny afternoon, spent sitting on a grass bank watching our new-look team win 4-0. I also went to St Albans, where I got to meet Mr Ardiles before our 6-0 victory.

I headed to The Hawthorns for our first League game full of optimism. I wasn't disappointed as newly-promoted Blackpool were beaten 3-1 with two goals from SuperBob and one from Bernard McNally. The ground looked strange with the roof removed from the Smethwick End, providing The Hawthorns with an uncovered terrace for the first time since the early 1960s. Our first away game took us back to Huddersfield. The atmosphere was completely different to five months earlier. Garner grabbed the game's only goal and we chanted: 'We are top of the League.' Ossie was our man.

We stumbled out of the League Cup against Plymouth but we were on fire in the League and another two home wins cemented our position. We travelled to Fulham in joyous mood. Craven Cottage, on the banks of the Thames, has always been one of my favourite grounds. We found a smashing pub and sat outside in the sun. This is one of the things I love about football. How different from that Tuesday night at Hartlepool last November. Our 1-1 draw was the least we deserved from another good performance.

Our next away game provoked further bad memories of the previous season. This time it was a night game at Burnden Park and two Bob Taylor specials saw us get the better of a decent Bolton side. Our celebrations with the players at the end helped build a bond that had been missing for a couple of seasons.

Everyone was on a high but we now had to get a result at Stoke. It was ten years since we had last won there but we had never felt so confident. Nearly 7,000 Baggies filled the entire away end and we witnessed a gripping game, real end-to-end stuff. In true Ardiles style, we went for it. Unfortunately, this style leaves gaps at the back and we came out second best by losing 4-3. It was our first League defeat and I was gutted.

Next up were Exeter at home. That meant another visit from Sharon and Steve and we had exciting news to share. Elaine was pregnant and I was going to be a daddy. A fairly straightforward 2-0 victory got us back to winning ways. We then had a major blip, with three defeats on the bounce and people questioning our new 'diamond' formation.

In the FA Cup first round, we had another possible 'banana skin' against non-League Aylesbury, but there was no messing about and Kevin Donovan scored a hat-trick in an 8-0 demolition job. Round two provided a new venue, Wycombe, who were Conference leaders. The game was chosen for live television and we ran out in ridiculously long 'baggie' shorts. Bobby Gould was spotted in the Adams Park commentary box and received plenty of stick. After taking a two-goal lead, we made hard work of it, allowing Wycombe to pull level and have us hanging on for a draw. Martin O'Neill's team then made a real good fist of the replay, SuperBob scoring the only goal. It was all in vain, however as West Ham knocked us out in the third round.

On our visit to Hull on the last day of October, Richie, Dubsey, Bill and I chose to sit in the home end. The performance was much improved and new signing Donovan looked the part. The game was heading for a 1-1 draw with just a few minutes remaining, when Darren Bradley unleashed a shot from some 40 yards that dipped, swerved and ended up in the back of the net. We had managed to stay fairly subdued when Garner got our first goal but this time we couldn't contain ourselves, particularly Richie Brentnall, who ran up and down the gangway in celebration. Apart from a few derogatory comments, we got surprisingly little hassle. Back to winning ways, we added another three points at home to Hartlepool with loan-signing Luther Blissett scoring our third.

A disappointing run followed, including a 1-1 draw on Preston's plastic pitch. On Boxing Day, we were at home to Chester and the fog was so bad that it was hard to work out what was happening. The game should never have been played but Paul Raven scored both in a 2-0 win, so we weren't complaining.

The game I had been looking forward to was Exeter away. This time we decided to make a weekend of it thanks to Steve, who invited five of us to stay. Another pleasant lunchtime session in The Victoria Inn was followed by an extraordinary match. At half-time Steve was giving us loads of stick as the Grecians went 2-0 ahead. It turned out to be a classic 'game of two halves'. With 20 minutes to go, Ian Hamilton pulled one back from the spot, then Gary Hackett and Carl Heggs added two more to make it 3-2. Our goals were from the three 'H's.

Albion fans had now established a new chant, jumping up and down shouting 'Boing Boing, Baggies Baggies.' I'm not entirely sure of the origins, but it certainly caught on. Even in the 'Vic' after the game, everyone was 'boinging' and an ancient bench collapsed under the weight of a rather large Baggie. The City fans had taken the defeat in good spirit and we were drinking together for over three hours. Steve then showed us round some excellent pubs in the beautiful city centre. The next morning, he had entered us into a five-a-side tournament. Considering our raging hangovers, our team of Richie, Dubsey, Neil Whitehouse and Neil Grainger didn't do too bad, resplendent in our new Albion barcode shirts.

Nearly 30,000 packed The Hawthorns for Stoke's visit and, just when we had chance to gain some new fans, we let ourselves down. A big game plus a big crowd nearly always seems to result in a disappointing defeat. The Potters won 2-1 and we left the ground to sounds of 'Delilah' echoing from the Smethwick End. Stoke had certainly become our bogey side. Not only did they take six points off us, they also beat us in the Autoglass Trophy quarter-final.

I was back working in London on the Waterloo Station development. It presented an ideal opportunity to travel to Bournemouth with fellow Baggie, Eddie Jarvis, for our midweek game. It was a horrible night, lashing with rain, so we opted to stand in the covered home end to watch an awful game which saw David Speedie fortunately give us a 1-0 victory.

We were struggling to put a run together, a poor 2-1 defeat at Blackpool being followed by an excellent 4-0 win against Fulham with Mickey Mellon scoring on his debut. Then the wheels really came off. We descended on Edgeley Park, with the nightmare of our previous season's 3-0 defeat to Stockport still clear in my mind. Ex-Baggie 'donkey' Paul Williams lined up in County's team and he was pelted with carrots before the game. After SuperBob gave us the lead, we just collapsed, big style, five bloody one. Predictably, even Williams helped himself to a goal and we dropped to fourth.

We took the lead again at Port Vale before losing 2-1 in front of 5,000 fuming Baggies – our fourth consecutive away defeat. Even the play-offs were now in doubt. Fortunately, The Hawthorns had become a bit of a fortress. Our loan signing from Newcastle, Andy Hunt, went on and scored our equaliser in a 2-2 draw at Bradford, then he had a 'mare' of a home debut against Brighton, but somehow managed to help himself to a hat-trick in our 3-1 win.

Even though Elaine was eight and a half months pregnant, she joined me for the trip to Chester, enabling me to visit a new ground – the newly-constructed Deva Stadium, half of which lies in Wales.

The ancient city was swamped with Baggies seeking lunchtime refreshment and our party found a great pub. We then headed to the out-of-town stadium. I have a photograph of my ex-wife sat in the stand and often tell my daughter Jade that this was technically her first Albion game! Raven, Donovan and Hunt got our goals as we beat the bottom club 3-1.

Next up we faced Plymouth in a televised game at The Hawthorns; another three points surely? But this is the Albion we're talking about and we somehow managed to lose 5-2. Maybe this was the kick up the arse we needed?

Another novelty away day next and 3,700 Albion fans descended on the East Midland outpost of Mansfield. The only pub we could find near the ground was the Lord Byron. However, when we arrived at 12.30 p.m., there must already have been 1,000 thirsty Baggies drinking there. We didn't even try to get served, we just sat outside soaking up the atmosphere. The game hadn't been made all-ticket so we didn't take any chances and walked up to Field Mill a good 45 minutes before kick-off. By 3.00 p.m., well over half the ground was rammed with Albion fans. It was a nice easy win, Taylor and Heggs both scoring and celebrating in their well-rehearsed, unique fashion. Hunt got the other in our 3-0 win.

I had a good excuse to miss our home game against Wigan on 24 April 1993. At 5.30 a.m., I was in Sandwell Hospital watching my daughter Jade Leigh Walton enter the world. It was an emotional experience and another baby 'born to be a Baggie'. We beat Wigan 5-1, with Bob Taylor's two goals making it 35 for the season and equalling Jeff Astle's record, thus grabbing the headlines in the Sports Argus. I was a happy daddy.

I still managed to get to Rotherham for our fourth end-of-season beach party. Our play-off spot was already secured so it was one big celebration at Millmoor. Unfortunately, the South Yorkshire police didn't want to share our fun and nearly every pub was forced to shut before the game. There seemed to be more inflatables, coloured wigs, balloons and beach balls than ever with everyone dreaming of Wembley. For the third away game running, Albion's support well outnumbered the home fans and we were rewarded with a 2-0 win.

For our final home game, against Hull, the programme included a Wembley voucher (just in case). They sold out long before kick-off as 20,000 sensed a trip to the Twin Towers. A straightforward 3-1 win followed. And so to the dreaded play-offs.

We finished fourth in the table, which meant we faced Swansea, who had finished fifth. The first leg of the semi-final was at the Vetch Field, all-ticket. I agreed to drive our minibus, and 3,000 ticket-less Baggies watched on a big screen at the NIA. We got to Swansea for midday and headed to the Glamorgan pub, which ran out of beer as kick-off approached. In terrible conditions and the rain teeming down, we were struggling to get any sort of grip on the game. Early in the second half, the Swans took the lead and worse was to follow as Martin Hayes beat Tony Lange to put us two down. Our Wembley dreams were disappearing in front of our eyes when a brave challenge from Daryl Burgess forced an own goal from McFarlane. Our dreams were rekindled.

The second leg was one of those extra special Hawthorns evenings, when everyone pulls together with one aim. West Bromwich Albion, when united as one, are a formidable force. Apart from 2,000 Swansea fans, the ground was packed with Baggies, every one prepared to scream themselves hoarse. Mission Wembley.

I was a nervous wreck as I took my seat in the Rainbow Stand. The atmosphere was something else and the Brummie Road End to my right was rocking, just a mass of boinging Baggies. I don't think I ever sang 'Come on you Baggies' with so much gusto. We *had* to do this.

After just seven minutes, Andy Hunt settled our nerves by levelling the score on aggregate. Ian Hamilton put us 2-0 ahead and everyone went ballistic. The Brummie Road stand seemed to move as every fan boinged in unison. In the second half, Mickey Mellon was sent off and panic briefly set in. To huge relief, ex-Baggie Colin West also saw red for the Swans. Towards the end the noise was deafening. 'Boing Boing, going to Wembley,' we chanted, counting down every second until the final whistle blew. We were going to Wembley for the first time in twenty-three years. The fans invaded the pitch and the players were chaired off. The scenes were incredible. Ossie and the players even returned for a lap of honour. I stood there savouring every minute and didn't want to leave.

Life was great; I had just become a father and now my team were going to Wembley. Jade was having a few problems, so I volunteered to drive down to the final, so I could get straight to the Birmingham Children's Hospital afterwards.

Wembley, 1993

We could have filled Wembley by ourselves, but Port Vale wouldn't release any of their tickets despite only being able to sell 11,000. As it turned out, 42,300 Albion fans headed to London on 30 May, 1993; the club's biggest ever away following. I was only nine on my previous visit to see Albion at the stadium and I savoured every minute this time as a thirty-two-year-old.

By the time we had parked, we didn't really have time for a drink, so our party just headed down Wembley Way to absorb the atmosphere. We sang our hearts out to try and roar our side to victory, but the first half was a stalemate. The turning point was Vale defender Peter Swann's foul on Bob Taylor and resulting sending-off. The fans turned up the volume and the players responded. Andy Hunt directed a header into the net and the vast majority of Wembley erupted. We urged the team on for more and, when full-back Nicky Reid blasted in his only Albion goal with 7 minutes left, there was no doubt about it. We were going up. In mid-boing, Kevin Donovan added a third and we carried on jumping up and down for the rest of the game. I stayed to see Darren Bradley lift the trophy and the subsequent lap of honour, then I had to get back. I dropped the lads off to celebrate in West Bromwich and headed straight to the children's hospital to give Jade a special hug. I just knew that next time we made it to Wembley, she would be with me.

Then the bombshell. Ossie's beloved 'Tottingham' (as Ardiles pronounced it) came calling and he was off. His assistant Keith Burkinshaw stayed put and took over.

1993/94

Back to Barnsley for our first League game, the only new face in our line-up was Kieran O'Regan. Kevin Donovan's goal earned us a point. In the League Cup, we beat Bristol Rovers 4-1 on aggregate before Chelsea knocked us out at Stamford Bridge (3-2 on aggregate).

Our good home form continued from the previous season. Oxford were despatched 3-1, followed by a draw with Southend and success against Wolves in a great derby memorable for Darren Bradley's 25-yard screamer into the Brummie Road net, triggering off possibly the best 'boinging' ever on the terraces in our 3-2 victory.

After a euphoric win, typical Albion, we lost at Notts County the following week. This was followed by horrendous performances and defeats at home to Crystal Palace (4-1) and at Derby (5-3). We lost five away games on the bounce, including 3-0 to Tranmere on my first visit to Prenton Park. Fortunately, we salvaged some pride at home, beating Peterborough 3-0 and Portsmouth 4-1, Paul Mardon making his debut in the latter.

I caught the train on 11 December to Southend. Most of the nearby pubs were closed to away supporters, so we had to resort to a military operation to gain entry. We spotted a back way in for regulars only, so one by one we went over a wall, through a hedge, into the back garden and inconspicuously entered. Once inside, we would take it in turns on look-out duty and give the next one the signal once the doorman was otherwise occupied. Twelve of us made it into the home-fans-only pub. The team put on one of their better performances, winning 3-0 with Hunt, Hamilton and Taylor on target.

Two new signings, defender Neil Parsley and winger Lee Ashcroft, didn't have much impact and we went ten games without winning, even suffering the humiliation of being knocked out of the FA Cup by Halifax Town at The Shay in a tie broadcast live on television. At Blundell Park, Grimsby, SuperBob and loan signing Graham Fenton were on target in a 2-2 draw. Ex-Blues man David Smith made his debut in this game.

Fenton scored again in our 2-1 win over Sunderland, on his home debut. I purposely got a ticket on the front row of the Halfords Lane Stand for this game as I wanted to do some filming with my camcorder, recording the Brummie Road End as a terrace before the bulldozers moved in at the end of the season. We were starting to pull away from the relegation zone and followed up with a good 1-0 victory at Watford.

There were the usual crazy antics at Molineux on 26 February. For some mad reason, I didn't go by train and decided to take a carload. It was the first time I had sat down in the South Bank and, with the game heading for a 1-1 draw, 'Captain' Mardon – International (Captain Scarlet speak) pounced to secure all three points. We went wild and the 'Dingles' were not impressed. As we stayed inside celebrating, Wolves fans gathered on the grass bank above the subway, waiting for us to exit. When we finally made our way, thousands of natives had gathered on the banks surrounding the subway. Bricks came raining on us from all directions. The police completely lost control, initially trying to herd us back inside. We ended up stuck between a police cordon and the external wall dodging the missiles that continued to be hurled in our direction. Some Albion fans retaliated and started returning the compliment. It was chaos. Eventually, the police decided to escort everyone to the railway station. To have broken the escort would have been suicide, so we agreed to abandon my car in Wolverhampton, go back to civilisation on the train and collect it next day. I still go to the 'Custard Bowl' whenever the Baggies are in town, but I know some who pledged never to set foot in there again after what will forever be known as 'The Stoning'.

For the game at Bristol City over Easter, we stayed overnight at Weston-Super-Mare. After our 0-0 draw, we attempted to have a drink in every pub at the resort. Come closing time, we stumbled into the Midland Hotel, where we spotted a bar still serving. Just as we were about to be thrown out, the landlord spotted an Albion shirt and agreed to serve us. Our hosts were Mr and Mrs Mardon, the Albion captain's parents.

We were not playing well and proceeded to lose three successive games in a row, including a horror show at home, 4-2 to our relegation rivals Blues. Our final home game against Grimsby was an emotional one. I stood on the Birmingham Road terraces for the final time. We had a shiny new Smethwick End and now it was the Brummie's turn to be replaced. Kevin Donovan scored the only goal as we said our farewells. I still have an exit sign on the wall in my garage.

We were in grave danger of returning to the third tier (rebranded Division Two after the Premiership's launch). We had two away games to complete the season and points were needed. We failed the first test, disappointingly losing 3-2 at Luton, so it went down to the wire. We had to win at Portsmouth in our last game to guarantee survival.

Baggies invasion of Pompey

Times like this make me proud to be a Baggie. When the going gets tough, we all pull together to achieve what is required. Pompey didn't have time to make the game all-ticket, so 12,000 of us invaded the naval city. Steve and Sharon from Exeter joined Elaine, one-year-old Jade and myself for the trip. We dropped the girls off at HMS *Victory* and headed towards Fratton Park at midday. Every pub we passed was packed with Albion fans. Even some of the notoriously rough home-fans-only pubs were heaving with thirsty Baggies. We parked at our usual watering hole and made our way to the ground a good hour before the start. It was a wise decision as, even at 2.00 p.m., the queues were enormous. As kick-off approached, the away end couldn't hold any more, so police let Albion fans into the side terrace, normally the domain of Pompey fans. They continually moved the 'ticker tape' temporary cordon along until they eventually reached the half-way line. The opposite stand was also half full of noisy Baggies.

It was like a time-bomb waiting to go off as drunken Albion supporters taunted their Portsmouth counterparts, separated by a few police and a thin line of tape. As the teams came out, up it went. The two sets of fans spilled on to the pitch, punches and boots flying everywhere. Fortunately, order was restored and we roared on the Baggies in the hope of the right result. Our Freddie Mercury look-alike in goal, Tony Lange, pulled off a string of fine saves before and after Lee Ashcroft connected with a header to put us ahead. With Albion fans in full voice, we held on and a pitch invasion followed. Go, West Bromwich Albion got its first airing and we celebrated as if we had won the League. This was a massive result, preventing a return to the third tier, which didn't bear thinking about. We finished fourth from bottom, level on points with Birmingham, who were forced down on goal difference.

18

The Italian Job, Part I

Albion had last played in the Anglo-Italian Cup in June 1971. We re-entered the competition in 1993 under Keith Burkinshaw after a break of more than twenty seasons. I had never been to Italy, so defeats in our first two group home games against Pescara and Padova were not going to stop me travelling.

We agreed that the cheapest way was to drive to the game against Fiorentina, so, together with Tony Jones, Michael Silvester and Exeter fan Steve Conabeer, I set off on 14 November. As we had soon established in Acapulco the year before, Steve's love of football and travelling provided an instant bond. We have continued to travel the world together to this day.

I decided to give Albion's FA Cup game at Halifax a miss as it was on the Sunday before the midweek date in Florence, but watched our defeat live on TV. Good decision not to go!

Jade was just six months old, so saying goodbye was heart-wrenching as I hadn't spent more than one night away during her lifetime, although I would later work on and off in Hong Kong and Dubai for several years, unfortunately missing chunks of her early childhood.

We caught the overnight Dover-to-Calais ferry and Steve, Tony and I agreed to take it in turns to drive. Our route took us through France, Belgium and Luxembourg. In Switzerland, we detoured to revisit our 1981 UEFA Cup destination, Zurich, and called in at the Hardturm Stadium. Seating had replaced the terraces at both ends, otherwise it was largely unchanged. We also called in at FC Zurich's 25,000-capacity Letzigrund Stadium.

A new country visited when we stopped off for lunch in Vaduz, Liechtenstein. Apparently, this tiny country's biggest export is false teeth! The area of the entire country amounts to only 62 square miles. The population is 37,000. Walking round the streets of Vaduz, it certainly didn't feel like a capital. I was informed it gets busy when the snow comes and it becomes a popular winter sports destination.

We were soon heading through the Alps into Italy. Driving in Europe was new for Steve, so as a special treat, we gave him the Milan rush hour to negotiate! Apart from a couple of wrong turns, he did a good job and we were soon heading out towards the Mediterranean coast. We entered the province of Genoa and pulled into the little seaside resort of Recco Beach (far away in time) – apologies to Martha & the Muffins. We booked into La Giaria guest house. Recco was stunning. Situated in the Liguria region, it is known for its focaccia al formation (flat bread with cheese). It's certainly an area I would like to visit again.

We were starving and promptly ordered pizzas and beers; all except Silve, who, for some reason, requested spaghetti bolognese. He has a rather large appetite and little did he know that the Italians tend to have 'spag bol' as a starter rather than a 'main'. He was almost in tears as our massive pizzas arrived alongside his tiny saucer of spaghetti, complete with dollop of sauce. The only way we could cheer him up was to each give him a slice of pizza.

Back at the digs, our hosts Toni and Edye gave us more beer. They were an eccentric couple and Edye sat there writing a poem about us while Toni kept getting sentimental, talking about his previous wife, who had died. Each time he started to cry, we changed the subject but, sooner or later, he was back on to his ex-wife and the tears would once again flow. It was a mad evening. Incidentally, Edye's poem translates as follows:

My magnificent four people
Four nice English people
Look at the sky, the mountains and the valleys.
The little ones in the fountain, two feet from me.
It likes our company.
The fountain makes waves in the water,
Murmurs and dances, accompanied by the wind.
All is in silence
In many thousands of forms.
This silence is broken by laughter.
Four young men running bare-footed in the street
And the fresh grass bouncing
Going against a thousand light years.

Hmmm! I'm not sure what kind of mind-bending drugs our landlady was on, but imagining us all 'running bare-footed in the street with the fresh grass bouncing', she must have been taking something.

Next morning, after more tears from our hosts, we were in good spirits as we drove along the coast in the Italian sunshine with The Drifters' greatest hits blasting out. Although we were going at a steady 90 mph, we seemed to be the slowest car on the road as numerous others bombed past us. Our first port of call was Pisa, where we pulled into Arena Garibaldi, home of Pisa SC. The 20,000-capacity stadium was completely locked, so we rang the front door bell and were welcomed in. Built in 1919, the stadium was certainly showing its age. It was excluded from Italian football in 2009, when it failed to collect enough money to pay off the club's debts. The club was then refounded under its current name of Associazione Calcio Pisa 1909.

Next stop was the famous leaning tower situated behind the cathedral. It is the third oldest structure in Pisa's Cathedral Square, having being completed in 1372. The tilt began during construction, caused by inadequate foundation on ground too soft on one side to properly support the weight. Prior to restoration work, it leaned at an angle of 5.5 degrees. It now leans at about 3.99 degrees. The top is displaced horizontally 3.9 metres from the centre.

After the obligatory 'holding up the tower' photographs, we had a quick look round the other buildings in Cathedral Square before encountering a group of Bolton fans who were also on Anglo-Italian Cup travels.

On to Florence, capital of Tuscany, described in the Forbes guide as 'One of the most beautiful cities in the world.' It is known for being the birthplace of the Renaissance and has been labelled 'The Athens of the Middle Ages.'

We located the 47,000-capacity Stadio Comunale Artemio Franchi, home ground of AC Fiorentina, and parked in a good position for a quick getaway after the match. During an impromptu unguided tour, Steve and I wandered down some steps trying to locate the entrance to a large tower overlooking the ground. Coming in the opposite direction were loads of schoolchildren we presumed had been on a stadium tour. It turned out we had entered a school. Tony takes up the story:

Two teachers appeared, turned the lights off and were about to lock up. Dean and Steve were nowhere to be seen, so I tried to explain there were two people still in the building but they assured us in broken English that it was lunchtime and all the children had gone home. I tried and tried to convince them they shouldn't lock up but they were having none of it. Suddenly, just as one of the teachers was turning the key, out of the darkness came Steve and Dean. The look on those teachers' faces is something I'll never forget.

We walked along the river towards our rendezvous point with mates who had travelled separately. These were pre-mobile phone days, so everything had to be pre-planned. Our instructions were to meet at 3.00 p.m. in the first bar on the city centre side of the famous Ponte Vecchio bridge. The bars in Italy tend to double up as cake shops and we very nearly walked past the first one, when we suddenly noticed the rest of our motley crew perched drinking. We joined Dubsey, Richie, Bill, Neil Whitehouse and Gary Penn for a few beers before having a wander to see the instantly recognisable cathedral and the Palazzo Vecchio, where we bumped into more Albion fans including Dave and Julia Foxall. For good luck, I put a coin in the mouth of 'Il Porcellino' (The Piglet), the famous bronze statue of a wild boar in The Piazza del Mercato Nuevo, and rubbed its snout to ensure a return to Florence (I'm still waiting).

We caught the bus to the ground and got comfortable in the Stadio Bar opposite. It doubled as a ticket office as well as a cake shop. I was on photographer duty for The Baggies newspaper, so popped across to the stadium to collect my press pass.

A crowd of 7,808 braved a cold evening to see Albion put up a moderate display against the 1990 UEFA Cup runners-up. 'The Viola' had now slipped into Serie B but were still far better than our lot. Goals from Banchelli and Antonaccio either side of half-time secured a 2-0 victory while Bob Taylor, Lee Ashcroft and Carl Heggs went close for us. The Albion contingent in the away section was boosted by a few England supporters in Italy for the San Marino game due to take place in Bologna the next evening.

Fiorentina actually went bankrupt a few years later before reforming in 2002. They are now back in Serie A and continue to be one of the best-supported teams in Italy.

On exiting the stadium, we were freezing, so we called in the bar for a warm drink before driving overnight back through the Alps. Once thawed out, we each took it in turns to sleep as we made our way to Strasbourg, a destination we visited during our previous Albion in Europe road trip twelve years earlier. This time we went to see Tony's now mother and father-in-law who bestowed a splendid lunch on us. It was Tony whom we had left behind in Strasbourg in 1981, he had long since married Claudine. After dinner, Tony's brother-in-law Christophe took us to the 29,000-capacity Stade de la Meinau, where his home town team Racing Club de Strasbourg played. Then a member of Ligue One, they were relegated to the fourth tier of French football at the end of 2010/11 after going into liquidation. They currently play in the Championnat National (Tier 3).

We said farewell to Tony's in-laws and headed back to Calais. It had been a very enjoyable few days with great memories. It was so tempting to return to Italy for the final game against Cosenza in December, but I had no holiday entitlement left. Incidentally, Albion made it four losses out of four with a 2-1 defeat in this meaningless game played in front of just 139 spectators.

19

Something Fishy Going On

After working so hard at Waterloo Station, I was invited to join the Queen, Margaret Thatcher and John Major for the opening of the Channel Tunnel rail link. I also moved house; Elaine, Jade and I uprooting to Ray Hall Lane, Great Barr. It was a much bigger house and almost opposite the entrance to the Birmingham County FA ground, handy for watching Albion's youth team on Saturday mornings.

1994/95

I attended what were to become regular pre-season fixtures at Halesowen Town and Kidderminster Harriers. New signings included Paul Edwards and Mike Phelan. As the new-look Hawthorns wasn't quite ready, we played our first five League games away and didn't garner a single victory. Our opener was at Luton and I now had an official photographer's permit for away games. So I watched the first half from pitch-side before joining the injured Andy Hunt in the Kenilworth Road press box. Bob Taylor scored in our 1-1 draw. Our second game took us back to the scene of 'The Stoning'. No hassle this time as it was Wolves' fans that stayed behind celebrating their 2-0 win.

I was on photography duty at the New Den, Millwall's new ground, to see goals from SuperBob and Jeroen Boere on his debut in a 2-2 draw. Boere passed away in 2007. The ground wasn't as intimidating as the old Den but it was still Millwall and not the most welcoming of places.

We finally played a home game on 17 September and, although my season ticket was for a seat in the new Birmingham Road End, I was temporary located in the Smethwick End while the new stand was under construction. We could only manage a 1-1 draw with Grimsby and it was clear that we had another relegation battle on our hands. We beat Burnley the following week but sunk to the bottom with four successive defeats. We were in turmoil and the presence of chairman Trevor Summers in the dug-out with manager Burkinshaw at Tranmere was farcical. Football chairmen should never get involved in team matters – it made us a joke.

Burkinshaw was relieved of his duties on 16 October and former Walsall star Alan Buckley was unveiled as our new boss four days later. His first game ended in a 2-0 defeat at Barnsley. It wasn't long before he started 'collecting' players from his former club Grimsby Town. First to arrive were Paul Agnew and Tony Rees.

Our form continued pretty much as before; win one, draw one, lose one. Consistently inconsistent. After the game at Sheffield United in December, I was returning my photographer's bib when I found myself outside the away dressing room. I stood and listened to Buckley going absolutely berserk after our 2-0 defeat. He was known for his tantrums and apparently threw a teapot against the dressing room wall on one occasion.

On Boxing Day, the new Brummie Road stand was officially opened and I took my new seat, No. 64 in Row JJ, which I have retained ever since. Around ten of us have seats together and the banter is always good, even if the game isn't. It was a winning start in our new surroundings as we beat Bristol City 1-0 thanks to an own goal. The Hawthorns was now a modern stadium, apart from the Rainbow Stand.

A 2-0 win at Reading aside, it was mostly doom and gloom until March and we were again in relegation trouble. Then a 2-1 win at Portsmouth was followed by a memorable victory in the Black Country derby. Our average attendance nearly doubled to see us get revenge for our early-season defeat at Molineux. Goals from Lee Ashcroft and Bob Taylor gave us a 2-0 win, not a bad scalp seeing as Wolves were pushing for promotion at the time. Then true to form, we lost our next home game 5-2 to Swindon.

Andy Hunt grabbed a hat-trick in our 3-0 win against Millwall and the manager enjoyed a successful return to Grimsby, where Donovan and Hunt were on target in our 2-0 success. Our last home game saw us finally put on the style, winning 5-1 against a Tranmere Rovers side bound for the play-offs. Lee Ashcroft helped himself to a hat-trick.

The curtain came down on yet another disappointing season with my last ever visit to Roker Park. Steve had driven up from Exeter straight from a night shift to join me. Once again, Albion's contingent wore beachwear and, as we both had photographers' permits, we watched from all four stands during the course of the 90 minutes. The spoils were shared in a 2-2 draw. I loved Roker Park; loads of character and a far better atmosphere than the bland 'plastic' grounds of today.

How times change. Premiership Coventry City had the audacity to knock us out of the FA Cup, beating us 2-1 at The Hawthorns after we had held them 1-1 at Highfield Road. We also fell at the first hurdle in the League Cup, embarrassingly losing 1-0 over two legs to Hereford. At least I ticked off a new ground with our first visit to Edgar Street.

We finished eleventh in the table and the future wasn't really looking any brighter. A ridiculous eleven different players had been captain during the season and we said goodbye to our former skipper Darren Bradley, who joined Walsall after 288 appearances. Tony Hale had replaced Trev the Shed as club chairman.

At work, Tarmac had decided to close Briggs Amasco Curtainwall. Fortunately, one of my contacts, Gary Summers, had just bought Alumet Systems, but didn't want to let go of his cladding fixing company GSL Installations, based in Southam, Warwickshire. He gave me a call, we had a chat and I was employed as a Director, responsible for the installation of façades all over the country (later the world). As part of the deal, the company purchased an Albion Premier Share for me. This new share initiative included an eleven-year Hawthorns season ticket.

Cup victory on the Isle of Man

Pre-season, Albion entered the Manx Cup – a tournament on the Isle of Man. Along with Dubsey, Anil Shiyal and Yhaia Haffidh, we booked on the 'King Orry' – the Isle of Man Steam Packet ferry from Heysham to Douglas. Yhaia (from the Yemen) hadn't done much travelling, so we wound him up beforehand by telling him to visit his doctors to find out what injections he needed. We also told him he needed a visa and reminded him to buy some Isle of Man currency.

Before boarding, we visited Christie Park, home of Morecambe FC. It was demolished in 2010. On arrival in the capital Douglas, we collected a hire car and located our guest house. It soon became obvious the island had been taken over by Albion fans. We established a 'local', The Quids Inn, a novel pub with turnstiles at the entrance where you paid a pound to enter. Then all drinks, crisps and anything else on sale cost a pound. Any bad behaviour led to a yellow card and further drunken stunts resulted in a red and banishment from the premises. Apart from odd stragglers, there didn't appear to be any fans on the island from the other competing teams; Wrexham, Bury, Port Vale and Wigan. Just Baggies, everywhere.

Our first game was at the Ballacloan Stadium in Ramsey against ex-Baggie John Deehan's Wigan Athletic. In a typical pre-season friendly, watched by 1,445, Albion scraped a 1-0 victory thanks to a goal from Paul Groves, our latest recruit from Grimsby. A good drinking session was had afterwards and we ended up in a night club well into the early hours. Most of the players were also there, including new signing Paul Peschisolido, who bought us drinks and did his best to win us over, fearful of his previous reputation, gained when he regularly scored against us for Stoke or Blues.

Next morning, we watched Alan Buckley and his assistant, Arthur Mann, putting the players through their paces on Douglas beach (Arthur was tragically killed in a fork-lift truck accident in 1999). Part of their routine involved getting the lads to stand in the freezing sea. We also visited the island's main tourist attraction, the Great Laxey Wheel, the largest working waterwheel in the world, built into the hillside above the village of Laxey in 1854. In the afternoon, we went to the National Sports Centre ground in Douglas to watch Bury v Wrexham. There were more Baggies there than fans of the two competing teams put together.

Our game against Port Vale meant a 30-minute drive across the island to Castletown. Dubsey decided to walk from Douglas and just made the pub in time for a 'super swift' drink before kick-off. In front of just 843 spectators at the windswept Castletown Stadium, well-taken goals from Andy Hunt and Bob Taylor earned our second victory in two days. Peschisolido made his debut and went close several times. We had a great laugh behind the goal, having banter with our 'keeper Nigel Spink and urging 'Pesch' to score, telling him: 'You would have put that away if you were playing against us.' Some Albion supporters had plastic football rattles. In Douglas afterwards we celebrated our appearance in the final. Bob Taylor scored the winner against Bury at the Douglas Bowl in a scrappy game. He was also our captain and lifted the Manx Cup for the first and only time.

1995/96

I took my young nephew-in-law Andrew to the usual friendlies at Halesowen and Kidderminster. Thanks to my photographer's license, I was able to 'snap' him acting as mascot with the team group before kick-off. He was the latest recruit to the Albion family and loved it from his first game, subsequently becoming a regular. Some 16,000 turned up for our 1-0 friendly home win against Villa.

Our campaign kicked off at home to Charlton and yet another signing from Grimsby, 'Diddy' David Gilbert, scoring the only goal. Just like last season, we were at Wolves for our second League game and Taylor scored in a hard-fought draw. September started off well enough with home wins against Sheffield United (3-1) and Blues (1-0) and a good victory at Oldham (2-1). After a couple of defeats, we hit a purple patch, beating Reading (2-0), Luton (2-1) and Portsmouth (2-1).

Then we went on the worst run in the club's history, losing an incredible thirteen of the next fourteen. Our only point in this horrendous sequence came in a goalless home draw against Wolves. Most managers would have been sacked but, amazingly, Alan Buckley was rewarded with a new contract! I could not get my head around this decision.

We had plummeted towards the bottom of the table, a situation thankfully halted by strengthening the defence. Paul Holmes and Shane Nicholson came in and Nigel Spink took over in goal. On 10 February, we won in the League for the first time for nearly four months, beating Southend 3-1 at home, and this was followed up with three points at Sheffield United and three more at home to Oldham.

We desperately needed someone to share goal-scoring duties with Hunt and Taylor. Enter Dutchman – Richard Sneekes, signed for £400,000 from Bolton. He became an instant hero, scoring on his debut in a crazy 4-4 home draw with Watford, a game that saw Bob hit a hat-trick. Sneekes, with his distinctive long hair, scored again four days later, netting our second in a 2-1 win against Barnsley. He was on fire and added a further eight goals before the end of the season, giving him a brilliant tally of ten in just thirteen appearances. It was real Roy of the Rovers stuff. His goal at Leicester was spectacular, a 25-yarder so powerful that it stuck in the stanchion in the net. He was being worshipped by Albion fans and our 2,500 following at Norwich chanted 'Sneekers, Sneekers' during the pre-match warm up. He duly obliged with our second goal there after SuperBob had scored the first in a 2-2 draw.

Apart from a few Sneekes wigs, there was no end-of-season theme. A midweek game at Barnsley, hardly providing much scope for a beach party. We finished in style with a 3-2 win against already-promoted Derby in front of 23,858, the biggest Hawthorns crowd of the season. Our goals were scored by the usual three; Taylor, Hunt and Sneekes. Our final position of eleventh was remarkable considering our campaign contained that fourteen-match run mid-season when we managed just a solitary point.

We were dumped out of the FA Cup by Crewe. On my first visit to Gresty Road, a young Neil Lennon stole the show in the Alex's 4-3 victory. The League Cup first round took us to Northampton. I had seen a game at their old ground when working at Milton Keynes. However, they had now moved to out-of-town Sixfields, where I saw us progress 5-3 on aggregate. We then crashed out to Reading by losing 4-2 at The Hawthorns after drawing 1-1 at Elm Park.

Fourteen players or backroom personnel based at The Hawthorns in the season had previously been with Grimsby. Certainly something fishy going on there!

At work, we had secured a contract in Hong Kong to install eight miles of glass balustrade at the new International airport. I visited Asia for the first time, a trip I was to make over twenty times in the next few years. On our first few flights, we landed at the old Kai Tak airport which was a traumatic experience. The runway was situated between numerous skyscrapers and mountains and jutted out into Victoria Harbour. It was ranked as the sixth most dangerous airport in the world until closure in 1998.

I would occasionally have to miss Albion games so would head to Champions Bar in Lan Kwai Fong at 1.00 a.m. along with fans from all over the UK for the results. I also had to take the *Sports Argus* with me for Albion-supporting ex-pats over there. To get my football fix, I went to watch South China FC or Happy Valley. I even saw Chelsea play an exhibition game at the National Stadium.

I loved it in Hong Kong, which provided the perfect base for exploring that part of the world. I would often catch the hovercraft to the Portuguese territory of Macau or a train into China to Shenzhen or Guangzhou (Canton). I even visited Guangzhou Apollo FC, a stadium where Albion played during their ground-breaking 1978 tour.

20

The Italian Job, Part II

In 1995, Albion had another crack at the Anglo-Italian Cup. I couldn't make the opening fixture, away to Salernitana, where we drew 0-0 in hurricane-like conditions. I attended the next two games at The Hawthorns – a 2-1 defeat against Foggia and victory over Reggiana by the same score – and we needed a win against Brescia Calcio in Italy to qualify for the next stages.

I didn't want to miss out on another trip and Exeter Steve was also up for it, our car load being completed by good mates and Red Admiral regulars Dave Foxall and Alan Harvey. On 11 December, we once again headed for Dover for the night ferry to Calais and arrived at the Kent coast in time for beer before boarding. We took a different route this time, through France, Belgium, Luxembourg and Germany, making our first 'ground-hopping' stop at Bundesliga club Karlsruher SC, where fog moving in from the Rhine made photography of the 45,000-capacity Wildpark Stadion difficult. Next stop was Stuttgart and the impressive Neckar Stadium then onwards before the first snow appeared. It was 4.00 p.m. on arrival at Bayern Munich's magnificent Olympic Stadium, where our plans completely changed. In just 10 minutes, the pitch disappeared under a white carpet several inches deep.

We had planned to cross the Alps and make it to Venice that evening but, as we drove away from the stadium, it was obvious we weren't going to make it far. We were sliding everywhere and narrowly missed several parked cars. The locals were tapping the windows, telling us we needed snow chains. We spotted a parking place and I decided to abandon the car before we crashed. Off we trudged in search of a hotel. As luck would have it, we walked round the corner and into a fantastic Christmas market, a hotel, a bank and several bars. This was an unscheduled detour, so we hadn't got any German marks – just Italian lira (no euros then). Fortunately, we got to the bank just before closing and got some beer money. Hotel booked, we sampled the delicious Munich wheat beer while discussing how on earth we were going to negotiate the Alps next day.

We got the underground to Munich railway station and enquired about catching a train to Brescia. It was just about do-able but very expensive. At least we had a back-up plan. So it was off to the famous Hofbrauhaus, a three-floor Bavarian beer hall dating back to the sixteenth century, to sink a few steins. When we mentioned that we were planning on driving to Italy, we were met with roars of laughter and mutterings of 'Crazy English.' During the evening's unexpected session, we were entertained at our table by a magician who rolled up a newspaper, poured Alan's beer into it, and unrolled it to reveal a completely dry paper with no trace of beer from the now empty glass. I know we had downed a few, but we were totally mystified. His trick became even more impressive when he rolled up the newspaper again and poured the beer back into the glass. How he did it became such a talking point that we almost forgot about the enormous task ahead of us.

With hangovers from hell, we peered through the curtains as daylight broke to see that, although white over, it wasn't snowing any more. Over breakfast, a decision was made to give it a go. It took a couple of hours just to get out of Munich, but we made it to a clear autobahn and headed through Innsbuck via the Austrian Alps into Italy. The scenery was incredible as we drove through snow-capped mountains.

The drive along Lake Garda was also spectacular and we arrived in Brescia in the Lombardy region of Northern Italy during late afternoon, soon locating the distinctly unimpressive

16,000-capacity Stadio Mario Rigamonti. We had managed to secure four press passes and the steward kindly let us park inside the main gates in a space reserved for visiting directors. On viewing the pitch, we didn't think the game could possibly be played. It was covered in a thick snow and we feared the worst. It was dark, grim and freezing cold as we wandered into the centre of the so-called 'Lioness of Italy'. Brescia is considered Italy's industrial capital with metallurgy and the production of firearms particularly important. It is also the homeland of Italian caviar. The drab, featureless centre is rendered colder still by the brutal block-and-column architecture from its fascist days. We eventually found refuge in a bar for a warm drink and something to eat. A few other travelling Baggies soon joined us and we shared stories with familiar faces Richie Brentnall, Kenny Hazel, long-haired Mick Hamblett, Carlo from Darlo and Fraser Allen – Chairman of the Sutton Branch of the Albion Supporters Club.

Back at the stadium, we were invited into the VIP lounge for complimentary drinks and snacks. Albion director Clive Stapleton looked amazed as we received the same hospitality as the Baggie hierarchy. Coach John Trewick kindly gave us some badges to exchange for Brescia souvenirs.

Unbelievably, the pitch was deemed playable and the match was on. I even ventured out and rounded up the players for a team photo in the snow. The game was played in a blizzard as we watched from the comfort of the press box. Just 196, including around sixty Albion fans, saw us scrape a narrow victory, with the ball increasing in size as it gathered snow. A win was essential and we were heading out of the competition until the 87th minute when Bob Taylor pounced on Ian Hamilton's through pass after David Smith had hoisted a long ball downfield following a goal-line block. The ball just made it over the line as it collected more of the thick stuff. At the end, we jumped around as if we had won the League. The players joined us in a celebratory snowball fight before it was time to head back across the Alps. Manager Alan Buckley told the press: 'The lads were magnificent. The snow made the game a lottery and we had to contend with some of the worst physical intimidation I've seen. But everyone showed tremendous commitment to the cause and it was good to see Taylor score.'

With great trepidation, we commenced our journey home and it was certainly memorable. First, we pulled into a petrol station, where we were approached by several ladies wearing fur coats. They opened their jackets to reveal that they had nothing on underneath. This was obviously a regular stop for lorry drivers on entering or leaving Brescia, but the ladies of the night soon realised we were not going to give them any custom from my Ford Orion. Then, at the foot of the Swiss Alps, with the windscreen wipers on maximum speed as the snow came down in lumps the size of golf balls, the wiper on my side suddenly blew off in the blizzard. Fortunately, we managed to recover it, but I had to drive for a while with one arm out of the window clearing the windscreen by hand. We soon found a garage where, even though it was the middle of the night, a mechanic kindly fixed it back on for a small fee. Phew! We had been informed that the roads through the Swiss Alps were more passable than the Austrian route, so we drove through the night towards Basle. By daylight, the snow had abated and we continued our tour of the Bundesliga by diverting to the 51,000-capacity Waldstadion, home of Eintracht Frankfurt. But it was too late to make our planned stop in Cologne after we suffered a puncture in Eintracht's car park.

Thanks to there being no speed limits on the autobahn, we made it to Calais for the 10.10 p.m. crossing and were back in Great Barr for 3.30 a.m. on the Friday. We had visited eight countries, covering 2,335 miles at a total cost of just £107.50 each, including petrol, insurance, ferries, AA cover and a quality hotel in Munich. The car had to be fumigated afterwards but it well was worth it. Another top trip: so many memories with great company, brilliant laughs and an Albion victory. N.B. We bumped into a load of Port Vale fans on the way back. They had played in Perugia and won 5-3 to also qualify, but their coach made it only as far as Bologna before being beaten by the snow. 'Two hundred quid just to play snowballs in Italy' was one of the more printable comments. Their only compensation was the fact that Stoke's match in Italy had been abandoned – permanently. We tried not to mention our victory at Wembley in 1993, although I think it may have slipped out!

Our victory in Brescia took us through to the English semi-finals and to St Andrew's to face Birmingham. It finished all square at 2-2 after extra-time and the players held their nerve to win the shoot-out 4-1, with Dave Smith, the ex-Blues man, putting away the decisive kick. Wembley was in sight and we only had to overcome Port Vale in the English final to secure another visit. After a 0-0 first-leg home draw, several thousand Albion fans travelled up the M6 to cheer the lads over the line ... or so we thought. Disappointingly, we were beaten 3-1. Those remarks to the Vale fans in Italy certainly came back to haunt us. Genoa progressed from the Italian section and won 5-2 at Wembley in front of just 12,683. The organisers must have wished for an Albion victory to ensure Wembley was somewhere near full.

21

Coast to coast – Kirkcaldy to Birkenhead

Tony Jones, Anil Shiyal, Steve Conabeer and assorted other mates had been joining me for regular trips to Scotland. We were attempting to see a game on every Scottish League ground and would try and get two midweek matches in on each visit, calling at other grounds en route and mixed in with the odd beer or two. 1995 was no exception and our selected first game was Raith's first ever UEFA Cup appearance against GI Gota from the Faroe Islands. I had applied for press permits for us under the guise of the 'British Association of Faroese Football Supporters'. On arrival at Starks Park, we were given our passes and welcomed into the executive lounge, where Kevin Keegan and Terry McDermott, the managerial team at Newcastle, were present, presumably on a scouting mission. The names on our passes were hilarious. I had given us all Scandinavian-sounding surnames (all ending in 'son'). Three of them were just about passable, but Anil is of Indian heritage and his badge name 'Anil Gunndersson' really shouldn't have fooled anyone!

Raith play in the coastal town of Kirkcaldy, Fife, on Scotland's east coast. It just happened to be the home of Willie Johnston's pub 'The Port Brae', so, after the match; we joined him for several pints. As ever, he was a brilliant host and soon donned an Albion shirt for 'team' photos with his Scottish caps and hat-trick match balls. It was great to see plenty of Albion mementos in his trophy cabinet. I visited 'Wee Bud' three times over the years and he couldn't have been more welcoming, I even interviewed him for the Baggies newspaper. Sadly, the brewery closed the Port Brae down in 2010 and Willie's memorabilia was locked inside.

1996/97

My first visit to Walsall's shiny new Bescot Stadium was pre-season for Chris Marsh's testimonial. It was all very nice and 'plasticy', but lacked the character of Fellows Park, which is now a Morrisons Supermarket. We started the season with a disappointing home defeat to Barnsley despite Andy Hunt's penalty. We then had three away games in a row – all in London. We drew at Charlton and Crystal Palace before beating Queens Park Rangers, back on grass, 2-0, with goals from Taylor and Peschisolido. Hunt helped himself to a hat-trick as we edged the home game with Reading.

During our annual Scottish football trip, we saw Dundee play Aberdeen in an exciting Cup game. For our second match, on our way back down south, we agreed to go to Middlesbrough's new Riverside Stadium to see Hereford play in the League Cup. My friend Dean Smith was Hereford's captain and kindly sorted some tickets for us. He was due to mark 'Boro's new signing – Italian international Fabrizio Ravanelli. We sent Dean a good luck fax message from East Fife FC earlier in the day saying 'Keep Ravanelli in your pocket'. The result ... Middlesbrough 7 Hereford 0 and Ravanelli got four!

Next up at The Hawthorns were the Wolves. Their new signing from Leicester, Iwan Roberts, grabbed a hat-trick as we were outmuscled 4-2. Fortunately, we bounced back at Tranmere the following week, winning 3-2 with Paul Groves, Dave Gilbert and Pesch on target. We had a new goalkeeper, Paul Crichton, another recruit from our 'B team' at Grimsby. Let's just say he didn't exactly fill me with confidence.

Six of our next seven games were drawn, the exception being our usual defeat by Stoke, this time 2-0 at home. A brief flicker of good form at Swindon saw us gain a 3-2 victory with Pesch making a fantastic run from the half-way line before finishing in style. I was working in London at the time and there was a rail strike on, so London cabbie and fellow Albion fan Tony Nash agreed to take Andy Miller, Steve Munday and myself to the County Ground in his black cab. Just for fun, he switched his meter on and, by the time we arrived, it showed a cost of £104.

As per usual, we followed a good win by getting stuffed, this time 4-0 at Portsmouth – a defeat that ended our 244-day, seven-month unbeaten away run.

Among the dross served up over the next few weeks, we actually managed a few decent victories, like Southend away (3-2), Norwich at home (5-1) and QPR at home (4-1). Our esteemed 'keeper Mr Crichton then had a horror show at Molineux. It had been an accident waiting to happen and the Wolves fans made the most of it, forcing him into numerous errors in our 2-0 defeat. His kicking was atrocious and a Black Country double defeat left a very sour taste. My patience with manager Buckley was wearing a bit thin. He had assembled a team of Grimsby rejects. Were we really going to achieve anything better than mid-table in Division One? Simply not good enough for a club with the standing of West Bromwich Albion.

Buckley was running on borrowed time and a shocking 5-0 reverse at Ipswich sealed his fate. He was rightly sacked and in came Ray Harford, who immediately appointed former Baggies favourite Cyrille Regis as chief coach. They identified our defence as the main problem. Crichton was soon replaced in goal by the experienced Alan Miller, back for his second spell, from Middlesbrough. Defenders Shaun Murphy, Andy McDermott and Graham Potter were also introduced.

Harford injected discipline and we at last seemed to have a game plan. His first away game was at Norwich, where we witnessed a brilliant Albion display and a well-deserved 4-2 win. Pesch got a hat-trick and Sneekes also got in on the act. Despite a couple of defeats, things were looking a lot better, with good wins against Southend (4-0) and Blues (2-0).

We finished with three wins from our last six games, the highlight being our 2-1 success at Sheffield United, with SuperBob and Stacey Caldicott on target. Our final fixture took us to Stoke for the last ever game at the Victoria Ground. In a big crowd, I was fortunate to have a photographer's permit. It was great to be on the pitch beforehand with the legendary Sir Stanley Matthews, who led the farewells in front of the Boothen End. Our 2-1 defeat didn't really matter as it felt like we were gatecrashers at someone else's party. By coincidence, Albion were also Stoke's first visitors at 'The Vic' some 109 years earlier (September, 1888). We finished sixteenth in the League as yet another disappointing season ended.

In the FA Cup, a huge Albion following to Stamford Bridge was housed in the lower tier of the main stand – and the view was terrible. The football on show wasn't any better as we didn't put up any kind of a fight, succumbing to a 3-0 defeat against Premiership giants Chelsea, who didn't even get out of first gear.

The good old League Cup presented me with the opportunity to visit my only new venue of the season; Layer Road, home of Colchester. I made a night of it, booking a B&B near the ground. The beer always tastes better after an Albion win and Hamilton, Hunt and Donovan scored in a 3-2 victory. David Gilbert was presented with his man-of-the-match award, a bike, on the pitch at the end. Inexplicably, we lost the second leg 3-1 and went out 5-4 on aggregate.

1997/98

Pre-season in 1997, I went to Hednesford's new Keys Park. Albion marked this visit with a 1-0 win. A testimonial was staged at The Hawthorns for Albion legend Ronnie Allen, who wasn't in the best of health, and 16,864 turned up to see us lose 2-1 to Villa.

New signings Kevin Kilbane (from Preston) and Albion fans Lee Hughes (from Kidderminster) and Sean Flynn (from Derby) were in place for the start of the season, 'Killer' Kilbane scoring on his debut – a 2-1 home win against Tranmere on the opening day. 'Hughesy' certainly made an instant impression the week after. We were trailing at Crewe when he went on as a second-half substitute and completely changed the game, scoring twice and celebrating with Albion fans packed behind the goal. We won 3-2. When interviewed afterwards, he said: 'I spotted my mates in the crowd and wanted to join them.'

We made it three wins out of three when Wolves came to town. In a close game, Keith Curle scored an own goal to give us another three points. He was named as the Albion Supporters' Player of the Year at the end of the season.

On our trip to Ipswich, I collected my photographer's documents and headed off to the pub to meet my mates. I noticed on the permit that it just had '1' filled in where it stated 'number of permits'. I changed it to '4' and all of us walked into Portman Road for nothing, with just one camera between us. A 1-1 draw kept our unbeaten run intact.

Pesch got a hat-trick in our 3-1 win at Bury and another good win came at Portsmouth, where a Paul Mardon goal and Andy Hunt brace saw us home 3-2. Our form was excellent. We briefly topped the table and were thinking about promotion. Ray Harford had got us playing positive attacking football and in November we put four straight wins together – against Norwich, Charlton, Port Vale and Birmingham. Our performance against Blues wasn't one of our better ones and they had much of the possession. We managed just one shot on goal in 90 minutes and Richard Sneekes put it away. 'One shot, we only need one shot,' taunted the Brummie Road.

Jade and I went to Middlesbrough to see Albion at the Riverside, it was a welcome change from the horrible experiences at the old Ayresome Park. We met up with my good friend, 'Boro fan Richard Harrington for a lunchtime drink on a boat anchored next to the stadium. We lost 1-0 and a repeat scoreline at home to Man City was overshadowed by the news that Ray Harford had quit as manager to take over at QPR. It seemed a strange decision as Rangers were in no better shape than Albion and certainly weren't a bigger club. Harford sadly passed away in August 2003.

On Christmas Eve, Denis Smith was unveiled as our new manager, joining us from Oxford. Not exactly the best present I've ever had.

We lost three and drew two of his first five League games, a run halted at Molineux of all places. Andy Hunt's goal gave us a much-needed 1-0 win over Wolves. New signings Mickey Evans and Matt Carbon scored the following week in our 2-0 win at Swindon. We had to wait a ridiculous eleven matches for our next victory, this horrendous run including a 3-0 home defeat to Portsmouth and a nightmare 5-0 thrashing at Charlton which saw us plummeting down the table.

When we finally won, it was on 4 April against high-flying Middlesbrough, new forward James Quinn getting both goals, including a penalty, in our 2-1 win at The Hawthorns. A 1-0 defeat at Huddersfield provided a new ground. The Terriers' had moved from Leeds Road to their three-sided McAlpine Stadium in 1994. New Albion players on display were the veteran defender Steve Nicol, Australian full back Jason Van Blerk and centre-half Paul Beesley. Young Chris Adamson was in goal and appeared to be well out of his depth. With just one success in our last five games, a thrilling 4-2 win at Sheffield United, we finished tenth, one place below Wolves.

A 3-1 victory against Stoke in the third round of the FA Cup was sweet for Denis Smith but, in the fourth round, a massive Albion following at Villa Park saw us embarrassingly beaten 4-0, our old nemesis Stan Collymore milking every minute of this humiliation.

Cambridge and Luton were both despatched over two legs in the League Cup before Liverpool outclassed us in the third round, comfortably winning 2-0 at The Hawthorns. Nigel Spink played in goal at Cambridge at thirty-nine years, then the record.

I was devastated on 31 July 1998, when I received a call from my dad informing me that Mom had passed away peacefully at their bungalow in Hednesford. She had been suffering with breast cancer for some time and her body couldn't take any more chemotherapy or radiotherapy. She was adamant she wasn't going to end up in hospital and, when she didn't wake one morning, Dad told her an ambulance was on its way. On hearing those words, she just switched off. I'm sure she knew what was happening and had made her mind up to die with dignity at home. We were very close and her death hit me hard. She had been a good mate as well as everything else and it was

Top Left: Mom's handmade rosette that she wore at the 1954 FA Cup Final when Albion beat Preston North End 3-2.

Top Right: My best friend in the '60s – my Grandad Jack Warren.

Left: With my mom, dad and brother Alan on a day out in Stourport, 1965.

Bottom Left: My denim waistcoat covered in Albion sew-on patches that I used to wear to all Albion games in the mid-seventies.

Installing curtain walling and windows for Allan H Williams on site in Milton Keynes 1983. Left to right: Dave Stinson, Big Alf, Neil Stinson, Dave Loats, Kenny Foster and me.

Scott Arms FC – League Champions 1985. A great Sunday league mixture of good footballers and maniacs! Back row L to R: Andy Stubbs, Dave Loats, Dave Foxall, Godfrey MacLean, me, Warren Jones, Michael Silvester. Front Row: Andy Norton, Micky Winnitt, Conrad Jones, Chris O'Nyan, Steve Brennan and Steve Scriven.

En route to Albion's World Club Championship game against Dumbarton 1988. We called in at several Scottish football grounds on the way including St Mirren's old Love Street ground in Paisley. Left to right: Dave Foxall, me, Paul Dubberley (Dubsey), Michael Silvester (Silve) and Chris Edwards. We lost 2-1.

At the home ground of KePS in Kemi, Finland 1989. Albion were due to tour Scandinavia but cancelled at the last minute – we still went! Left to right: Dubsey, me, Silve, Neil Whitehouse and Tony Jones.

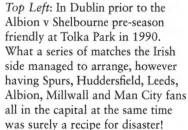

Top Left: In Dublin prior to the Albion v Shelbourne pre-season friendly at Tolka Park in 1990. What a series of matches the Irish side managed to arrange, however having Spurs, Huddersfield, Leeds, Albion, Millwall and Man City fans all in the capital at the same time was surely a recipe for disaster!

Top Right: Me and Dave Loats (Skin) on the terraces at Selhurst Park before Albion's game against Crystal Palace in 1981.

Middle Left: My nephew Stuart Walton in the Rainbow Stand paddock at The Hawthorns in 1990.

Left: The Albion team before the game against Newry Town in Northern Ireland, 1990. We had to drive past a burned-out bus to get to the ground and the pitch was surrounded by armed police. Back row L to R: Shakespeare, Naylor, Raven, Burgess, Bradley, Hodson, Goodman, Foster. Front row: Robson, Harbey, Bannister, Hackett, McNally, Ford.

With my all-time hero Jeff Astle – The King – in 1991 before the game against Bristol Rovers, which was played at Twerton Park in the Roman city of Bath that condemned us to the third tier of English football for the first time in our history. The end of season theme was Togas at Rovers. Left to right: Dave Foxall, Martin Davies (Davel), Jeff Astle, Andy Miller, Steve Power.

On Wembley Way outside the famous old twin towers to see Albion beat Port Vale 3-0 in the 1993 play-off final. We were joined by 43,000 other Baggies. Left to right: Chris Edwards, Me, Silve and Dubsey.

Me on the terraces at Oakwell, Barnsley for Albion's second end of season beachwear party 1990. Last away game theme parties were to become a big part of Albion's fixtures.

Me with new Albion Manager Ossie Ardiles, the Argentinian World Cup winner, at Clarence Park for Albion's pre-season friendly against St Albans in 1992 – we went on to win promotion via the play-offs in Ossie's first season.

Me with Jade on the last remnants of the Brummie Road End terraces at The Hawthorns in 1994. At least Jade can say that she went in the Brummie Road when it was still a terrace!

In the Artemio Franchi Stadium, Florence in 1993 after driving to Italy to see Albion play Fiorentina in the Anglo-Italian Cup. Left to right: Tony Jones, Silve and me.

Baggies' invasion of Portsmouth.

Life as an Albion missionary. With two of the Brisbane Baggies, Australia, 1999. Left to right: me, Steve Barlough and George Holland. Steve kindly gave me the keys to his house for a couple of days.

The famous Little Mermaid statue in Copenhagen gets 'Baggiefide' during Albion's Danish tour 1999. I paddled out to the statue much to the amusement of the watching Japanese tourists.

Passing through Austria on our way to see Albion play Brescia in the Anglo-Italian Cup, 1995; shortly after this photograph was taken, we got snow-bound in Munich and had to continue the journey the following day. Left to right: Dave Foxall, Alan Harvey and me.

Wearing my colours at the Gambia v Sierra Leone game 1999. We thought that the home side had won until we were in the pub later that night – it turned out that Sierra Leone fans made up the majority of the crowd.

My daughter Jade meets Albion mascot Baggie Bird before the Gillingham v Albion game in 2003.

The players pose for me in the snow before the Anglo-Italian Cup game in Brescia, Italy 1995. The game should never have been played, but I didn't complain ... we won 1-0.

Goalkeeper for the Albion supporters' team to face The Blue Wave (Greve FC supporters) in 2000. A game was also organised in 2001. Some life-long friendships were formed during our Danish trips.

With our good friends from The Blue Wave – The Greve FC supporters group in 2001. A great bond was forged between our two sets of fans during our three pre-season tours to Denmark.

A brilliant after-game barbecue with the Slagelse FC fans – the Red Vikings after our pre-season game in Denmark, 2001. The home fans raided the club shop to kit us out with souvenirs. The Greve fans laid on a coach and accompanied us on the trip. A three-way supporter's football tournament took place prior to the main event.

A proud moment – meeting The Queen at Buckingham Palace in 2004. Alumet had received the Queen's Award for Enterprise. Along with Gary Summers and Julie Robinson, we had a ten-minute private audience with Her Majesty.

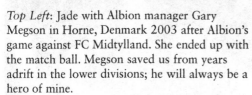

Top Left: Jade with Albion manager Gary Megson in Horne, Denmark 2003 after Albion's game against FC Midtylland. She ended up with the match ball. Megson saved us from years adrift in the lower divisions; he will always be a hero of mine.

Top Right: My step-son Oliver's first match in 2003; Jade looked after him at The Hawthorns for the Premier League game against Chelsea.

Above Left: My kids Ollie and Jade at Glanford Park before Albion's game against Scunthorpe United in 2007. The pair of them get on really well together and both love the Baggies.

Middle Right: Former Albion striker Andy Hunt at his home in Belize, Central America 2003. I went to visit him with Glenn Robinson and Anil Shiyal via Mexico and Guatemala after he featured in an Albion programme. Andy and his wife Simone made us very welcome.

Right: Holding the FA Cup before our cup-tie at Bournemouth in 1998. My biggest regret is not seeing Albion lift the trophy in 1968. Maybe someday?

Me and Jade outside the new Wembley Stadium for our play-off final defeat against Derby County in 2007.

Ollie's 11th birthday present – to be Albion's mascot for the game against Barnsley on 1 September 2007. I was as excited as him!

Ollie at Wembley for our FA Cup semi-final defeat against Portsmouth in 2008. That's two trips to the new Wembley and we haven't seen Albion score yet!

First Division Champions and the birth of Mask-arade, with Chris O'Nyan in keeping with the superheroes theme outside Loftus Road before our 2-0 victory against Queens Park Rangers in 2008. We sold 300 Kevin Phillips masks before the game and launched Mask-arade immediately afterwards.

Champions! The first time that I had seen Albion win a major trophy: QPR 2008 – I told the kids to take in every second as it's not very often that you see the Baggies with silverware. A brilliant day.

Chris and me with the First Division Championship trophy at The Hawthorns.

With my fellow Alumet directors. I worked in the construction industry for thirty-eight years and at Alumet for twenty-two years. Left to right: Paul Summers, Damien Bradley, Gary Summers, Steve Smith and me. I retired in 2016.

Albion manager Tony Mowbray with Ollie and Jade on Albion's pre-season tour to Germany 2008. I flew to Dusseldorf for just 5p!

Top Left: Wearing Tony Mowbray masks at Blackburn in 2009. The Albion manager received tremendous support from the Albion fans even though we had just been relegated. He left for Celtic shortly afterwards.

Top Right: England v Sweden, Japan 2002.

Middle Left: With TV presenter and staunch Albion fan Adrian Chiles in Dinamo Zagreb's ground on our way to Varazdin for Albion's friendly in Croatia, 2009. We ended up getting drunk together and nearly missed the match!

Middle Centre: With Steve Conabeer in Bloemfontein at the Japan v Cameroon game, South Africa World Cup 2010. We flew into Johannesburg and drove over 1,000 miles to Cape Town via Botswana and Lesotho.

Middle Right: The Three Mask-ateers: Chris O'Nyan, me and Ray Duffy. From Chris's crazy idea to a million-pound business in a just few years, including an appearance on TV's *Dragons' Den*.

Bottom Right: In my dreams! With the Premier League trophy in Barclays Bank, Leamington Spa.

Ollie with Albion manager Roberto Di Matteo before our pre-season game against Venlo in the Netherlands 2010.

Having some fun with our masks in Venlo centre before Albion's pre-season game in the Netherlands 2010. We produced masks of all the players.

Do you know the way to San Jose? Before our game against San Jose Earthquakes on Albion's pre-season tour of the USA, 2011. Left to right: Dave Bending, me, Kevin Wainwright, John Tkaczuk (Sauce), Neil Reynolds and Norman Bartlam. This, for me, is what football is all about.

Roy Hodgson Day at the Reebok Stadium, Bolton, 2012. Roy had accepted the England manager's job and so an England theme was our way of saying thank you.

The Roy Hodgson triplets! Having some fun with the manager at a Player of the Year night.

Outside the Swedbank Stadium before our pre-season friendly in Malmo, Sweden, 2012. The guy on the far right is Malmo fan Hubert Sarnandt – one of Dubsey's travel friends.

The Albion fans converge on Harry's Bar in Malmo on the day of our game in Sweden 2012. The camaraderie on the pre-season tours is first class.

With my good friend Benny Andersen, reunited in Copenhagen before Albion's game against FCK in 2012. I first met Benny when he was chairman of The Blue Wave on our first trip to Greve in 1999. Benny and his brother Martin came over for my wedding in 2005.

Ian Tinsley and I with the 'Scandies' in Malmo, 2010. The Norwegian and Swedish Baggies were brilliant company and their Albion knowledge is incredible. Left to right: Torbjorn Allund, me, Ian Tinsley, Henrik Skaalvoid, Robert Jensen, Geir Andreassen and Stian Boe.

Mask-arade-sponsored Albion mascot Baggie Bird for three years; here goalkeeper Boaz Myhill presents Chris and me with our framed shirt.

A proud moment in my business career – after receiving the West Midlands Director of the Year award, I was then named UK Director of the Year for Leadership in Corporate Responsibility 2012. Jade attended the ceremony to see Michael Portillo present me with the award. I was runner-up as overall UK Director of the Year.

Top Left: With some of the usual suspects in the players' tunnel at Gleisdorf FC before our pre-season game in Austria 2013.

Above: Cover star! It was weird to see myself on the cover of the *IoD West Midlands* magazine after representing the area and winning in the London final.

Middle Left: Outside a poster advertising our game against Puskas Academy in Sopron, Hungary 2013.

Left: Ollie and Jade flew out to Vienna to meet me on Albion's pre-season tour to Austria and Hungary 2013. Here they are at our match in Sopron, Hungary.

Bottom Left: As official suppliers to Manchester United, Mask-arade were invited as special guests at their Champions' League game against Bayer Leverkusen. Here we are with ex-Albion legends Bryan Robson and Mickey Thomas. Robson surprised us at half-time when he brought the Premier League trophy and the Community Shield into our executive box.

Another great pre-season trip, this time in Cork, Ireland. Having a few beers after the match in the excellent Franciscan Well brewery pub.

Jade and me with Albion manager Pepe Mel. The Spaniard's tenure was short-lived, a shame really as he was a lovely bloke and he had good footballing principles.

Outside the Rosaleda Stadium before Malaga's game against Levante in 2014. We went to Spain to remember our great friend Richie Brentnall. Left to right: Davel, me, Dubsey and Tony.

Raising a few glasses for Richie Brentnall in Fuengirola, 2014. Richie sadly passed away in Spain the year before and this was the first of our annual memorial weekends. Right to left: Silve, me, Davel, Tony, Dubsey and Bill.

With the Pittsburgh Baggies before our game against Richmond on our USA East Coast tour 2015.

With my ever-supportive wife Ruth in Pula, Croatia 2014.

This could never happen at The Hawthorns! With various USA-based Albion fans having a tailgate party outside the ground, before the match against Richmond Kickers in 2015.

Enjoying the good times with family and mates; it's half-time at Villa Park and we're 1-0 up against our arch rivals. Being brought up in Great Barr, Villa have always been the enemy as far as I'm concerned. Victory is always sweet. (Action Rewind Photography)

The next generation: my nephew Stuart and his son Joel. Joel attended his first Albion game in 2015 ... it's in the blood.

Gone but not forgotten, Albion fan extraordinaire and good friend Richie Brentnall. Richie sadly died in a freak accident in Spain, 2014... Seat HH 69 in the Brummie Road End is much quieter these days. RIP big fella.

A proud dad – Jade's graduation ceremony at the Symphony Hall in Birmingham, 2015.

Another classic old ground sadly gone forever. We visited the Boleyn Ground for the last time to see Albion play West Ham in 2015. The Irons moved to the Olympic Stadium in 2016.

emotional at the funeral when many of my friends turned up unexpectedly. They knew she had been a season-ticket holder with me in the early 1970s.

1998/99

A testimonial game at Bromsgrove pre-season was a good excuse to visit their Victoria Ground for the first time and I attended our 2-0 win with my Bromsgrove based ex-school mate Paul Hutchinson. Rovers were dissolved in 2010 and a new club Bromsgrove Sporting, were formed from the ashes. Next up was St George's Lane, where we won 3-2 against Worcester City. The bulldozers moved into this lovely old ground in 2014.

I met our new signing from Cagliari, Enzo Maresca, before another 3-2 friendly win, this time at Notts County. I also went to The Hawthorns to see Albion play Jamaica in a testimonial for club record breaker Tony 'Bomber' Brown. An incredible 20,358 attendance was the biggest for a friendly since Norman Heath's testimonial in 1954. We lost 1-0, much to the joy of thousands of Jamaicans present.

The new season was Albion's 100th in League football and Barnsley (fresh from relegation from the Premiership) were our opening-day opponents for the third time in six years. A 2-2 draw at Oakwell in front of 18,114 was followed by three straight wins. Sheffield United were destroyed 4-1 and Italian signing, Mario Bortalazzi (from Genoa), made his first start in our impressive 3-0 win at Port Vale; Hughesy grabbing his first Baggies hat-trick. Our new striker from Osasuna, Dutchman Fabian DeFreitas, made an impressive home debut, coming on as substitute against Norwich and scoring two second-half goals to seal our 2-0 victory.

Just when I was starting to think this might be our season, we travelled to Grimsby and gave their manager Alan Buckley the last laugh as they spanked us 5-1. We lost again the week after at home to Bolton (3-2) as reality set in.

A fine 3-1 win at Bristol City gave us fresh hope, but at the end of September we were on the wrong end of a 3-0 result at Oxford. Then, just five days later, we thrashed Watford 4-1 at The Hawthorns. Wolves came to town on 29 November and goals from Shaun Murphy and Kilbane sent them packing 2-0. The following week, we lost 2-0 at Bury with 'keeper Phil Whitehead making his debut. Typical Albion.

My second visit to the McAlpine Stadium was a pleasing one, James Quinn (2) and Hughesy sealing our 3-0 win against Huddersfield. We also pulled off a good 2-0 away win at Watford, where Sneekes and new winger Mark Angel grabbed goals. But a disastrous 4-0 defeat at Birmingham in April triggered off a terrible run which resulted in just one more victory in our last nine games. We became a laughing stock on Easter Monday when DeFreitas failed to turn up in time because he thought our home game against Crewe was an evening kick off. We were humiliated 5-1 and it seemed Smith had lost the plot.

Our 2-1 loss at QPR was our fifth defeat on the trot and, despite earning a point at Molineux, the season ended with a whimper at Tranmere Rovers, when a huge Albion following (many in fancy dress) converged on Birkenhead to see us lose 3-1. A final league position of twelfth was extremely disappointing, especially after such an encouraging start.

The FA Cup draw dealt us a trip to the seaside. On arrival at Bournemouth, the first thing I noticed was an enormous queue for the away end that snaked all the way round the ground and car park. A few thousand Albion fans sought to gain entry to the small open terrace. I managed to get my photograph taken holding the trophy before the game, which was more than the team did. We deservedly lost 1-0 in a pitiful performance.

We also fell at the first hurdle of the League Cup, throwing away a 2-1 lead in the second leg at Brentford, The Bees won 3-0 on the night and 4-2 on aggregate.

In my personal life, things hadn't been going too well between Elaine and me. We went on holiday with Jade to Jamaica to try and sort things out. But, despite a nice few days in Ocho Rios, we both knew our twelve-year marriage was over. Once we were home, we decided to separate. The hardest part was telling Jade I was leaving. I moved into a flat in Leamington Spa and took myself off to Australia to think things through and make some decisions about my future.

22

Baggies Down Under

Not having been to Australia before, I decided to fly to Sydney and travel up the east coast to Cairns. I would be travelling on my own, so I put a request out on the BOING (Baggies on the Internet Group) chat line asking if there were any Albion fans over there who fancied a beer during my stay.

To my surprise, I was inundated with replies. Dave Payne was first to get in touch, inviting me to a bar in Sydney for a meet-up with several other Baggies. George Holland also made contact from Brisbane and then ex-Smethwick Baggie Tony Mole threw a spanner in the works by saying in an email: 'I'm fed up of Albion fans going to Australia. Why doesn't anyone visit me in New Zealand?' Now there was an offer I couldn't refuse! New Zealand was another country on my hit-list, so I promptly responded and he recommended a cheap flight from Sydney to Wellington, which I added to my itinerary.

I was working in Asia, so it made sense to head Down Under from there. GSL had secured a contract to provide management for the glass façade installation on the large PB Com Tower development in Manila. My good mate David Loats (Skin) was based there and I flew to the Philippines to stay with him and his family for two days. Skin showed me the sights of Manila, including some very 'interesting' bars. There is a large ex-pat community in the capital and I met some great lads on a memorable night out.

My next port of call was Singapore for some meetings, Luckily, one of my business associates gave me the keys to his luxury apartment on Orchard Road, just round the corner from one of my favourite Singapore bars, Muddy Murphys. I was also taken to Orchard Towers, more commonly known as The Four Floors of Whores.

I packed my work stuff into a large suitcase and deposited it in the luggage office at Singapore airport. I could now travel with just a backpack to Australia. My itinerary now read: London – Hong Kong – Philippines – Singapore – Sydney – Wellington – Brisbane – Townsville – Cairns. Just for good measure, I added Papua New Guinea on the end.

I managed a few beers in Sydney before crashing out. Next day, I went on a boat trip around the harbour and visited The Rocks, the football stadium, Sydney Harbour Bridge, the Opera House and Bondi Beach. I had arranged to meet Dave and his wife, Ann, in the Union Hotel, Newtown, at 7.00 p.m. When I walked in, I could hardly believe my eyes. The whole bar was packed with people in Albion shirts. Dave and Ann introduced me to various members of the 'Sydney Baggies', including Mike Saunders – brother of BOING website master Finbarr, Michael Trigg, Jeremy Barnes, Julian Floyd and Mike and Gaye Wilson. They had descended on Sydney from all over New South Wales. One had driven 200 miles. I felt like a minor celebrity as I was bombarded with questions about the current state of affairs at the Albion.

After several pints of Victoria Bitter, we went to the Indian Fantasy restaurant next door, where a table had been booked. It was a brilliant evening. Just as I was starting to flag a bit and people were heading home, young Julian announced: 'You aren't going anywhere. You're coming with me to The Rocks.' I explained that I had an early flight to New Zealand, but Julian was having none of it. He was determined to make my night in Sydney memorable. Several bars later, I finally got back to my hotel at 3.00 a.m., booking a 5.00 a.m. wake-up call as I passed reception.

With a raging hangover and very little sleep, I headed for Wellington. Tony had agreed to meet me at the airport, but I was wondering how I would recognise him. I need not have worried. As soon as I was through customs, the first thing I spotted was a large banner portraying a footballer in blue and white stripes, proclaiming 'Welcome Deano' It was Tony and his son George, whose middle name is Cyrille!

During the journey to Tony's house in Petone, Wellington, he explained what he had been through over the previous few weeks. He used the Internet at work and, after inviting me, he raised the subject with his very pregnant Kiwi wife, Claire, 'I've invited someone to come and stay for a couple of days in June' declared Tony. 'Oh, that will be nice' replied Claire, 'One of your friends from back home?' At that point Tony should have said 'yes', but instead explained how he had emailed me via the BOING internet group. Claire snapped: 'So let's get this right ... you've met someone on the Internet and invited them to stay with us?' Tony, realising how ridiculous this now sounded, added: 'But he's an Albion fan. He'll be alright.' I understood Tony's logic, but, knowing plenty of Albion fans who are far from 'alright', I could also see his wife's point. Apparently, Claire originally forbid it and told Tony I couldn't stay. After going close to a divorce, he eventually talked her round.

This confession cleared my hangover and I must admit I entered the house with certain trepidation. Fortunately, I got on really well with Claire and ended up laughing about the whole situation. The Moles proved to be smashing hosts and Tony had booked a day off to show me round Wellington in his Datsun Cherry, calling at Basin Reserve, Brooklyn and the Athletic Park Stadium, which closed down later in the year. We had a few beers in town at The Backbencher pub and I joined them both for a 'blues party' at a friend's house; a novel event where everyone had to wear blue, every record had blue in the title and all the drinks were blue cocktails. I spent a pleasant last morning in the capital, visiting the state-of-the-art 'Te Papa' national museum.

My next stop was Brisbane, where I was again greeted at the airport by an Albion-themed banner. Steve Barlough, one of the Brisbane Baggies, whisked me off to Dicey Reilly's Irish pub in Garden City to meet George Holland. I was starting to feel like a West Bromwich Albion missionary. After a few pints of Guinness, George explained that he had met another Albion fan from Great Barr at the recent Test Match. He described this guy leading the Barmy Army conga – it was Dubsey! Steve invited me back to his house in the suburbs, introduced me to his lovely family, gave me a set of keys and told me to stay as long as I wanted, to just come and go as I pleased. The international brotherhood of Baggies never ceases to amaze me.

I spent the next couple of days visiting the famous Gabba cricket ground, The Suncorp Metway Stadium, Mount Coot-tha Lookout and the downtown beach.

My next flight took me up the coast to Townsville, where I finally ran out of Baggies. However, displaying my colours always guaranteed conversation whenever I entered a bar. Just 8 kilometres offshore was the mountainous Magnetic Island. I got the ferry and hired a push-bike for the day to explore the national park and bird sanctuary. The name of the island came about because of the apparent 'magnetic' effect it had on Captain Cook's compass as he passed in 1770.

I caught a bus to the gateway to Queensland's tropical north, Cairns, and used it as my base to visit the Great Barrier Reef. I spent a full day sailing round the Reef, one of the seven wonders of the natural world and the 'largest living thing on earth.' It was breathtakingly beautiful and I visited the tropical Green Island – a Marine National Park with stunning coral cay and rain forests.

To finish my incredible trip, I flew to Port Moresby on Papua New Guinea. It was completely different to Australia's cities and something of a culture shock. At the Ambers Inn Hotel, I chatted to an Aussie guy, Phil, who was equally shocked. The hotel was fenced in with barbed wire and the neighbouring streets appeared to be covered in blood. I later discovered it was the bright red juice of the areca nut, more commonly known as 'betel nut' – a natural high seed that is chewed by the locals and spat onto the ground.

Phil and I were desperate for a beer, but were warned against it and told it was dangerous for two white men to be seen out after dark. Then I remembered that a black barman in Cairns had given me his brother's number in Port Moresby. I looked him up and explained our predicament. Mike agreed to pick us up and enquired how he would recognise us. I replied: 'Well, we're both white.' There was a long silence then, fair play, he agreed to collect us. He told us to keep our heads down, so we wouldn't be spotted as he drove us to his flat in a run-down suburb. He pointed out the numerous bullet holes in his windscreen and showed us the scenes of several murders. Mike and his mate were really good company and, after sharing a few beers, 'smuggled' us back into his car and dropped us back, agreeing to pick us up again in the morning.

Sure enough, next day he showed us all around the port, even taking us to his local to play pool, much to the amusement of his mates. To return the favour, Phil got us into the members-only Royal Papua Yacht Club. A good time was had by all and the whole trip was an adventure to remember. The experience made me realise how powerful the West Bromwich Albion brand is. I met some fantastic Baggie folk and numerous football fans with tales to tell about my team.

The Oz Baggies, a brief history by former president, Jeremy Barnes

In my early days in Oz, I became aware of an Albion Supporters Club in Melbourne run by a guy called Bryan Williams. This was an absolute revelation as it was the early-1980s pre-Internet days and all we had to rely on for updates was the BBC World Service. Unfortunately, after a few years, the club petered out after Bryan suffered a family bereavement. But, after a while, the early Internet revolution arrived, meaning access to online British newspapers and up-to-date news, scores and, most of all, gossip.

In 1986, with more and more information available, plus the introduction of highlights shows in Oz, I took up the mantle. I advertised in a newspaper called *British Soccer Weekly* under the Australian Supporters Clubs, along with the mighty Liverpool's, Manchester United's and Arsenal's which seemed to be the only teams that Aussies supported.

Slowly but surely, the club grew bigger and bigger. Baggies as far flung as Perth joined. I produced monthly newsletters, first in black and white, then full colour, and a logo was produced. I was the first president and we were listed in the *Albion News* and also sponsored players, Dave Gilbert being one of the first. T-shirts and car stickers were run off and we were up and running big time. The club went from strength to strength. We recruited around fifty members and one of the highlights was receiving a visit from Paul Thompson, Albion chairman at the time. He was a real gentleman and took time out from his business commitments in Oz to meet us in the Rocks in Sydney. I travelled from Melbourne, but was well and truly outdone by the Perth Baggies, who crossed from one side of the continent to the other; the equivalent of London to Moscow!

One of the great joys was being a contact for Baggies coming over for holidays and I was lucky enough to meet the legendary Dave Watkin (Mr Football Ground), the author Deano Walton, and Mark (Cuzer) Currie, who came over for the Ashes. I even had a visit from former-Albion keeper Simon Miotto in Melbourne. He was a lovely guy to talk to about all things Baggies related.

I'm now back in Blighty and a Hawthorns season ticket holder. I am very proud to say the club is still going strong and all the members will always welcome fellow Baggies to Oz.

I do sometimes laugh when I hear Albion fans here in the UK question how anybody can be a supporter from such a distance, but I challenge them to regularly stay up until 4.00 a.m. on a Sunday to listen to or watch a live game on television. It was never easy, but we did it because we have one thing in common ... the love of the Baggies!

23

Wonderful, Wonderful Copenhagen

For three seasons running, Denmark was the destination for Albion's pre-season tours. This appealed to me because our previous Scandinavian tour (without the Albion) covered only Sweden, Finland and Norway. The club had sealed some sort of nursery side deal with Greve Fodbold, a club in the lower reaches of Danish football.

1999

Before the trip, I was contacted by Benny Andersen, chairman of the Greve supporters group 'Den Bla Bolge' – The Blue Wave. He invited all travelling Albion fans to meet in the Tingstedet Bar before the first game. I travelled to Copenhagen with Neil Grainger, Neil Whitehouse, Bill Ahearne and Paul and Trevor Dubberley.

On the day of our first game, we arrived in Greve (21 km from Copenhagen) and made ourselves comfortable in the Tingstedet. Familiar faces soon joined us, including Mick Hamblett, John Tkaczuk (Sauce), Spock, The Grorty Dick team – Simon and Glynis Wright, 'Dancing' Dave Byrne, Kenny Hazel and his mate Steve. Stuart Hill also checked in, having driven from his home in Stourbridge. Benny introduced himself and other members of The Blue Wave; his brother Martin, Per Johansen and Mortan Martinsson – a mad bloke from the Faroe Islands. It was also the first time I had met some of the Scandinavian Albion fans; Olle Kanno and Per-Erik Bengtsson from Sweden, Stian and Marianne from Norway, and Danish Baggies Michael Morch and Bo Daugaard. Barman Frank kept the beer flowing and we almost forgot we had a match to attend.

It was a 15-minute walk from the pub and a steady stream of Baggies and Blue Wave members staggered along to the Idraets Center ground. There was great banter with Benny and his mates throughout and their garden shed-style club shop was even selling Albion shirts. The Blue Wave were joined on the terraces by members of the Red Vikings from Slagelse FC. Apparently, the rival fans once hated each other but ended up drinking together and became friendly. Denis Smith's side strolled to a 4-0 win in front of 686 spectators, two first-half goals from newly-wed Kevin Kilbane and second-half strikes from Mickey Evans and Adam Oliver emphasised the gulf between the teams.

A great night was had in Copenhagen afterwards and we headed back to the Hotel Centrum at 6.00 a.m. – just as locals were heading for work. We explored the lovely city over the next two days and discovered that, if you went through the Hard Rock Café, you could gain free entry to the world-famous Tivoli Gardens. We stopped off at a bar in Nyhavn, the seventeenth-century waterfront district, where Albion director John Wile and Secretary Dr John Evans bought us a drink.

A long walk to Langelinie took us to the Copenhagen icon *The Little Mermaid*, a bronze statue on a rock by the waterside. It has been a major tourist attraction since 1913 and, much to the amusement of the watching Japanese tourists, I waded out and adorned it with an Albion shirt.

Our hotel was near the railway station in an area containing more than its share of extreme sex shops. I consider myself to be a man of the world but couldn't believe some of the magazines blatantly on window display; titles like *Gay Dog* and *Twat Loving Eels* were not your average newsagent's top-shelf fare. There was also the delightfully named 'Spunk' bar!

It was time to get back to football and the same venue as the first game. This time the opposition was Danish Superligaen team Odense Boldklub. Our new Greve fans joined us and we met again in the Tingstedet. We gifted Odense two goals through mistakes from Graham Potter and Jason van Blerk, Mickey Evans pulling one back in our 2-1 defeat.

It had been a good trip. I had made lots of new friends and another country had been crossed off.

2000

Word had got around about how good the 1999 tour had been, so numbers doubled as we returned to Copenhagen and the Hotel Centrum. This time, I was joined by the three Neils – Reynolds, Grainger and Whitehouse, plus Dubsey, Anil and Exeter Steve. Benny had booked time off to act as 'tour guide'.

The first night was spent showing the Copenhagen 'virgins' the delights of the city. One bar didn't actually open until 5.00 a.m. – now there was a challenge. Sure enough, in we went as the doors opened … blood-splattered walls in the toilets, drug addicts, winos, pimps and prostitutes in the bar. Lovely!

During a very drunken evening, we were stood outside Rosie McGee's pub in the town square, by a bus stop. As each bus pulled in, we challenged each other to board it through the front door and get off again via the other one before it pulled away. This soon developed into the 'International bus-running tournament' with competitors representing England, Denmark, Sweden and Norway.

The tour's first game, against Næstved BK, meant a 90-minute train journey. The stadium was in the middle of a nice housing estate. Benny came with us as translator and around 100 Baggies made up much of the crowd of 267. Gary Megson fielded Danish trialist Kasper Rasmussen at right back and young Elliot Morris kept goal in a drab 0-0 draw. We had over an hour to wait for the return train and thankfully, there was a smashing little bar next door.

In between games, a group of us caught the ferry across the Oresund Strait to Malmo in Sweden. We wandered round town and visited the 26,500-capacity Malmo Stadion, home of Malmo FF until the construction of the Swedbank Stadion in 2009. Numerous photographs of their former manager Roy Hodgson adorned the walls in the entrance hall.

Benny had organised a football match between Greve and Albion fans to be played at the 'Hullet' behind Greve's home ground. Our line-up included Norwegian Baggie Torbjörn Alund, Michael Morch, Chris Saunders, Dubsey, Per-Eric, Neil Whitehouse, Wayne Ferris (Bear), Jay Poole, Stian Boe, Neil Reynolds, Neil Grainger, Darren Tranter and myself (in goal). We narrowly lost but Dubsey had a 'chested' goal ruled out for hand-ball. Several crates of beer were consumed *during* the game and a great afternoon's bonding continued well into the night at the Tingstedet.

The second game was back in Greve against FC Copenhagen – managed by the aforementioned Roy Hodgson. It was good to meet in our local with yet more familiar faces; Sutton Baggies Fraser Allen and Andy Hodgson (Bubs), Warwick Baggie Andrew Freeborn (Boo), Graham Dring, Brian Thurlow (Lava), Tony Fathers and Mark Bird. New Zealand resident Kevin Buckley was camping nearby and Stuart Hill had once again arrived by car. London cabbie Tony Nash also joined us along with Richard Ryan, Dave Watkin, Norman Bartlam, Kevin Elcock, Chris 'Finbarr' Saunders and his girlfriend Kerry, and the usual suspects. Copenhagen won 1-0 thanks to a 49th minute Nicklas Jensen goal. We could have drawn if the usually reliable Bob Taylor and James Quinn had shown more composure when it mattered. Darryl Burgess was captain, and Brian Jensen (born in Copenhagen) was recalled in goal. It was good to see young Adam Oliver get a run out.

The next day, we took a boat around Copenhagen and visited Freetown Christiana, a self-proclaimed autonomous neighbourhood of about 850 hippy residents in the borough of Christianshavn. I was amazed to see many illegal substances blatantly on sale. In the afternoon, we caught a train to the beach and spent a nice sunny afternoon relaxing.

Our final game was against Greve Fotbold, back at the Idraets Center. We followed the familiar routine of drinks in the Tingstedet and stroll to the ground. Fraser managed to get into the commentary box before kick-off and a chorus of 'Slap a Dingle' was heard over the PA system. In a repeat score line from the previous year, we beat our favourite Scandinavian opponents 4-0, with 324 present to see Jason van Blerk score our first goal of the tour. This prompted Andrew Freeborn to stage a one-man pitch invasion in celebration. Further goals followed from Quinn, Justin Richards and Hughesy. Back at the pub we said our goodbyes to our good friends from The Blue Wave.

2001

For the third year running, Denmark was our destination and this time I shared a room at the Centrum with Exeter Steve and Neil Reynolds. We were back in family territory in Greve, with everyone clocking in at the Tingstedet as we greeted our Scandinavian counterparts again.

We hardly had to break sweat in winning the opening game against our so-called nursery club 6-1. That made it fourteen goals against Greve in three meetings. We led 2-0 at the break with goals from Neil Clement and Lee Hughes. Debutant Scott Dobie added a third eleven minutes into the second half and a fourth came from Adam Chambers. A James Quinn penalty and sharp finish from Bob Taylor completed an easy victory.

Steve and I visited Carlsberg's Elephant Brewery on our day off. It was free to enter and, after a 30-minute self-conducted tour, we collected tokens entitling us to two pints in the brewery bar – a drinker's dream!

Match two involved a 40-mile trip to Greve's friends, Slagelse. The Greve lads had organised a coach for us and arranged a three-way fans' tournament beforehand. Representing the Baggies were Kev Buckley, Olle Kanno, Chris Saunders, Torbjörn Alund, Paul Lindgard, Stian Boe, Paul Dubberley, Dave Watkin, Neil Reynolds, Jay Poole, Steve Conabeer, Matt Wright, Matt Stephens, Tim Davies, Chris Trickett, Shane O'Callaghan and Colin Fisher. Torbjörn's young sons were also given a run. The matches were refereed by former lightweight boxing champion Jesper D. Jensen – nobody was going to argue with him. Unfortunately, the games were overshadowed by a horrific injury to Neil Reynolds, who was taken to the medical centre in Glynis's wheelchair, with a snapped Achilles tendon. Not wanting to miss the Albion match, Neil talked the doctor into delaying the operation until after the game.

Albion beat Slagelse 3-1 before a 607 crowd. Ruel Fox opened the scoring, with Bob Taylor and a Jason Roberts penalty making it three. All nineteen players were used, including 'keeper Chris Adamson and Portuguese midfielder Jordao.

We were invited back to a barbecue at the supporters' clubhouse. It was a memorable evening and the Slagelse fans must have emptied their club shop to kit us all out as 'Red Vikings'. The biggest cheer was reserved for Neil when a taxi dropped him off with his leg in plaster. Adding to Neil's misery, next morning, he received a call saying his mom was seriously ill and advising him to return home immediately. Sadly, she passed away before he made it back.

Two days later, we set off by train again, with Benny on guide duties, this time to the seaside resort of Aabenraa in Southern Denmark. We had to catch a bus to the borrowed ground for our game against Haderslev. The stadium was in a forest in the middle of nowhere. Derek McInnes captained the side in a hard-fought 1-0 win in front of 815 spectators, Jason Roberts' 73rd minute goal deciding it. Michael Appleton was sent off for an outrageous tackle on substitute Haysen. On checking the timetable, it became apparent there were no buses to get us back to the station afterwards. Negotiations with Albion's staff led to permission for us to use the team coach to take us while the players were getting changed. The offer was gratefully accepted and our happy band made our way back to Copenhagen.

In between Albion matches, Dubsey and I went to the Superligaen game between Bronby and AGF at the almost full 29,000-capacity Vilfort Park in the capital's suburbs.

Our final game of the tour took place a short train ride from Copenhagen, in the town of Hvidovre. Jordao became the hundredth player to be sent off in an Albion first-team match when he was dismissed against Peter Schmeichel's former club who were now managed by the former Walsall boss Jan Sorensen. Bizarrely, the referee allowed Megson to send on Ruel Fox in Jordao's place. In a hotly-fought contest, we also had three players booked, including both Chambers twins. Lee Hughes captained the side and Scott Dobie scored in the 1-1 draw.

N.B. Several of the Scandinavians I met during those tours have become firm friends. I often see Norwegian Baggies Stian, Marianne and Torbjörn. Swedish pair Olle and Helena are also regular visitors – in fact, they attended my wedding in 2005, along with Greve lads Benny and Martin Andersen.

24

New Millennium, New Hopes

I was now happily living alone in a detached house in Southam, 5 minutes from my Alumet office and with Jade coming to stay most weekends. As a single man, I had the travel bug well and truly and joined my good friends Dubsey and Bill Ahearne for a week in Africa:

The Gambia

We travelled through Senegal into the Gambia and the local newspaper in Banjul informed us that an international football match between Gambia and Sierra Leone was due to take place. It had to be done, so we called at the stadium to purchase tickets and stumbled across a little bar called The Oasis in the middle of a mud-hut village. What happened next was surreal. There, behind the bar were Albion pennants, a mug, programmes and several copies of the Baggies fanzine *Grorty Dick*. It turned out that the owners were Baggies from Cannock! Needless to say, they made us very welcome. At the Katchikally crocodile pool, another strange experience occurred where we walked among the live crocs; no fences or barriers.

On match night, we headed for the 30,000-capacity Independence Stadium in Bakau and took our seats. I was wearing my Albion shirt, which received plenty of inquisitive looks. Half way through the second half, the only goal was scored and, judging by the celebrations, we left believing Gambia had won. Later, when enthusing with two Gambia fans, they informed us their side had lost and the team in white was Sierra Leone. Apparently, the Gambia is full of Sierra Leone refugees who are football-mad. They massively outnumbered 'home' fans and caused our confusion.

1999/00

Denis Smith left on 27 July and we were manager-less for the start of the season. I went to Highfield Road pre-season for Cyrille Regis's testimonial, which we lost 4-2 to Premiership Coventry.

We kicked off in Division One with a 1-1 home draw against Norwich. Ex-Villa player and manager Brian Little was then appointed as our new boss. I was really disappointed – another conspiracy? I couldn't stand him as a player, now here he was in charge of my team. He had previously managed Stoke, where, ironically, he was replaced by Gary Megson.

His first game was at Port Vale, where we won 2-1 thanks to goals from Hughesy and Killer. We won our next away game 2-1, too, this time at Swindon; Killer was on target again with Mickey Evans grabbing our other goal.

The new manager brought in Larus Sigurdsson and Andy Townsend to add experience. A share of the spoils (1-1) at Wolves in October concluded a run of five draws. By Christmas, we had managed only three more wins; Crystal Palace away (2-0), Portsmouth at home (3-2) and Stockport at home (2-0). The football, in general, was awful and our performances at Tranmere (0-3) and Crewe (0-2) saw the fans starting to turn. We also lost our little Italian, Enzo Maresca, who joined Juventus for a club record £4.5 million.

So to the new Millennium and were on a terrible run of eleven games without a victory. Little was slaughtered by the travelling Baggies as he left the pitch after our 1-0 defeat at Fulham. He was duly sacked the day after.

Manager-less again, we were spanked 6-0 at Sheffield United and 3-0 at home to the Blues. We were in free-fall, heading towards the relegation trap-door again. Then it was another case of 'cometh the hour, cometh the man'. Gary Megson was appointed and things were about to change for the better.

His first game was at Edgeley Park against one of his previous clubs, Stockport County. Our new Danish 'keeper Brian Jensen made his debut in our 1-0 win. Hughesy got our goal in a much better performance. Unfortunately, despite an improvement, we didn't win again for another eight games. Megson had dipped into the transfer market and brought in Georges Santos, Des Lyttle, Neil Clement, Peter Butler and the biggest coup of all – the prodigal son, Bob Taylor returned.

It wasn't long before SuperBob was among the goals, scoring in our 2-2 draw at Barnsley and in an amazing 4-4 draw at home to Bolton. Our 2-1 reverse at Walsall (completing their double against us) saw us back in the relegation places with just three games to go. The first was at home to fellow strugglers Grimsby. Taylor did the business, scoring both goals in our 2-1 win. We clawed out of the bottom three with a valuable point at QPR but still needed to win our last game, against Charlton, to be sure of safety. A Hawthorns crowd of 22,101 roared the lads on to a 2-0 victory, Sneekes and Taylor ensuring another season in Division One. Ex-Albion man Andy Hunt played for Charlton and appeared to be trying to help our cause. Top man.

Walsall went down.

We were knocked out in the third round of the FA Cup, losing 2-0 at Premiership Blackburn Rovers in a replay after an encouraging 2-2 draw at The Hawthorns.

In the League Cup, we beat Halifax 5-1 over two legs, then overcame Wycombe 5-3 on aggregate before a disappointing 2-1 home defeat to Fulham in round three.

Albion's disciplinary record wasn't good, with thirty-five yellow cards and six red. Those sent off were Sigurdsson, Carbon (twice), Burgess (twice) and Sneekes. Paul Thompson moved in as chairman, taking over from Tony Hale.

Dubai

The construction industry was winding down in Hong Kong after the transfer of sovereignty to the People's Republic of China in 1997. GSL had gained a good reputation as a provider of experienced glass façade installation supervisors, so I was pleased to spend a month in Dubai, working on the new Emirates Towers development with fellow Albion fan Nick Peach and recruiting around a dozen supervisors. I visited Dubai numerous times over the next couple of years, attending a football match on one trip. It was impossible to tell the rival fans apart as they all wore the same long white robes (dishdashes). At half-time, the whole crowd disappeared to various prayer rooms beneath the stands. I could think of many times when I needed to pray at half-time at The Hawthorns! On another visit, I went to the rugby sevens, followed by a massive open-air concert headlined by Ian Dury and the Blockheads. I also saw the Hothouse Flowers at my local out there – The Irish Village, set into the walls of the national tennis stadium.

Jordan

Dubsey and I headed out to Jordan for a road trip. We flew into the capital, Amman, for the Jordan v Kyrgyzstan football match at the national stadium. We treated ourselves to tickets in the main stand, which we shared with the newly-crowned King Abdullah, whose father King Hussein had died the year before. The two teams formed a heart shape in front of the king before kick-off and, when Jordan scored their goals, the whole team came over to the main stand to lift their shirts and reveal a picture of the two kings. The atmosphere was great and a cheerleader with a drum ensured that the crowd continued chanting throughout.

Iceland

In complete contrast to the Jordan trip, I joined my new Leamington mates Ray Duffy and Ed Buckley for a long weekend in Iceland. It was certainly different, and incredibly expensive. A taxi from the airport to Reykjavik cost us £75 and beer was over a fiver for a pint. We had a mad afternoon visiting nearly every bar in the capital. I even managed to get another football stadium in – Laugardalsvöllur, the home of Iceland's national football team.

On our last day we spent the afternoon at the Blue Lagoon, a geothermal spa located in a lava field in Grindavík. We were due to fly home at midnight but, because of the extortionate prices we made the decision to get a taxi direct to the town of Keflavík, which is close to the airport. We were looking forward to having a few beers on our last night so, as we entered the town, I asked the taxi driver to drop us off at the nearest bar. He then uttered those never-to-be-forgotten words 'There are no bars in Keflavík' What! We got out of the taxi in the middle of the main street and just stood there with our bags, we looked to the left ... nothing, we looked to our right ... nothing, just tumbleweed blowing along the road. Reykjavík was too far and a £150 round taxi trip so we wandered around until we found a pizza restaurant that was open. We ended up at a cinema watching Coyote Ugly. Rock and Roll!

2000/01

After the dramatic end to the previous season, I was eagerly looking forward to this one. Jason Roberts became our first £2 million player, signing from Bristol Rovers and the experienced Derek McInnes came in from Rangers.

I travelled to Nottingham Forest for our first League game full of anticipation. I should have known better. We lost 1-0 and followed up with two more defeats, including a humiliating 4-1 reverse at Barnsley. Things had to get better. Fortunately, they did, as Megson started to organise his troops. We ground out narrow wins against QPR (2-1) and Crystal Palace (1-0); McInnes scoring his first goal in the stripes.

Our League Cup campaign lasted two rounds. We made it past Swansea (2-1) over two legs, before bowing out to Premiership Derby, losing 4-2 at home following an impressive 2-1 win on my first visit to the new Pride Park. I was back there in the FA Cup when Derby came out on top (3-2) in a cracking tie, in which Hughesy and SuperBob were on target.

Hughesy scored our winner at Crewe and Roberts bagged his first Albion goal in an excellent 1-0 victory at Portsmouth. He followed up with a brace in our 2-1 win at Sheffield Wednesday. It's always sweet to win a Black Country derby and our home game on 17 October was no exception. Hughesy put away a penalty for the only goal. At our midweek 3-1 home win against Wimbledon, the stewards outnumbered the away supporters. I counted only fifteen travelling Dons fans in the Smethwick End.

Lee Hughes hit top form in November, scoring the opener in our 2-0 win at Huddersfield, then becoming the first Albion player since Jeff Astle to score hat-tricks in successive League games, taking home the match ball after our home wins against Gillingham and Preston. Benny Andersen came over from Greve for the Preston game and I contacted Albion director John Wile, who kindly organised VIP hospitality for us before presenting Benny with a signed shirt to take back to Denmark. It was also the day after my fortieth birthday bash at Southam Rugby Club and both Benny and I had sore heads as we settled in the directors' box.

Chile

On 2 December, I jetted off to Chile with Dubsey for a mid-season break. We enjoyed a couple of days in Santiago, calling in at the Estadio Nacional Julio Martínez Prádanos, a stadium that hosted the World Cup final in 1962. We flew to Arica, Chile's northernmost city, close to the Peruvian border and hired a car for a journey across the Andes towards Bolivia. Because of the high altitude, we were warned to stop overnight half-way up the mountain range to acclimatise. This proved to be sound advice as we walked around like zombies in the mountain town of Putre and sought a bed for the night, we didn't even have a beer!

The next day we reached the summit. On the way back to Arica, heading towards our half-way stop over we were running very low on petrol and spotted a town called Guallatire on the map, but it was a forty mile detour. When we finally got there, we were horrified to find the place completely deserted, just a couple of stray cats wandered about in what had become a ghost town. We had hardly seen any cars at all during our journey and the prospect of sleeping in the car was becoming a distinct reality. The car was literally running on fumes as we turned the engine off to freewheel down the mountains, at long last we spotted the lights of Putre in the distance as we rolled along. I have never been so pleased to see civilisation, we eventually made it and managed to purchase a container of petrol from the village store.

Back in Arica we called in at the Estadio Carlos Dittborn. This tiny 9,746-capacity stadium surprisingly hosted seven games in the 1962 World Cup tournament.

Before heading home I caught the train to one of my favourite ever football stadiums. With the Andes Mountains as a backdrop the 47,347 capacity Estadio Monumental David Arellano is the home ground of Colo Colo FC. I would have loved to have experienced a match at this fascinating venue. Maybe one day I will.

Good wins at home to Nottingham Forest (3-0) and at Bolton (1-0) put us in a play-off position at the end of the year and we stayed in contention. A memorable away day on 7 April, it was Richie Brentnall's fiftieth birthday and we were at Fulham. Without Richie's knowledge, we had liaised with landlord Dave Chapman at the Albion pub in Goldsmiths Row to put on a surprise party and had even booked accommodation for the night. At the game, I managed to get a birthday card signed by Cyrille Regis and Brendon Batson as well as Fulham chairman Mohammed Al Fayed.

After our 0-0 draw, we convinced Richie that we had to head to Liverpool Street to meet our mutual friend Robbie from Portsmouth. From there, we all caught a bus following London cabbie Tony Nash's instructions. After a short journey, he announced that we should get off, so we piled off and walked down an alleyway towards the Albion pub. We had been walking for a few minutes when Dubsey asked: 'Where's Richie?' I presumed he must be having a wee somewhere, then it dawned that we had left him on the bus. He had been reading his programme near the front and hadn't heard Tony instructing everyone to disembark. After general hysterics, reality kicked in and we realised that he didn't know where we were heading.

We called in the pub and explained to Dave the gaffer. The bar had been decorated with posters of Richie and 'Happy 50th birthday' bunting everywhere among the array of Baggies memorabilia. Dubsey's brother Trevor had his car with him and we sped off in an attempt to find the bus. When we did catch up, the driver explained that a man answering Richie's description had got off a few stops back. He didn't have a mobile, so we tried to put ourselves in his mind and guess what he could have done. We thought he might have gone to the nearest pub, so we called in about a dozen rough places, to no avail.

We gave up eventually and made our way back to the pub. About twenty of Richie's friends had turned up and we had to have his party without him, even cutting his specially produced birthday cake. Afterwards, we were invited to another party. It was just a shame Richie wasn't there to join us. His hotel bed stayed vacant. It turned out he thought we had left him on the bus on purpose, so he got off, caught a bus back to Liverpool Street and went back to Birmingham (in a sulk) for a birthday drink.

Jade and I drove down to Kent for our game against Gillingham on 21 April. She was chuffed to have her photo taken with Baggie Bird just three days before her eighth birthday. Neil Clement and Hughesy scored in a 2-1 win, which pretty much confirmed our place in the play-offs. After a 1-1 draw at home to Huddersfield, sixth spot was ours. The last away game, against Preston, was meaningless, so a party atmosphere prevailed as fancy-dressed fans packed out Deepdale's main stand as we signed off with a 2-1 defeat. Along with many other Baggies, we stayed overnight in

Blackpool. What a place that is! It's as though the dregs of society from every town in the UK have been dumped in one place.

In the play-offs, we had to face third-placed Bolton and, in the first leg at The Hawthorns, we stormed into a two-goal lead thanks to Roberts' strike and a Hughesy penalty. Just as we were dreaming of Wembley, the 'Trotters' stuck twice towards the end, making it honours even.

The away end at Bolton's new Reebok Stadium was packed to capacity on the Wednesday night, with Albion fans ready to roar the lads on. I had even booked a room next to the ground in anticipation of some celebratory beers. Sadly, we were outclassed and we couldn't complain about the 3-0 defeat. However, it was one of those nights that made me proud to be a Baggie. For the whole of the second half, we sang our heads off, completely drowning out the celebrating Bolton fans. Everyone sensed we were on the verge of turning a corner and let out ten years' worth of built-up emotions in those 45 minutes. In the final quarter, Gary Megson just stood there, facing us in disbelief. The noise was deafening and anyone would have thought we were heading for Wembley. While Bolton's fans headed home, every Baggie stayed in the ground applauding the team, who returned the compliment.

At the hotel, the locals couldn't believe the passion of our supporters and wished us well for the following season.

During a lads' weekend in Moscow, our pre-trip homework informed us that Dynamo Moscow were due to play CSKA in the Moscow derby. We all agreed to go, eventually locating the Dynamo Stadium via the underground – not easy when they use the Cyrillic alphabet. The ground seemed unusually deserted for a match day and the girl in the club shop explained that, because of crowd trouble, the match had been relocated to a neutral ground – Torpedo Moscow. What I found interesting in the official club shop were cassette tapes on sale depicting images of Dynamo's rival fans with their faces battered and covered in blood.

The shop girl couldn't have been more helpful. She locked up and escorted us to the underground station, where she indicated which trains we needed to catch. On board, we got talking to two Russian punk rockers that were in awe of us being English. One thanked us and said: 'I live for football hooliganism and the Sex Pistols'. We all felt wrongly proud!

On exiting the underground, we found that the police and army had formed a human corridor all the way to the Torpedo stadium. We didn't see any trouble, but there was certainly nastiness in the air. Souvenir sellers displayed Union Jack scarves imprinted with the words 'Dynamo Ultras' and 'Hooligans'. Football violence was still very much alive and kicking in Russia.

25

Arise, Sir Gary

2001/02

Just before the new season kicked off, I visited Whaddon Road, home of Cheltenham Town to see our 2-1 win. Our opening League game took us to the Bescot Stadium, where Walsall beat us 2-1 on Scott Dobie's debut – not the start we had hoped for. Things didn't get any better the following week when Grimsby came to The Hawthorns and left with all three points. The rot was stopped with a 1-1 draw at Sheffield Wednesday, Dobie grabbing his first goal for us.

On 11 September 2001, the world changed forever. I was in Scotland for our annual football trip and we watched the whole drama unfold on TV in a Forfar pub during the afternoon. We looked on in horror as two planes were deliberately crashed by al-Qaeda terrorists into both towers of the World Trade Center and a third into the Pentagon. To my amazement, the pub regulars seemed unfazed by events and barely lifted their heads from their drinks.

Our chosen game at Forfar went ahead, but the atmosphere at Station Park was very strange, with everyone speculating as to what would happen next. On the same evening, Albion beat Swindon 2-0 at The Hawthorns in the League Cup. This followed our win on penalties at Cambridge in the first round. Our run was to end against Premier League Charlton at the third stage.

The Hawthorns redevelopment was now complete and a new £8 million East Stand had replaced the Rainbow Stand. It transformed the ground, creating 8,800 additional seats, increasing the capacity to 27,700 (all seated).

Our season was back on the rails. New centre-forward Danny Dichio scored in our 1-0 victory against Gillingham, and we thumped Manchester City 4-0 with goals from Neil Clement (2), Derek McInnes and Dobie. Another two wins, Watford (2-0) and Preston (2-0), made it four on the bounce. Young Dobie was in fine form, scoring all four in those games. He was proving the perfect replacement for Lee Hughes, who had left for Coventry.

More new players came in; midfielder Andy Johnson from Nottingham Forest and centre-half Darren Moore (Big Dave) strengthened the defence after arriving from Portsmouth. We were accumulating lots of points, clocking up wins at Pompey (2-1), at home to Burnley (1-0) and at Stockport (2-1). Only our second draw of the season came on 25 October when a Clement free-kick special rescued us against high-flying Wolves.

Loan signing Uwe Rosler bagged the winner against Forest and a Johnson strike earned all three points at Blues, we followed that with a great 'six-pointer' win at Molineux on 2 December with Jordao netting. Then, as usual, we stumbled through the festive period, but recovered in style at The Hawthorns on New Year's Day, hammering Stockport 4-0.

We also embarked on a good FA Cup run. In the third round, we triumphed against Premiership Sunderland at the Stadium of Light. An early kick-off meant a 6.00 a.m. start, it didn't prevent a massive Albion following to see 'Clem' and 'AJ' on target in our 2-1 triumph. Another Premier League team in round four … Leicester came to The Hawthorns and a near-full house roared us home 1-0. The ground was full to capacity against Cheltenham in the next round and Dichio's winner put us through to the quarter-finals. We put up a good battle against yet another top tier team, Fulham, but they scraped through to the semis 1-0. Oh well, time to concentrate on the League.

We catapulted ourselves among the promotion contenders with four more successive wins, starting with a Midlands double against Walsall and Blues. Jason Roberts was on fire and scored the only goal in both games. He struck again as a brace at Burnley earned a 2-0 victory. Our fourth win came against Norwich, with Dichio chipping in with the decider.

The Walsall victory was overshadowed by the terrible news that Jeff Astle had passed away. The King had been my boyhood hero and the news hit me hard. He was only fifty-nine and his death was proved to be the result of brain injuries caused by repeatedly heading the ball. The whole Walsall game was tinged with sadness and it was a nice touch from Jason to lift his shirt to reveal a t-shirt printed with Jeff's image when he scored.

With Dubsey, Bill and Richie, I travelled to London for a night game at Millwall on 19 February, booking overnight accommodation. As I was on photographer duty, I left the lads and agreed to meet under the railway tunnel after the match. I stood with Millwall's fans on the side of the ground during the second half, astounded that none of them were watching the game. They were just looking up at Albion's fans, gesticulating and shouting threats, even though they beat us 1-0.

At the end, I headed for our agreed rendezvous point and looked round for my mates. They were nowhere to be seen, so I phoned Dubsey concealing my accent. I enquired as to his whereabouts. To my surprise, he said: 'Underneath the railway tunnel. Where are you?' I looked round again. The tunnel was now deserted. All became clear when Dubsey said: 'We're by the police horses.' We were in two different tunnels. I told him to stay put and I would make my way round. I was then faced with a raging mob of Millwall fans trying to get to 'Dubsey's tunnel' and the Albion fans. The police had pulled a gate across to prevent access and I was stuck in the middle of the mob, on the wrong side of the gate. I could see the lads in the distance behind the horses. When the police finally let everyone through, the main gang charged past my mates with me bringing up the rear. As I reached them, we just gestured to each other and kept walking, hoping nobody would spot us. A bus pulled up and we jumped on it. We had no idea where it was going, we just needed to get away. When we were far enough from The New Den, we got off, flagged down a taxi and made it to the digs for last orders. Oh what fun these Millwall trips always turn out to be!

My Pompey mate, Robbie Welch, joined me for the home game against Portsmouth. He left for the pub well before the end as we destroyed them 5-0 with goals from Igor Balis, Larus Sigurdsson, Dobie and Roberts (2).

Battle of Bramall Lane

16 March, brought a game that will forever be known as the Battle of Bramall Lane. I was on photographer duty on the side of the pitch and couldn't believe what I was seeing, or indeed hearing from Sheffield United manager Neil Warnock. The game was abandoned in the 82nd minute by referee Wolstenholme after the Blades had gone down to *six* men – three sent off and two taken off injured.

It was always going to be spicy. Megson was a Wednesdayite and there was no love lost between him and Neil Warnock (anagram Colin Wa**er).

United 'keeper Tracey was dismissed as early as the 8th minute for deliberate handball outside his area. Dobie then put us 1-0 up with a fine header. After some heated exchanges, we scored again after 63 minutes. Warnock then sent on ex-Albion man Santos, who had suffered a broken jaw courtesy of Andy Johnson's elbow in a previous game when AJ was at Forest. Santos was on for barely 30 seconds before being dismissed for a two-footed premeditated lunge on Johnson, causing him to spin up in the air in agony. Just 90 seconds later, United's second sub, Suffo, who hadn't touched the ball, head-butted McInnes and was also shown the red card.

I witnessed Warnock gesticulating at his players to get sent off and get the game abandoned. Their captain, Keith Curle, was running round kicking Albion players, but the ref was having none of it. In the 78th minute, Dobie scored again and, soon afterwards, their midfielder Brown was 'taken off for his own good' by his manager. With Albion 3-0 up and strolling against seven men, United's Ullathorne dramatically collapsed with a supposed muscle spasm. He went off, leaving the referee no alternative but to abandon proceedings.

Back in our favourite Ward's Brewery pub, the Devonshire Arms, we were lost for words; there were so many questions. Had we won 3-0? Had we got three points? Nobody knew. What we did know was that Dubsey was setting off to Japan for the World Cup, travelling overland. I said goodbye and arranged to meet him at the Ireland v Cameroon game in June. Little did he know our season was about to get really interesting.

After an enquiry, our result at Bramall Lane was allowed to stand and we banked the points. Wolves were now in our sights as we headed to Nottingham Forest for a Friday night game. Just when a goalless draw looked likely, up popped Bob Taylor with a diving header near the end; another great win. Next up were Crewe at home and, no messing; they were sent packing 4-1.

Four days later, Barnsley came to The Hawthorns and we won 3-1. Wolves were panicking and dropping points. We had the momentum. Surely, nothing could get in our way? Thousands of Albion fans took over Highfield Road for our 1-0 win over Coventry on Easter Monday, with SuperBob again on target.

Rotherham United next and an expected three points. Not so. Although Jordao's shot was a good two feet over the line, the referee ruled it out and another Taylor goal couldn't prevent two points being dropped. I did the maths. If we won our last two games, we could overtake Wolves and grab second place. Baggies fans made up the majority of the 20,209-strong crowd at Bradford City. I was walking round the pitch in my photographer's bib beforehand and spotted more Albion fans in the home sections of Valley Parade than City supporters. I was a nervous wreck and Bradford were giving it all they had in Stuart McCall's farewell appearance.

As injury-time approached, Taylor was fouled in the area in front of the Albion fans and the referee pointed to the spot. First elation, then silence, as reality set in. We had missed an incredible *eight* penalties throughout the season. Who would take it? Up stepped our Slovakian man of mystery – right back Igor Balis. We held our breath. I tried to focus my lens but my hands were shaking. We need not have worried. Balis coolly put it away and the Albion fans went bananas; numerous supporters in fancy dress spilled on to the pitch and it took several minutes before a restart was possible. Sensing a pitch invasion, the ref soon blew the whistle. What a win! Now all we needed was a win in our last game and promotion was ours. I got done for speeding on my way out of Bradford. I was dreaming of the Premier League and not concentrating. Six points on my licence and a hefty fine for doing 79 mph in a 50 limit contra flow. Ouch!

Manchester City had already won the title. Second place was between us and Wolves, who had Sheffield Wednesday away. A win for Albion would do it and we roared the team on from first whistle to last on an emotional afternoon against Crystal Palace at The Hawthorns. I'm so glad Jade was with me to witness it, just three days before her ninth birthday.

We took the lead on 17 minutes when a Clement free-kick was headed up by Darren Moore. Dichio challenged two defenders and, when the ball dropped, Big Dave side-footed home. The Hawthorns erupted in sheer relief. At half-time, Megson's team talk was summarised with his final words 'Right now, you are still First Division players. When you come back in, I want you to be Premier League players.'

On 54 minutes, just as Wednesday went in front against Wolves, SuperBob pounced on a goalkeeper's fumble to put us two up. The Hawthorns 'boinged' in unison and word has it that the Wednesday fans did the same at Hillsborough. Wolves scraped a draw but we won comfortably to earn our place with the elite. The pitch was consumed with celebrating Baggies; the after-match scenes of joy will remain with me forever. The players eventually emerged with their families to rapturous applause. The biggest cheer was reserved for 'Sir' Gary Megson, who was rightfully named First Division Manager of the Year and deserved a knighthood as far as I was concerned.

The celebrations continued with an open-top bus tour. Thousands of joyous Baggies packed the streets of West Bromwich and the square outside the Council House in Oldbury, where the players were introduced to the crowd.

World Cup in Japan

It was time to fly to Japan. I had two match tickets, one for Ireland v Cameroon and one for England's opening game, against Sweden. Luckily, on the flight, someone had a spare ticket for England v Nigeria, so that was another in the bag. As I disembarked in Tokyo, I was met by a posse of Japanese press and film crews. I had a microphone shoved in my face and was asked: 'Hello, are you a hooligan?'

I had 30 minutes to catch my train to Niigata, which would enable me to get to Ireland's match at half-time. I had purchased a two-week rail pass, which proved to be a sound investment. I made my connection and, in true Japanese style, arrived bang on time. A quick jog to the Big Swan Stadium and I entered the Cameroon end just as the referee signalled half-time. Among the Cameroon flags, there was a massive St George flag with the words 'West Brom' emblazoned on it – it was Dubsey's. It had taken him over four months to travel overland, whereas I had flown it in around 15 hours. I presented him with a Baggies in the Premier League t-shirt and spent the second half telling him all about Albion's amazing end to the season. Oh and the match taking place in front of us ended 1-1.

It was great to catch up and we drowned ourselves in beer afterwards, drinking into the early hours with the Irish fans. Next morning, it was time to catch a train to Tokyo and then out to Saitama for England v Sweden. The Japanese seemed to be supporting England. Everywhere we went, people wanted to take our photo and we constantly heard shouts of 'England' and 'Beckham' aimed at us. In the fan-zone outside the Saitama Stadium, the atmosphere was fantastic. Among 25,000 England fans, we met Chris Kamara from Sky Sports, who was happy to have his photograph taken with my Albion flag.

I had obtained my ticket from Olle the Swedish Baggie, who had secured it via his country's FA. My seat was in the middle of the Swedish fans and my 'Astle is The King' t-shirt somewhat blew my cover. No worries. They were really friendly and we had some great banter throughout. Sol Campbell put England ahead but Sweden deservedly equalised in the second half. The ultra-efficient trains had us back in Tokyo in no time.

A great night followed in the bars of Roppongi – an entertainment area in the district of Minato. I had an unbelievable stroke of luck in Tokyo the next day. I was mooching around a market when an old lady stepped out from one of the stalls. She muttered 'England v Argentina?' and held up a VIP ticket for the forthcoming game 516 miles away on the island of Hokkaido. I was expecting her to ask silly money, but she just wanted the £150 face value. I snapped her hand off.

Dubsey and I spent the next day visiting the temples in Osaka and caught up with Albion fan Simon Handy, who worked over there. He showed us round, took us to a sushi bar and then to a good pub to watch some football.

The overnight train journey to Sapporo was exhausting, with very little sleep in our carriage. It was full of fans from all over England. The few who did manage rest were entered into the 'English snoring championships', with Dubsey a strong contender, representing West Bromwich.

Sapporo was great and we explored it on a lovely summer day, together with Dubsey's brother, Trevor. We caught a cable car up Mount Okura, which had been used for skiing events at the 1972 Winter Olympics. It provided excellent views of the landscape. Back at ground level, we visited the Sapporo TV tower before crashing out in the sun with Robbie, my mate from Portsmouth. A couple of geisha girls walked past and happily posed with our Albion flags.

The match took place at the 41,580-seated indoor arena, the Sapporo Dome; the first time I had watched an indoor game on a full-size pitch and one to remember. David Beckham scored the winner from a penalty and I celebrated among the suited VIPs. Mine was the only flag on display in this section and I was certainly the odd one out in my England shirt and shorts. How on earth did that old lady in Tokyo get this ticket? The after-match party went on well into the night and I had a drink in one bar with Kammy and his TV mates.

To break up the train journey back to Tokyo, Dubsey, Robbie and I stopped off in Miyagi to take in Mexico v Ecuador. We thought that tickets would be readily available and didn't expect 30,000 Mexicans to be in town; the match was a total sell-out. Our train had departed, so we were stuck. Time for Plan B ... We found out where the official party from Ecuador were staying and coolly walked into reception past their fans, who had gathered outside, and the security guards. We spotted a guy with an Ecuadorian FA badge on his blazer, so I asked him about obtaining three tickets. I explained that my grandad originated from Quito! He said he would send 'Capitan Lunar' down to see us and that we should wait in the lobby.

A few minutes later, an ex-player in an Ecuador tracksuit appeared from the lift, and asked 'Are you the three English guys?' and handed us tickets. We shook hands with every player, wishing them luck as they boarded the coach.

We became honourable Ecuadorians for the afternoon and, again, the atmosphere was incredible for a game the Mexicans won 2-1. We sat next to a girl who had travelled alone as her brother had been struck ill. She joined us for a drink afterwards and gave me her brother's ticket for Ecuador v Croatia in four days' time.

Our next match was England v Nigeria back in Osaka. Again, the Japanese lined the streets to welcome us. They nearly all carried England flags and had their faces painted with the flag of St George. The game was a disappointing 0-0 draw, but a point was enough to see us through to the next stages.

We met up later with Baggie mates Bill Ahearne, Trevor Dubberley and Richie Brentnall. Robbie also hooked up with his Fulham mate, Danny. We had a brilliant night in various bars. When we entered the first, the locals appeared apprehensive of us, probably because the media had portrayed all English as hooligans. We solved this problem by buying a bottle of Sake and sending it over to the Japanese contingent, courtesy of the English. It broke the ice immediately and they made us very welcome, buying us numerous drinks and taking us to other bars. The language barrier was solved by singing Beatles songs! At the end of a very drunken evening (some unearthly hour the next morning), they wished us luck and handed us their ties and other gifts as a show of gratitude and friendship.

Richie was a right character and I could write a book based on his stories alone. He was hilarious without knowing it. In Japan, we had forewarned Robbie and Danny about him and, on their initial meeting with the 6-foot 5-inch giant, he lived up to his reputation. He joined them to watch a match on TV in their hotel room and gratefully accepted a few beers. To return the compliment, he popped out to a vending machine for another eight cans. When drinking the first one, he commented: 'I don't think much of this beer.' Robbie took a swig and replied: 'That'll be because it's green tea, Richie!'

Dubsey had obtained tickets for all Cameroon's games and I joined him for the one against Germany. We proudly displayed our Albion/England flags among the Cameroon fans in the Shizuoka Stadium. Only a few thousand Germans had made the journey and it was the Africans who made all the noise. Unfortunately, two second-half goals secured their defeat.

I had one final game to attend, making use of my free ticket for Ecuador v Croatia in Yokohama. The International Stadium was to be the venue for the final, so it was a perfect opportunity for me to cross it off, as I had to return home and wouldn't be in Japan for the latter stages. I celebrated with Ecuador's fans as their team pulled off a surprise 1-0 win.

I was sad to be going home. The other lads stayed and Dubsey even attended some games in South Korea. As I had tickets for only two matches when I set off, I hadn't done too badly. I attended seven games, in seven different stadiums, in fourteen days. It had been my best ever holiday; great company, a new country, lots of beer and World Cup football. Life doesn't get much better than that.

26

Back in the Big Time (Briefly)

There was no overseas tour for Albion in the summer of 2002, so I joined Steve in Helsinki, Finland for one of Exeter City's pre-season games. Steve Stanier and Glenn Robinson also came along.

Tallinn was only a short hovercraft journey away, so, after checking in at the Helsinki Marriott, we spent our first afternoon and evening in the Estonia capital. We propped up the bar over beers as it meandered out of port. Just as we ordered a second, the locals took their seats and looked at us intrigued. We didn't have to wait long to find out why. The engines were turned to full throttle and the vessel bounced off the waves, sending our beer everywhere but in our mouths.

As we disembarked, stinking of alcohol, the first thing we saw was a man sunbathing naked on a grass bank. It was 5.00 p.m. on a Friday and rush hour, yet the roads were almost deserted. We had a pleasant stroll around the pretty city, which resembled a mini Prague. We had a few drinks in the picturesque town square, then a few more until it got dark, so we continued in a conveniently situated Irish pub. We were due to catch the hovercraft back at 9.30 p.m., so we agreed to drink up just before nine but then had a 'super swifty' and reached the point (pint?) of no return. We were too comfortable, there was a good band on and the beer was flowing. We missed our crossing and continued well into the night. We had nowhere to stay and our enquiries revealed that everywhere was full. Luckily, I convinced a receptionist that I was good friends with the manager and we finally obtained a room. Our bags spent a quiet night, unpacked in the Marriott in Helsinki, which we eventually reached next morning.

Our Helsinki city tour included the Olympia Stadion – the largest in Finland and home to the national team. We also visited the neighbouring Sonera Stadium, which housed the Finnish FA. After lunch, we headed to the tiny ground of PK-35 in the Pukinmaki area. We pigged out on the excellent hot dogs in the afternoon sunshine and watched Exeter win 3-1. After the game, we had a photograph taken on the pitch with the whole Exeter team, including ex-Albion man Kwame Ampadu.

We bumped into the players again in one of the city bars later in the evening and had good banter with Kwame, singing his name to the tune of Xanadu … 'It's Ampadu, Kwame Ampadu'. Ok, the beer may have played a part.

2002/03

Coincidentally, the furthest Albion ventured was to Devon and our first game was a 3-2 win against Exeter. To cement further relationships, Steve's son Lewis was City's mascot and my cousin, Paul Rejer, was the referee. While in Devon, I saw our 2-0 win at Tiverton Town and our 1-0 win at Torquay United. My love of new grounds also took me to our friendly at the Memorial Stadium, the third different Bristol Rovers ground I had seen a match after Eastville and Twerton Park. On this occasion, we lost 3-2. Our final friendly was at Broadhall Way, Stevenage, where we strolled to a comfortable 4-0 victory.

What a game to start our first Premier League season. Jade joined me at Old Trafford to see us compete with eventual champions Manchester United. Tickets were hard to come by, so the game was beamed back live to 7,693 fans at The Hawthorns. I felt enormous pride as Derek McInnes led the Baggies out in the August sunshine but, sadly, he was harshly sent off with the scores level and we lost 1-0. Summer signing Sean Gregan made his debut, with Jeremy Peace having taken over as chairman.

During the game, Albion fans had been singing the 'yam yam' song to the Dambusters tune. It involves holding your arms full stretch and doing a plane impression. To the home fans it looked as though we were disrespecting the 1958 Munich air crash and after the match things started to turn nasty. Dubsey acted as peacemaker, attempting to explain to hundreds of angry United supporters that it had nothing to do with the disaster. Incredibly he got away with it.

The following week, Leeds came to The Hawthorns. New signing Lee Marshall scored our first ever Premier League goal but it didn't prevent a 3-1 defeat. I sat next to Adrian Chiles at our midweek game at Highbury to see us thumped 5-2 by Arsenal. Three defeats in three games – the season was going to be tough.

Respectability was restored with our first victory when Darren Moore bagged the only goal at home to Fulham. Ex-Man United player Ronnie Wallwork was one of two debutants against the 'Cottagers'. Lee Hughes made his second bow after re-signing from Coventry. Jason Roberts then scored our winner at West Ham and yet another new signing, Jason Koumas, made his debut. The Boleyn Ground was much safer now and I even managed a celebratory drink in a pub near the ground. This would have been unthinkable twenty years ago. We made it three wins out of three with another 1-0 home win, against Southampton, with Sean Gregan on target.

Surely it couldn't last? Next stop Anfield, and Russell Hoult became the first Albion keeper to be sent off in 107 years. Joe Murphy went on and his first job was to face a Michael Owen penalty, which he duly saved. Unfortunately, our ten men still lost 2-0. We appeared to be facing twelve men every week with referees clearly favouring established Premiership teams.

There was a rare new ground to visit in the League Cup, Wigan's new DW Stadium – certainly a contrast to Springfield Park. Nathan Ellington, who would later sign for Albion, got a hat-trick as we slumped 3-1.

We were sinking fast and our next win in the top flight didn't come until a Danny Dichio goal ensured a home success against Middlesbrough on 30 November. After that, we continued to struggle. We were often losing to just one goal but we couldn't stack up enough points.

On Friday 13 December, 2002, on a stag night in the Warwickshire village of Harbury, I met my future wife, Ruth. So much for Friday the 13th being unlucky! She was in The Dog pub on a rare night out with her friend, Janey. We got chatting and it turned out we had much in common. We had both been married and each had a young child. However she had no interest in football. I said: 'Surely you must have watched the World Cup?' Ruth replied: 'Why? I'm Welsh'. I had no answer to that. Christmas was discussed and, as Ruth's son Oliver would be with his dad and Jade with her mom, we agreed to spend Christmas Day afternoon together. We actually saw each other nearly every day up to the festive period and we have been together ever since.

For a present, I gave Ruth a ticket for Albion v Arsenal on Boxing Day and, for six-year-old Ollie, bought a Baggies strip. I was determined to show my new girlfriend the match-day experience. She had never been to a game, so I wanted it to be a good one. We started off in The Vine for a chicken tikka, before taking our seats in the Brummie Road. We actually opened the scoring with a Dichio goal, though their class showed and we went down 2-1. Ruth said that she enjoyed the day, but expressed no desire to go again!

In the FA Cup, a Dichio hat-trick saw off Bradford at The Hawthorns before we departed at Watford in round four, losing 1-0.

We pulled off a surprise 2-1 win against Manchester City on our last ever visit to Maine Road in February. They would shortly move to the City of Manchester Stadium, built for the Commonwealth Games.

Ruth's son Ollie liked football, but didn't support a particular team – I soon put paid to that! I took him to The Hawthorns for his first game, against Chelsea, and he was really excited. En route I asked him how many people he thought would be there and his first response was: 'A lot, about

200?' I told him there would be more than that, so he said: 'A million?' I guess 27,000 was more people in one place than he had ever experienced. Fortunately, he was hooked and my daughter Jade kept him entertained throughout the game. He came again a few times that season and it made me proud a few months later when he brought home his school project. It was a cushion he had designed with the Albion badge and the statement: 'WBA till I die'. Ruth said, 'Look what you've done to him.' Mission accomplished!

Ruth and I bought a house in March, 2003, selling our own properties and moving in to a lovely cottage in Harbury. Ruth joined me for our trip to Sunderland and an overnight stay in Durham. Although she witnessed a 2-1 away win, we were already relegated despite having four games left to play. A reality check came at home to Liverpool. The Reds hit us for six with no reply.

Refs at Rovers

The theme for our last away game, at Blackburn, was 'Refs at Rovers' – our protest against all the ridiculous decisions that had gone against us that season. Everyone wore black and hundreds of Baggies got hold of proper referees' outfits. A mickey-take of referee Uriah Rennie was the funniest on display. A fan with a toilet seat round his neck called himself 'Urinal' Rennie. The Grorty Dick gang gave large red and yellow cards to every fan entering the away end. This provided hilarious entertainment as every challenge was greeted with thousands of cards being brandished and numerous whistles causing chaos on the pitch. Many fans had opted for their own form of fancy dress and a great conga took place near the end, involving an assortment of large animals including a brilliant 9 foot giraffe. We actually played well and thoroughly deserved the 1-1 draw that Jason Koumas's goal brought us.

We signed off with a 2-2 home draw against Newcastle. Scott Dobie scored both goals in Bob Taylor's 377th and final Albion game. Over 16,000 fans attended his testimonial game 48 hours later to say farewell to the legend that is 'SuperBob'.

We finished nineteenth and went down with Sunderland and West Ham.

At Luton Airport ready to board the flight to Valencia to see Albion in the UEFA Cup, 1978, aged 17. Left to right: Me, Tony Jones, Barry Swash, Kevin Pitt with Nigel Bellmore behind us. The game in Spain is one of my best Albion memories.

With the lads in Zurich, 1981, venue of Albion's UEFA Cup game against Grasshoppers. We had just arrived by car with very little money between us. Left to right: Malcom Llewellyn (Sweat), Me, Andy Payne, John Skeen (Skeeny) and Tony Jones. Michael Silvester (Silve) is at the front.

Before the match in Brescia in the dug-out with Albion players Paul Mardon (centre) and Andy Hunt (right), 1995.

In my second home, The Hawthorns, with the old Brummie Road End and Woodman Corner terraces in the background, 1982.

My daughter Jade (born 24/04/93) wearing her Albion bib, gets to grips with Baggies fanzine *Grorty Dick*.

On one of my regular pilgrimages to Albion legend Willie Johnston's pub The Port Brae in Kirkcaldy, Fife, 1995. Left to right: Dave Jones, Steve Conabeer, Anil Shiyal, Willie Johnston, Tony Jones and me.

27

The Andy Hunt Tour

'Ole ole, ole ole Andy Hunt, Hunt Hunt'. I couldn't get that song out of my head as we went in search of the former Baggies striker in Central America in 2003.

When he started writing his 'Postcard from Belize' column in the *Albion News* in 2002, I was intrigued. I emailed him to find out more and was surprised to receive an instant response with an invite.

Andy was born in West Thurrock in 1970 and trained in tourism management while playing for Ashill and Kings Lynn before signing semi-professional for Kettering. In 1991, he joined Jim Smith's Newcastle for £210,000. The 'Bald Eagle' was soon replaced by Ossie Ardiles, who set about rebuilding the team round a bunch of promising youngsters. This wasn't a quick fix and by October, 1991, the Magpies were bottom of Division Two. Ardiles was sacked and in went Kevin Keegan. Despite netting thirteen goals in fifty-one appearances, Hunt found himself surplus to requirements so his former boss enquired. Andy initially joined us on loan in March, 1993, going on as a substitute for Simon Garner and scoring on his debut at Bradford. He then scored a hat-trick on his home debut against Brighton, although he is first to admit that it wasn't one of his best performances. He said: 'I think I might be one of the only players to have been booed, and then cheered for scoring a hat-trick in a game.' In May 1993 he secured a permanent move for a bargain £100,000.

He went on to form a deadly partnership with Bob Taylor and become a crowd favourite, scoring eighty-five goals in 228 appearances (plus 12 as a sub). He will always be remembered for our winner in the play-off semi-final against Swansea, then that all-important first goal against Port Vale at Wembley before appearing very drunk at the civic reception next day.

After Albion failed to gain promotion in 1998, he was out of contract and Charlton snapped him up on a 'Bosman' free transfer. Relegation followed in his first season but, in his second, he finished leading scorer with twenty-four goals and Charlton were back in the Premiership. Following his tremendous record of thirty-two goals in eighty-six Valiants games, Andy was forced to retire in April 2000, through chronic fatigue syndrome. He moved to Belize where he turned out for Banana Bank FC and Belmopan Bandits.

Back to Andy's email, he stated those immortal words: 'You should visit sometime.' Now that was an offer I couldn't refuse. I mentioned it to fellow Albion fan Anil Shiyal and Hull fan and neighbour Glenn Robinson, who were both up for it. We agreed to make it a holiday, visiting Mexico and Guatemala while in 'that neck of the woods.' I got back in touch with Andy and he said he would meet us at a bar in the town of Belmopan as we would never be able to find his jungle retreat.

In January 2003, we flew to Cancun, Mexico, and checked into our hotel in time for a few local beers. We ended up in a bar allegedly used in the film *Cocktail* starring Tom Cruise. The resort wasn't really our sort of place. Every bar seemed full of loud Americans so we were pleased to be only there for one night. Next morning, we caught a 'Novelos' bus for the 300-mile journey to the Belize border. En route, we passed through the resort of Playa del Carmen and agreed it looked far more. We pledged to stop there on the return journey for our last couple of days.

I couldn't believe the films being shown on the coach journey. The passengers were all ages, including families with children, yet we saw extreme violence and graphic sex scenes on the screen. Just as well I wasn't travelling with my kids.

We reached the border town of Corozal and wandered the deserted streets for a room. Choices were limited, so we plumped for a scruffy little guest house called 'Nestors', complete with cockroaches in the shower. The only way we were going to sleep was to get drunk, so we headed into 'town'. One of the bars was in complete darkness with just a man on a plastic chair, a fridge full of beer and a really ropey prostitute. (No, we didn't.)

We caught a bus into Belize City next day and spent a pleasant few hours mooching round the fascinating markets. We also discovered some high-class bars just round the corner from some right flea-pits.

Andy had recommended we stay in a town in the Cayo district, San Ignacio, as his health food/travellers shop 'The Green Dragon' was there. He also recommended a nearby guest house, 'Rosas'. San Ignacio was a smashing little town, with plenty going on and lots of friendly bars. We even checked out the local football ground, the Norman Broaster Stadium, home of Belize Defence Force FC.

Andy's Dutch sister-in-law, Miriam, was the lovely host in the Green Dragon and she made us welcome whenever we called in to use the internet. She also rang Andy to check everything was on for the next day.

After grabbing some pies from Chunky's Cool Spot, we hopped on the bus next morning for the journey to Belize's capital, Belmopan. With a 16,000 population and covering just 12 square miles, Belmopan is the smallest capital in the continental Americas. It is, however, the third largest settlement in Belize, behind Belize City and San Ignacio. Founded as a planned community in 1970, it is one of the world's newest capitals.

I have no idea what meat was used in Chunky's pies but, when we questioned him next day, he just smiled. In Belmopan, we soon located the bar for our pre-arranged rendezvous and even managed a couple of cheeky beers while waiting for Andy. Exactly on time, unshaven, wearing shorts, shades and a sun hat, he came over to us. We didn't recognise him at first and it all seemed surreal, meeting our ex-striker in a small town bar in the middle of Central America.

Andy was really welcoming and introduced us to his brother, Ian, who was there for a holiday. We jumped in Andy's truck and headed for the supermarket to stock up with a couple of crates for the day. We were soon heading out of the city through the jungle and even had to drive on to a raft at one stage to cross a river. It was obvious why Andy had said we would never find his home, which was incredible – like something out of a film; it was a three-storey dome-like building surrounded by beautiful scenery with parrots and other tropical birds flying round.

He introduced us to his beautiful wife, Simone, a former MTV presenter, his new-born son, Lucas, and father, Terry. They all made us feel at home and we sat chatting and drinking beer on the verandah of the stunning property.

Terry was a real character and had an endless supply of funny stories. Andy told us about his typical day of jungle living, consisting of riding his horses, playing football with the locals and chilling. It sounded terrible ... he must really miss those trips to Grimsby and Barnsley!

He also told us the story of how he met his wife while at the Albion. He was a big pal of teammate Darryl Burgess and they often watched MTV together. Andy really fancied the presenter and went on and on about her. During an end-of-season break, he went with Darryl to a DJs' tournament in Rimini. They noticed that Simone was starring at one of the nightclubs, so Darryl tracked her down and got a signed photo for her 'secret admirer'. After one particular set, they met Simone – and Darryl spilled the beans about Andy's infatuation. The rest, as they say, is history; a brilliant love story which I suggested was worthy of a film.

During the afternoon, Andy pointed out about twenty Guatemalan men who had just finished their day's work in the fields. They were all heading to the full-sized football pitch which was conveniently situated on Andy's land. 'Do you fancy a game?' he asked. It took us completely by surprise as we'd had about six beers each. 'Why not?' was our unanimous response. So, over we went to where the Guatemalan lads were getting changed into their spartan gear. This was serious stuff. Two players shared one pair of boots, wearing one each with nothing on the other foot. Andy and his brother also joined in the semi-organised game in blistering heat. We were well out of our depth. The Guatemalans were super-fit and Andy was different class, helping himself to numerous goals. We were all relieved when full-time came and we virtually collapsed with dehydration.

We went back to Andy's for something to eat and even more beer. He showed us where his new pool was being built and also a cupboard where his football trophies were stored, along with the ball from his debut hat-trick for Albion. I was surprised none of his memorabilia was on display, but it became obvious he wasn't a massive football fan. He was more interested in mixing music demos on his computer these days.

At the end of a very enjoyable day, we said our goodbyes and wished everyone well. Andy took us back into Belmopan for the last bus. The journey through the jungle was even more intriguing than in daylight. The trees were lit up by fire-flies illuminating the branches like little blue fairy lights ... or was it the beer kicking in?

Next day, complete with hangovers, we got a taxi to the border with Guatemala, then another lift to Peten Basin and the UNESCO World Heritage site of Tikal National Park. Tikal is one of the largest archaeological sites and urban centres of the pre-Columbian Mayan civilisation. It was an incredible place, consisting of ruins of an ancient city found in a rain forest, remains of temples, royal palaces and pyramids, some of which tower over 70 metres. The site was discovered in 1853 when Ambrosio Tut, a gum-sapper, reported the ruins to the Guatemalan newspaper *La Gaceta*. Spread over 23 square miles, many of the pyramids and temples had not yet been cleared, mapped or excavated.

For a major tourist attraction, Tikal was very quiet and we were able to climb up some of the magnificent pyramids completely alone.

After crossing back into Belize, I realised I had left my camera in a taxi in Guatemala. While Anil and Glenn waited, I went back through passport control and back across the border. I explained my predicament to the posse of drivers hanging round immigration. They were really helpful and one took me to the driver's house. He was asleep on the couch but woke to see me standing on his doorstep and opened his vehicle. There was my camera on the back seat. Needless to say, I tipped both men handsomely.

We were sad to leave Belize. It's a lovely little country with very friendly people, but it was time to start the long journey home. As planned, we disembarked the ramshackle bus at Playa del Carmen. There were no X-rated movies this time, although we were soon to experience a live version. When trying to find somewhere to stay, we went to one hotel but couldn't find anyone on reception. We went outside, peered through a window and caught the manager and receptionist (we presumed) in an uncompromising position at the most inappropriate moment imaginable. There they were at full throttle! We left them to it in a state of hysterics and soon found a guest house with normal services on offer. Playa del Carmen was a great little resort and we had two days of sunshine and beer. Our journey home was broken up by a drunken night in Miami, where we consumed a couple of crates of Budweiser in Bayside Marina to finish off a memorable week.

It was great to see Andy again at The Hawthorns in September 2015, when he attended the Everton game. He appeared on stage in the Fan-zone and was welcomed on to the pitch at half-time, along with his old partner, Bob Taylor.

Andy has now opened a new resort called the 'Belize Jungle Dome' and I would urge anyone with a sense of adventure to pay him a visit. You certainly won't regret it. www.belizejungledome.com

Andy kindly sent me the following to include in this book:

I'm sure Dean and his friends were given a real culture shock visiting us in Belize at the Jungle Dome. In those days, the Jungle Dome was nothing like it is now. I am very thankful for their visit. I note that they have travelled extensively, much to do with the life and times of the Baggies, and I hope their Central American adventure added another exciting chapter to their stories. I would imagine they have as much knowledge of football as they do of beers around the world.

I shared some stories with them and, although my time at West Bromwich Albion was full of false dawns, I was always given a fond reception from the fans and felt I had given my best for the club. Unfortunately, the promotion season I was part of did not result in significant progress at the club. The momentum was lost when Ossie Ardiles left and, in subsequent seasons, I seemed to play under a different manager every year. I have always believed in long-term stability for the benefit of a club but that was absent in my time at the Albion. This ultimately led to my departure. However, I cannot thank the fans enough for the support I was given. I had some terrific partnerships with different strikers and scored some memorable goals and hat-tricks along the way. Life moves on and I wish everyone at the club well.

Regards,
Andy Hunt
Belize 2015

28

Vikings and Promotion

Rio de Janeiro

In 2003, on holiday with Ruth in Rio, I spotted a flyer in the hotel reception advertising the Brazilian Cup semi-final at the Maracana Stadium that night. She looked at me and knew exactly what I was thinking A few hours later, we were taking our seats to watch local side Flamengo play Sport FC. The crowd of 41,436 seemed to be made up entirely of home fans and, as in Russia, their 'Ultras' displayed Union Jack flags. The game ended 0-0.

Odense

It was Denmark again for Albion's pre-season tour. Jade and I flew to Aarhus (in the middle of our street – as Madness would say), hired a car and drove down to Odense on the island of Funen. There were plenty of other Baggies about in what turned out to be a very nice city, the third largest in Denmark. We visited the birthplace of Hans Christian Andersen and watched an outdoor show depicting his fairytales.

Albion had played two games before we arrived. Their third game was against Odense Boldklub at the 15,633-capacity Fionia Park. Ex-Odense player Busko Larsen escorted us, having contacted me beforehand and explained he had always supported Albion. He was a great guy and gave us some of his old Odense shirts. A 2,223 crowd saw the hosts win 2-1 and Jade had her photograph taken with most of our players as they boarded the coach.

In between games, Neil and Joan Reynolds joined us for a drive to Billund and a day at Legoland. Although the trip was essentially for Jade, I was impressed by the sheer scale of the exhibits, including models of whole towns.

Our final game was against Midtylland at neutral Horne. It was a nice drive to the neighbouring old port of Faaborg and we enjoyed a few hours before kick-off exploring the narrow streets lined with attractive old houses. The match, at Horne Stadion, attracted 1,500 spectators, including many from England. They watched Albion dominate against the Danish side and win comfortably 2-0 with second-half goals from Hughesy and Dichio. Jeremy Peace stood on the grass bank at the one end, mingling with travelling fans. Jade ended up keeping the match ball and Gary Megson kindly took it on the coach and got it signed by the squad for her.

2003/04

There were lots of new faces at The Hawthorns; Thomas Gaardsoe (from Ipswich), Swiss international Bernt Haas (Sunderland), Paul Robinson (Watford), Rob Hulse (Crewe), James

O'Connor (Stoke), Mark Kinsella (Villa), Joost Volmer (Fortuna Sittard) and Macedionian international Artim Sakiri.

What I expected to be a winning League start at Walsall turned into the Paul Merson show, the Saddlers' new player manager dictated the game and helped himself to two goals as we collapsed and went down 4-1 in a Bescot embarrassment. Merson took the plaudits, but still declared afterwards that Albion would be promoted.

We made amends the week after, beating Burnley by the same score at The Hawthorns, with Hulse, Sakiri and Hughes (2) on target. Another four straight wins catapulted us to the top of the table. Ollie, joined me for his first away game, on 23 August for our 1-0 victory against Watford. Further 1-0 wins followed against Preston and Derby before Ipswich were thrashed 4-1 at The Hawthorns.

It's always nice to win on the road and three points came from our long trip to Gillingham; Clement and Dobie scoring in our 2-0 win. Jade joined me and enjoyed meeting Baggie Bird on the pitch before the game. Our last trip to Millmoor, the former home of Rotherham, was another pleasing day, Hulse (2) and an own goal saw us home 3-0. Then a classic at West Ham: We were 3-0 down after just 22 minutes and ready to throw in the towel. An own goal triggered an amazing comeback; Hulse (2) and Hughesy made it 4-3 and the points were ours.

For my birthday, Ruth bought me a flight to Hanhoi, Vietnam, where Dubsey was pottering around South East Asia. During the trip, in Luang Prabang, Laos, after a very cheap, drunken night (20p a pint), we were itching to know how Albion had got on at Nottingham Forest. We had no reception on our phones so Dubsey went back into town at 3.00 a.m. to seek an Internet café. It was closed, so he knocked on the door, waved a few Laotian kip at the security man and was soon inside, returning with the great news we had won 3-0 with two brilliant goals from Koumas. We went back out to celebrate.

Back in the real world, we secured another 1-0 win at Bradford before the festive slip. I visited the National Hockey Stadium in Milton Keynes on 30 December to see us at the franchised Wimbledon's temporary home. We sat on a stand made out of scaffolding to witness a terrible, televised 0-0 draw. The stadium was built in 1995, closed in 2007 and demolished in 2010.

We clicked again with a 2-0 victory over Walsall and lost only twice in the next sixteen games to secure the second promotion spot with three games remaining. Our brilliant run included six wins on the bounce in March and April and it was just like the old days at home to Coventry, Hulse, Horsfield and Kinsella scoring in our 3-0 stroll.

Proposal

I was in Cape Town with Ruth when we beat Ipswich 3-2 at Portman Road. I found a pub on the Victoria & Albert Waterfront and watched with an Ipswich fan as Ruth went shopping. It was a brilliant game and Ruth joined me with the match poised at 2-2 and about to enter injury-time. Then Lloyd Dyer struck our winner and I went mental, hugging her and jumping around the pub.

We were staying in lovely Camps Bay, with the beach backdrop of the Twelve Apostles mountain range, it was perfect. Call me an old romantic, but I proposed on top of Table Mountain. My first attempt was thwarted when the cable-car was closed due to heavy fog but it cleared later on in the week and, fortunately, she said 'yes'. We went into town and chose a ring. After all, South Africa is famous for its diamonds.

I returned in time for our 1-0 win against Gillingham at The Hawthorns but it was our game at Sunderland that effectively clinched promotion. With the 'Mackems' throwing everything at us and a draw the limit of our ambitions, Lloyd Dyer broke away and, with everyone screaming at him to take it to the corner, he headed for goal and squared for Jason Koumas to put away for an unexpected 1-0 victory.

With news of results elsewhere filtering through before kick-off, our home game against Bradford City became a non-event. Second spot and automatic promotion was ours. Hughesy and Horsfield still did the business by scoring in a 2-0 win.

Vikings at Reading

Our game at Reading was chosen for our end-of-season theme – Vikings, in tribute to our Danish centre-half, Thomas Gaardsoe. Some 3,000 Baggies dressed in horned helmets, tunics and carrying various blow-up axes created a tremendous atmosphere at the 'Mad Stad'. Sadly, the players were already 'on the beach' and slumped 1-0.

This was further evident on my visit to the Britannia Stadium on the Tuesday night. I sat with my Stoke mate Sean Goodwin and TV star Nick Hancock to see the Potters thrash us 4-1. A near full house at The Hawthorns for our last game witnessed a third successive defeat as Nottingham Forest beat us 2-0. It appeared as though the squad had broken up for summer two weeks earlier.

Forest had put us out of the FA Cup, too, winning 1-0 in the third round at the City Ground. We had better luck in the League Cup by seeing off Brentford, Hartlepool, Newcastle (in front of 46,932 at St James' Park) and even Manchester United (2-0 at The Hawthorns, Cristiano Ronaldo and all). We finally exited the competition at the fifth hurdle with Arsenal's kids soundly beating us 2-0 at the shrine.

Gary Megson nevertheless became the first manager to lead Albion to promotion twice and the first to take the club back up in the top flight at the first attempt. He also became our longest serving boss since Vic Buckingham in the 1950s.

29

The Great Escape

Latvia

When the season ended, I went for a long weekend away with Glenn and Steve to Riga. While in the Latvian capital, we were treated like VIPs at the Skonto Riga v FK Ventspils game, being invited into the President's lounge at the Skonto Stadion simply because we were English. It was a very poor standard of football on a bitterly cold afternoon.

Royal Appointment

At Alumet, we had developed an off-site constructed insulated façade system called the Avon Drywall Beam. The company had received the Queen's Award for Enterprise in the birthday honours list. One of the biggest days of my life came when I joined my colleagues, Gary Summers and Julie Robinson, at Buckingham Palace to meet Her Majesty. The whole experience was surreal and made me feel really important when I drove up to the gates at the end of the Mall and they were opened to let us into the Palace courtyard.

We were introduced to the Queen and Duke of Edinburgh and instructed to wait in the corner of the dining room as 'she will be with you in a few minutes.' We wondered who 'she' could be. It couldn't be … could it? Then, to our amazement, accompanied by two of the staff, Her Majesty was reintroduced to us and we spent ten minutes chatting to her about our business. Fortunately, she led the conversation. Well, what exactly do you say to the Queen of England? She was very pleasant and a lot smaller than I imagined; a tiny, fragile old lady. Later, we met Princess Anne, Prince Edward and other members of the Royal Household. Edward was very friendly and seemed to be generally interested in our story; however Anne just turned her nose up and didn't really want to know. Philip was only interested in the females!

2004/05

Back in the Premier League, we made a steady start, with our first three games ending 1-1. Among the new faces were Hungarian captain Zoltan Gera, a signing from Ferencvarosi for £1.5 million, Jonathan Greening from Middlesbrough, Polish goalkeeper Thomaz Kuszczak from Hertha Berlin, Nigerian international Kanu from Arsenal, Martin Albrechtsen from FC Copenhagen, Rob Earnshaw from Cardiff for £3.6 million and Darren Purse from Blues. Lee Hughes had his contract cancelled when he was jailed for six years following a serious driving offence.

A dreadful performance at Layer Road ensured a 2-1 League Cup exit to Colchester and we had to wait until 2 October for our first League win. Kanu and Gera were on target in our 2-1 home success over Bolton. After two bad defeats in a week in December – 3-0 at Crystal Palace and 4-1 at home to Chelsea – Gary Megson was sacked. He had transformed the club over four years and I will be forever grateful. Former Albion star and ex-England skipper Bryan Robson returned to take over and struggled to stop the rot, although we picked up a useful point at Arsenal, Rob Earnshaw scoring his fourth goal in three games in our 1-1 draw.

Back home, the usual Christmas nightmare unfolded, with embarrassing defeats at Birmingham (4-0) and at home to Liverpool (5-0). Chants of 'you don't know what you're doing' were aimed at Robson in the latter stages of the St Andrew's humiliation. We stopped the rot on our first visit to the City of Manchester Stadium when we came away with a 1-1 draw without managing a single effort on target. City's Richard Dunne generously scored an own goal.

In the FA Cup, an Earnshaw brace knocked Preston out in round three, but we bowed out 3-1 at Spurs in a replay after a 1-1 Hawthorns draw.

We actually beat Manchester City in the return match, the in-form Ronnie Wallwork and new signing Kevin Campbell finding the target in our 2-0 victory. We had propped up the table for most of the season and Robson had brought in Kieran Richardson, Richard Chaplow and Japanese World Cup star Junichi Inamoto together with Campbell in an attempt to survive.

Club sponsors T-Mobile had launched a 'Great Escape' campaign and a pleasing 2-0 home win against Birmingham was topped with a brilliant 4-1 success at Charlton, where Earnshaw bagged our first Premier League hat-trick and created history as the first player to score a treble in every division. He also scored one for Wales. All Albion fans got behind the campaign and our calculators confirmed that, somehow, we could stay up.

Gera scored a great goal in a 1-0 home win against Everton, and Robson's Army converged on Villa Park. We were trailing 1-0 into stoppage-time when full-back Paul Robinson got his head on the end of a cross and netted a brilliant equaliser in front of Albion's fans. We celebrated as if we had won the League and everyone started to believe we could do it.

More useful points came against Tottenham and Blackburn (both 1-1), but these were sandwiched between defeats at Middlesbrough (4-0) and at home to Arsenal (2-0). Our hopes were fading fast at Manchester United when we were trailing 1-0 deep into the second half. Earlier results elsewhere meant survival was still possible ... if we could get a teatime point. Amazingly, and almost unheard of at Old Trafford, the referee awarded us a penalty, which Earnshaw duly put away to ensure the season went down to the wire. Ruth had spent the afternoon shopping in Manchester and we went to see Rod Stewart in concert afterwards to round off a great day.

On what became known as Survival Sunday, we were at home to Portsmouth. On occasions like these, Albion fans can create an incredible atmosphere and become the 'twelfth man'. In our favour was the fact that Southampton, one of our relegation rivals, were Pompey's arch rivals. Portsmouth fans were even buying Albion shirts from the club shop sale before the match, with letters on the back stating 'Send the Scummers down'. It was the first time I'd experienced a Hawthorns full house ALL cheering for the same team.

Any three of four could go down. Norwich had thirty-three points, Southampton and Crystal Palace thirty-two and we were bottom with thirty-one. We *had* to win and hope other results went our way. Eleven years earlier, we had been in a similar situation – requiring victory at Pompey to avoid relegation to the third tier. No team had ever stayed up after being bottom at Christmas (as we were) and with other results going against us, and our game at 0-0 we went in at half-time still anchored at the bottom.

Geoff Horsfield went on after an hour and his first touch set The Hawthorns alight as he netted with a low volley. 'Feed the Horse and he will score' chanted the crowd. We still required a 'swing' elsewhere, so when Richardson added a second with 15 minutes remaining, the celebrations were muted. Our job was done. The players stayed on the pitch while fans crowded round radios. Norwich (6-0 at Fulham) and Southampton (at home to Manchester United) had both lost, so it was all down to Crystal Palace, who were leading at Charlton 2-1. News then filtered through that the appropriately named Jon Fortune had scored a late equaliser. The Hawthorns erupted. Jade and Ollie joined thousands of delirious supporters who stormed on to the pitch to congratulate the players. The tannoy blasted out 'The Great Escape' tune and

Robson was drenched in champagne. We finished fourth from bottom and had done it. What a result, what drama, what a day!

Stag weekend

It was the summer of our wedding and Ruth headed to Valencia for her hen weekend while I opted for the Slovenian capital, Ljubljana, for my stag bash. I was joined by best man Steve Conabeer, Ray Duffy, Chris O'Nyan, Gary Summers, Glenn Robinson, Adam Robinson, Steve Stanier, Tony Jones and Barry 'Basher' Baker. I got away lightly on the first night, but was forced to eat some dodgy cake that had me laughing hysterically when trying to order food.

Ljubljana is stunning and, before the madness started, I managed some sightseeing with a trip to the castle and the splendid old Bezigrad Stadium – home of NK Olimpija Ljubljana and host to some international matches. The stadium closed three years after our visit.

After lunch, we got comfortable in the main square and started drinking. We caused chaos as we played a game in which whoever was wearing the cowboy hat would blow a whistle and everyone had to get off the ground or pay a forfeit. We were diving on cars, tables, climbing lamp-posts ... anything to avoid being last. I was forced to drink a few glasses of the local fire water and attend a kangaroo court where I was found guilty and blindfolded. I had my top removed and felt another shirt being lowered over my head. I was horrified when I discovered my 'mates' had dressed me in a Villa shirt with 'DEANO' on the back! As the afternoon became evening, we ended up in the Cutty Sark pub, where the landlord unwittingly joined in our game. The whistle blew as we entered the bar and we all leapt on tables, causing glasses to smash and drinks to fly everywhere. The gaffer took it all in good spirit and provided a round of blueberry wine that triggered off several more rounds of the evil drink as the evening quickly deteriorated.

Everyone cheered when a couple of girls entered the bar. They promptly turned and walked back out. We had met up with a stag party of Millwall fans and I ended up on the dance floor with the groom, who was dressed as a Hawaiian girl. I felt pleased with myself when I swapped my Villa shirt for a bikini-top made of coconut shells. I was extremely drunk and proceeded to act out what became known as my 'Del Boy' moment, stumbling across the floor and trying to steady myself against the wall. It turned out to be a swing door and I went head first through it and ended up unconscious at the bottom of some steps. I was out for the count, strapped on a stretcher and taken to hospital, apparently to the applause of the watching Slovenians enjoying their evening meals. Gary Summers shouted: 'Now the party's starting' and the lads continued drinking while Steve accompanied me to hospital.

Glenn thought it was a great idea to take a photo of me, shirtless, face down on the stretcher, and texted it to his wife, Julie, who was at home watching the Eurovision Song Contest with Ruth and the girls. My future wife could see Julie's expression and demanded to see the photo. Julie texted back: 'Ruth is horrified,' to which Glenn replied: 'So are we. It was his round!'

Steve thought I had died when the doctor shone a torch in my eyes at the hospital and my pupils didn't move. Fortunately, I came round in the early hours and tried to get off the bed. I couldn't understand what was going on as I was strapped face down. I somehow managed to turn the bed upside down with me underneath it, creating a ridiculous amount of noise. At that point, the doctor decided to discharge me. He put me in a wheelchair and instructed Steve to take me down the corridor, turn right and pay the hospital charges. We turned left and disappeared out of an emergency exit.

Next morning, I noticed I had lots of missed calls from Ruth, so I phoned her straightaway. I insisted I was okay and had been discharged with just a few bruises. She was unaware I had been in hospital and shouted back: 'Discharged from where and what bruises?' I was digging myself into a deeper and deeper hole. As the lads were having breakfast, contemplating my funeral. I walked in.

My punishment on the last day in Ljubljana was to wear a Wolves shirt all day, even at the go-cart racing that Steve had organised. I was fortunately given a reprieve on the evening and was at last able to enjoy a few quiet beers.

I had a few days to recover before my second stag night – for my mates who couldn't make Slovenia. We did the Harbury pub crawl: The Crown, The Village Club, The Dog, The Gamecock, The Shakespeare and The Old New Inn. No hospital required this time!

Wedding bells

We had a hiccup in the lead-up to our big day when Ruth unveiled her chosen colour scheme: gold and black! I said: 'You're having a laugh, aren't you?' Not being a football fan, she was unaware of the sensitivity between Wolves and Albion. Needless to say, the outfit was soon changed.

We couldn't have wished for better weather for our big event. 18 June 2005 was the hottest day of the year so far, with glorious sunshine. Ruth and bridesmaids Jade and Rhiannon (Ruth's niece) were taken to All Saints Church, Harbury, by a local resident, Danny Killion, in his vintage Bentley. I joined guests for a 'nerve settler' in The Dog before the ceremony. Supporting Steve Conabeer were Glenn Robinson, Ollie and Rhodri (Ruth's nephew) as ushers. Ruth looked fantastic and was walked down the aisle by her brother, Pete. We were fortunate to have Ruth's mom and my dad present but sadly our other two parents were no longer with us.

Afterwards, it was back to the Village Hall, which we had been suitably decorated for the occasion. It looked fantastic. We had a great night and it was lovely to see Olle and Helena from Sweden, along with Benny and his brother Martin from Denmark, all of them friends that I first met on Albion trips to Copenhagen. We embarked on a very special honeymoon, with Ruth's first visit to South East Asia (my favourite part of the world) taking in Cambodia and Malaysia.

30

Sold Your Seats for a Pie and a Pint

Pre-season in Portugal

I obtained a cheap flight from Coventry to Faro to see Albion on their 2005 pre-season tour, basing myself in Albufeira on the Algarve and meeting up with Dubsey and his brother, Trevor, who had driven down from his villa in Spain. We were joined by Neil and Joan Reynolds and stayed at the Hotel California (I kid you not). As we checked in, the manager actually said: 'Welcome to the Hotel California' I was expecting him to follow up with: 'You can check in any time you like, but you can never leave.' It was such a lovely place!

Albion were taking on the might of Benfica at the Estadio Municipal de Albufeira for the Capital of Tourism Cup. As the match had been hastily arranged, not many Baggies had made the trip, just the usual suspects. As we settled in the main stand, I thought the bloke behind me looked familiar. It was Gazza, Paul Gascoigne himself; a smashing bloke who happily chatted to us. He was there due to his involvement with franchise club Algarve United and was catching up with his mate, Bryan Robson.

We were completely outclassed by Benfica – managed by Ronald Koeman and containing several Portuguese internationals including Nuno Gomes. It was embarrassing to watch. They wouldn't let us have the ball and everything they hit at our goal went in. We were very poor. Brazilian star Geovanni Diebersen scored a hat-trick for the thirty-one-time Portuguese champions as we were crushed 5-0 in front of around 4,000. Albion captain Kevin Campbell had a face like thunder when he collected the runners-up trophy, presumably thinking: 'Why are you presenting us with this after that shambles?' We didn't let it ruin a good night out, drinking with holiday makers until the early hours.

During our family holiday in Croatia, I met a chap at the hotel bar who turned out to be Football League referee Scott Matheison. We became good friends and, a few weeks later, he turned up on my doorstep with Geoff Horsfield's match shirt from one of our games where he had been an official at the match.

2005/06

Back home, I went to see our 1-0 friendly win against the newly-titled MK Dons at the National Hockey Stadium. The only new face in our starting line-up for our opening game was 'keeper Chris Kirkland, who was on loan from Liverpool. However, fairly soon, in came Curtis Davies from Luton, Diomansy Kamara from Portsmouth, Darren Carter from Blues, Nathan Ellington from Wigan and Steve Watson from Everton.

Jade and I travelled by train for the opening game at the City of Manchester Stadium and came away pleased with a well-earned 0-0 draw. Another good result came in our first home game as Horsfield hit a brace in our 2-1 win against Portsmouth. We were then thrashed 4-0 at Chelsea.

A few of us used Durham as a weekend base for our game at Sunderland, staying above Rosie Malone's Irish pub. After our 1-1 draw at the Stadium of Light, I was having a drink with Dubsey and Richie Brentnall. Now it's fair to say that Richie was renowned for his tightness; he could peel an orange in his pocket. Anyway, I got the first round in, our usual tipples of lager for Dubsey, bitter for me and cider for Richie. Dubsey then did the same and, when it came to Richie's turn, he returned from the bar with three ciders. 'What's this?' We questioned. Richie explained that he had bought us cider because he thought that our mouths might need refreshing. Although we complained vigorously, he refused to replace our drinks. When I went back to the bar, all was revealed. Chalked on a blackboard were the words: 'Special offer – cider 65p'. Richie refused to accept this as his reasoning and calmly quaffed all three pints. The argument continued back in Durham, where Dubsey and I were first to the bar in our digs. For a joke, we ordered Richie tap water and the barman played along by including a cocktail umbrella and sparklers. When Richie joined us, we said we thought 'his mouth might need refreshing'. Touché. Richie drank his water without a word and sulked all evening.

Our League Cup campaign saw us overcome Bradford in round two (4-1) before sending us to Fulham. I was working in London and staying in a hotel within walking distance of Craven Cottage. In a good game, Earnshaw put us ahead and Kanu scored on 90 minutes but Fulham equalised twice, the second time in injury-time. Junichi Inamoto stole the show in extra-time. He collected the ball on the half-way line, shook off a couple of challenges and unleashed a 35-yard screamer to win it.

George Best passed away on 25 November, at the age of just fifty-nine. We were Manchester United's opponents just five days later in the League Cup fourth round game at Old Trafford and coincidentally had also been their opponents for Best's debut in 1963. It was a night dedicated to the legend and Albion fans fully engaged in the pre-match tribute when the whole crowd held posters up of the former United ace. We lost 3-1.

An unexpected victory came against Arsenal at The Hawthorns as goals from Kanu (against his former team) and an absolute scorcher from Darren Carter (his first for the club) nailed our first home victory against the Gunners since 1973. A run of three defeats on the bounce was halted with our best performance of the season, an excellent 4-0 win against Everton. Ellington (2), Clement and Earnshaw shared the goals. This victory triggered off a mini-revival and a couple of points were added to our tally against Middlesbrough and Fulham before all three were secured with a superb 2-0 home win against Manchester City.

Our festive dip was reversed on 28 December, when Kanu produced his best Albion performance, scoring both goals in our 2-0 win against Spurs. Another rare win came at Wigan when Tomasz Kuszczak somehow hurled himself in front of former Albion striker Jason Roberts' point blank effort to produce the save of the season in our ten-man 1-0 triumph, Darren Moore having been dismissed. Reading dumped us out of the FA Cup, beating us 3-2 at their place in a replay.

Little did we know that our 2-0 win against Blackburn on 4 February, would be our last of the season. Nigel Quashie made his debut and goals came from Campbell and Greening. We lost nine of our thirteen remaining games, including a 6-1 hammering at Fulham. The only bright spots were our 0-0 draw at Villa and an exciting 2-2 draw at Everton once we had already been relegated, Uruguayan Williams Martinez scoring is only ever Albion goal. Jade joined me for this game and we stayed over in Southport then caught a 'ferry across the Mersey' before the game. Oh well, back to Division One.

World Cup in Germany

There was a bonus in June, when Alumet's supplier Schuco invited me to two games at the World Cup in Germany. It turned out I wasn't the only Baggie on-board. Josh Bowen was also a season-ticket holder, so he helped me hang my Albion emblazoned flag of St George in the back window of our coach. Our first game was Spain v Ukraine in Leipzig. The Zentralstadion had certainly changed since my previous visit many years before. Spain cruised to a 4-0 win, which didn't help the mood of Schuco's Ukranian staff, who we went out with after the game.

Next day, our coach transported us to Nuremberg for England v Trinidad and Tobago. It was a strange sight before the game to see the podium from the Nuremberg Nazi rallies festooned with

England flags. It was great to be back among England fans at a World Cup match and we won 2-0 at the Franken Stadion.

Kiev

On another weekend away, Ruth and I went to Kiev in Ukraine and I got a match in. We passed Dynamo Kiev's stadium during the day and saw a decorator's table set up on the car park ready for that evening's game with two old ladies selling tickets off a roll. One of them cut our tickets off with scissors; no complicated computerised ticketing system here! Watching the hosts beat Kpnbnn 2-0 was an enjoyable experience.

Scotland

There was no foreign tour for Albion in 2006. Relegation had probably taken its financial toll, so we had to make do with three games in Scotland. I missed our 2-1 defeat at Kilmarnock but Jade and I went to Motherwell and Dunfermline. It was decent weather, so we packed the tent and headed to a campsite on the Fife coast. We linked up with Neil and his family for the game at Fir Park to see a few new faces in the line-up; Swiss international 'keeper Pascal Zuberbuhler, striker John Hartson and defender Chris Perry. It was the first time we had played at Motherwell since Joe Wark's testimonial in 1978. Back then, the finest Albion side I have seen ran riot, winning 8-1. There would be no repeat this time, although a debut goal for Hartson and an own goal gave us a 2-1 victory.

In between games, we spent a nice day in Edinburgh and went to Kirkcaldy for another pilgrimage to Willie Johnston's pub. The Dunfermline game brought back many memories for some Baggies present – it was at East End Park on 15 January 1969, that we drew 0-0 in the first leg of the third round of the European Cup Winners' Cup before Athletic knocked us out at The Hawthorns the following month. This time, Hartson was on target to seal a 1-0 win, after which the players happily posed for photographs with Jade.

2006/07

As we kicked-off in a division now rebranded as the Championship, we had a straightforward home win against Hull, Hartson delivering another two goals. I travelled to Cardiff three days later for our final visit to Ninian Park; another classic ground that was about to disappear. Zoltan Gera was on target in our 1-1 draw. We beat Leyton Orient and Cheltenham in the League Cup before succumbing once again to Arsenal's youngsters, by the familiar Hawthorns score of 2-0. Three wins in our first eight games spelled the end for Bryan Robson. Assistant Nigel Pearson became caretaker boss and oversaw a great 4-2 triumph over Leeds. Tony Mowbray was appointed on 10 October and could not have wished for a better start as Kamara (2) and a hat-trick from new signing Kevin Phillips gave us a memorable 5-1 win at Ipswich.

Our form continued with a fine 2-0 win at Crystal Palace and, on a brilliant Hawthorns lunchtime, Wolves were destroyed 3-0. Goals from Greening, Kamara and Hartson (penalty) gave us Black Country bragging rights. Centre-half Paul McShane joined us to strengthen the defence and it was a familiar story against Coventry in December when we gave them a 5-0 stuffing. Phillips was fast becoming a fans' hero and was christened 'SuperKev'.

For once, Christmas didn't disappoint. Two home games brought two wins, over Preston and Ipswich. Mowbray had introduced a crowd-pleasing brand of attacking football. A rare new ground on 3 February, the KC Stadium, staged an Albion win over Hull thanks to a Kamara goal. The venue compared well with other new grounds. The architects had given it some thought rather than designing bland, identical 'plastic' stands. Still, all grounds appeared better following an Albion victory.

Just like buses, another one came along shortly afterwards, The Walkers Stadium had replaced Leicester's old Filbert Street home and I was there to witness our 1-1 draw. Again, this arena was pleasing on the eye and a large Baggies following added to the surprisingly good atmosphere. In the FA Cup, we beat Leeds 3-1 and then out of the hat came Wolverhampton Wanderers v West Bromwich Albion. What an afternoon we had at Molineux. FA Cup rules dictated Wolves were obliged to give us fifteen per cent of the capacity and the only way this could be achieved was to give us the whole of the South Bank – the recognised Wolves home end. The Dingles were not amused and, to calm them down, their chief executive Jez Moxey offered relocated season ticket holders a free pie and a pint. Before the big game, there was a social media appeal for all Albion fans to take Tesco carrier bags with them (in recognition of the name Wolves fans often give us). As the Baggies sang 'You sold your seats for a pie and a pint', we put Wolves to the sword, hitting top form in a 3-0 win with goals from Kamara, Phillips and Gera. At the end, our stand was covered in blue and white plastic that was a vast improvement on the orange. Unfortunately, we lost on penalties to Middlesbrough in the fifth round after drawing 2-2 at the Riverside.

We were pushing for automatic promotion, our side further strengthened by Slovenia captain Robert Koren and defender Sam Sodje. Maybe nerves kicked in, but some disappointing defeats meant we had to settle for the dreaded play-offs. However, we had another away game first, at yet another new ground – Coventry's Ricoh Arena. This time, it was an Irish theme and fans dressed up in green with ginger wigs as a tribute to our red-headed Irish defender, Paul McShane. A nice drink at the superb canal-side pub, The Greyhound, put us in good spirits before a rare Paul Robinson goal gave us a 1-0 win in the lovely sunshine. We signed off the League campaign in real style at The Hawthorns the following week by thrashing Barnsley 7-0 thanks mainly to another SuperKev hat-trick.

In the play-off semis, we were paired with our old adversaries, Wolves. Chris and I set off in my car for the first leg at Molineux, where we had already played twice that season. We were full of confidence and it turned out to be another cracking game, just like a cup-tie. Two goals from Phillips and a Kamara classic gave us a 3-2 lead for the second leg. A full house generated a red-hot atmosphere three days later, when another SuperKev goal sent us to the new Wembley for the first time to face Derby County.

Wembley '07

As it would be Albion's first visit to this spectacular arena, I decided to take my whole family, getting tickets for Ruth, Ollie and Jade. We travelled on a packed train from Leamington, meeting other family and friends on board. It was cold, really cold, and, after walking down Wembley Way, I went in search of hot drinks to keep the girls warm. The kids were having a great time, singing along to 'The Liquidator' as it was blasted out, although Ruth was shocked to see them singing the swear words to this Albion anthem. Sadly, the team just didn't perform and a poor Derby side edged it 1-0. I think we would have given a better account of ourselves in the Premier League than the Rams, who came straight back down ingloriously.

31

Boing Boing

South Korea

I went with the lads for a week in Seoul and my football fix came with a trip to the Sangam Stadium – constructed for the 2002 World Cup. We were allowed in and also visited the World Cup museum.

Cape Verde

My family holiday was on the African island of Sol in Cape Verde, where we stayed in a purpose-built resort. I wore my Baggies shorts on the first day and it soon became evident that around a dozen Albion fans were there. A crowd of us set off to the local town to watch our game at Sheffield United but Sky TV had not yet reached this African island. It was noticeable that we had picked up some local fans because I spotted WBA sprayed on a wall. Clearly, our new Cape Verdean signing, Pedro Pele, was an influential figure.

Slovenia

I travelled with Geoff Waters, Bill Ahearne and Scott Waters to Slovenia to see Albion take on Red Star Belgrade on our pre-season tour. We flew into the Austrian city of Graz and shared a 90-minute taxi journey to take us 72 miles to Murska Sobata in the Prekmurje region, where the game was to be played.

It was a nice little town, with many fine bars. The match took place at the Mestni Stadion, Fanzanerija, home of Mura '05. In front of around a thousand spectators, on-loan striker Sherjill MacDonald made his first senior start and Shelton Martis was our new defender on show. Paul Robinson headed us into a 19th minute lead before Belgrade's Stanic beat Dean Kiely with a superb free-kick two minutes from time. We had a brief chat with Curtis Davies and it was painfully obvious he wasn't going to be with us much longer. Sure enough, he went off to Villa shortly afterwards for an astonishing £10 million. A few weeks into his career there, he described himself as a 'pub player'.

Very few Baggies made the trip and, after a heavy session with the Albion regulars, we caught a flight back from the local airport in Maribor next day. Albion's players were also at the airport, although on a different flight. Slovenia became another country that I had seen my team play in.

2007/08

I drove to Burnley for the first League game. It appeared much more relaxed than our 1990s visits when Turf Moor was stuck in a 1970s time warp. New faces in the starting side included full-backs Carl Hoefkens (a Belgian international) and Tininho from Mozambique, centre-half Leon Barnett, midfielder Felipe Teixeira and striker Craig Beattie. Our new signing from Middlesbrough, James Morrison, was on the bench. Despite a Kevin Phillips goal, we were beaten 2-1. Ollie was Albion's mascot for the 2-0 home win against Barnsley, he was taken into the dressing room to meet the players before leading them out with Jono Greening onto the hallowed turf. I joined him on the pitch to get his photo taken with every member of our team. He enjoyed every minute of his fantastic experience. I so wished that they'd had mascots in the '60s, I would love to have led Graham Williams out of the tunnel and had a kick around with Bomber and The King.

Happily, The Hawthorns became a fortress as we won six of our first seven home games, including an impressive 4-0 victory against Ipswich, with Chris Brunt making his first start and new signing Ishmael Miller on target, and a 5-1 thrashing of QPR. There was an enjoyable day on the road and a new ground on 22 September. Goals from Brunt, Barnett and Teixeira gave us a 3-2 win on a cold afternoon in Scunthorpe, who had only moved to Glanford Park in 1988 and they now appear to be on the move again.

After knocking out Bournemouth and Peterborough in the League Cup, we were shocked to be beaten 4-2 by Cardiff at The Hawthorns.

I ventured with the kids to a more regular venue – Vicarage Road, Watford, where a superb performance and goals from Miller, Phillips and Albrechtsen secured a 3-0 win. Another stroll at the Ricoh followed as we smashed Coventry 4-0, and then came a 2-1 victory at Plymouth with Roman Bedbar bagging both goals on his first start.

Wembley '08

In an epic FA Cup run, we beat Charlton on penalties in a home replay and there was no messing about at Peterborough in round four thanks to a routine 3-0 win. In round five we were drawn away to Coventry – joy! A massive Albion following made up a large part of the 28,163 crowd to see us demolish the Sky Blues 5-0, making it seventeen goals against them in two years. Jade accompanied me to Bristol Rovers in the quarter-final and we sat in a strange marquee structure to see Miller bag a hat-trick in a 5-1 triumph. So we were off to Wembley again for a semi-final against Portsmouth. This time, the weather was good but the result was disappointing, a lucky goal by ex-Baggie Kanu gave Premier League Pompey a 1-0 win. Ruth's nephew, Rhodri, had won a competition and was one of the mascots leading the Albion out. At least my kids had seen us at Wembley twice in just two years. It took me twenty-three years to achieve that feat.

In the League, apart from a shock 4-1 home defeat to Leicester, things were progressing well. Fantastic comebacks against Colchester at home (4-3) and at Blackpool (3-1) saw us clinching important late victories. A Zoltan Gera strike in our 1-0 win at Wolves set us up nicely for the final three games. After a fine 2-1 win at Norwich, we just needed a point at home to Southampton to guarantee promotion. On a nerve-wracking night, we were trailing 1-0 when the ball ran nicely for Chris Brunt, who lashed it into the Brummie Road net. The ground erupted. The 1-1 draw ensured we were back in the Premier League, but, to clinch the title, we still needed a point from our final game, at QPR.

Champions and a new business

A few nights beforehand, my good mate, Chris O'Nyan, arranged a meeting with Ray Duffy and myself in the Hamstead pub, Great Barr. He pitched his new business idea to us – personalised face masks. After much discussion, we decided to give it a trial at Queen's Park Rangers. The game had been given a superheroes theme and there wasn't an outfit left in any Midlands fancy dress shop. Chris and Ray made 300 Kevin Phillips masks, which Chris and I, appropriately dressed as Batman and Robin, sold outside the Loftus Road stadium.

The masks proved really popular and added to the fantastic atmosphere. The away end was packed, with every kind of superhero imaginable being celebrated. The players responded and goals from Kim Do Heon and Brunty gave us a 2-0 win and the title. It was emotional at the end; great to see Albion win silverware – the instantly recognisable old First Division League championship trophy and fantastic for my kids to witness Jonathan Greening lifting it directly in front of them. I said to them: 'Take in every moment. Believe me; you won't see us win a trophy very often.' And our new product had made it on to the pitch at the end, with Robinson and Gera both wearing 'SuperKev' masks while Phillips himself donned three!

We sold 300 masks at the game, taking £600 from a £20 investment in card, printing and elastic. It was a no-brainer. Chris, Ray and I became the 'Three Maskateers' and Mask-arade was born.

Germany

I had never seen Albion play in Germany, so, when I heard the pre-season tour news, it had to be done. Jade and Ollie wanted to join me but didn't break up from school until after the first game. Problem solved – I got a return flight to Weeze for only 5p. Yes, *five pence*. I could commute!

My biggest expense was driving to Stansted and parking. I flew out on my own for the first game against Borussia Mönchengladbach, played at the Hubert-Houben Stadion in Goch, close to the Dutch border. The tiny ground is the home of lower-division club SV Viktoria Goch and it was only a 30-minute drive from the airport. I sat on a grass bank under an umbrella in the rain. We went behind early but Graham Dorrans, making his debut as a second-half substitute, set up Sherjill MacDonald for our equaliser. Our joy was short-lived as the Monchengladbach substitute scored the winner. There was a smattering of Baggies around the ground but we were heavily outnumbered in the crowd of 3,000.

I stayed in Goch overnight and enjoyed a few beers in the market square with some very boisterous Albion fans. Next day, I flew back home for the night, collected the kids and drove back to Stansted. Unfortunately, I couldn't obtain 5p flights this time, but still paid just £23 each. We arrived in Düsseldorf early evening, in time for a few drinks. Our hotel was in a red-light area, so it was an eye-opener for Jade and Ollie to look out at the numerous sex shops. This was when I first encountered Dave Thornhill; 'Stockbroker Dave' as he is known. He was stumbling around blind drunk, complaining of a broken arm. SBD was to become a good mate.

Neil and Joan shared our hire car for the hour's drive to Euskirchen, where we faced our second opponents, FC Köln. It was a beautiful little town and we soon found the travelling Albion fans when we spotted Sauce's flag outside a quaint bar. We had a smashing lunchtime, sitting in the sun drinking German wheat beer. It seemed a shame to call a halt but we got to the Erftstadion in time for the kids to have photos taken with the players near the team coach.

At the home of SC Kappellen-Erft, it soon became clear Koln were in a different class. We were battered in the first half, conceding four times in 38 minutes, including an own goal from Roman Bednar. Fortunately, the drunken Koln fans in the 3,866 crowd kept us entertained at the beer tent behind the goal. Craig Beattie finally gave us something to cheer by making it 4-1. Our flight home was at 5.00 a.m. next morning, so we headed for Weeze town, where a festival in the main square kept us occupied until the early hours. It was then off to the airport for a couple of hours sleep in the car before check-in. The things we do to follow our team.

2008/09

The one new face in our first line-up was defender Abdoulaye Méïté. However, he was soon joined by £4.7 million signing from Real Mallorca, Borja Valero, Dutchmen Ryan Donk and Giovanni Zuiverloon. Chris and I drove down to London for our first visit to Arsenal's new Emirates Stadium. It was the best English club stadium I had visited. Outside, we sold the new Mask-arade range of Albion fridge magnets. Comedian and well known Baggie, Frank Skinner even helped us with a sales pitch.

A 60,071-strong crowd saw us put up a good battle but fall just short, Arsenal winning 1-0. I didn't go to Hartlepool to see us exit the League Cup in a disgraceful 3-1 defeat. We did, however, manage three wins in our first seven League games – against West Ham (Jonas Olsson's debut), Middlesbrough and Fulham to keep hopes high. But we were brought back to earth with a bump by losing eight of the next ten, including some shockers; 4-0 at Manchester United and Sunderland, and 3-0 at home to Hull, at Liverpool and against Chelsea at The Hawthorns. The 75,451 attendance at Old Trafford was the highest we had ever played in front of in the League.

This horrendous run sent us to the bottom and that's where we stayed for the rest of the season. We were playing half-decent football but just couldn't compete against established Premier League teams. Goals were hard to come by despite the signings of forwards Luke Moore and Jay Simpson (loan). Wins were even rarer; Middlesbrough (3-0), Sunderland (3-0) and Wigan (3-1) were all we could muster after the turn of the year.

In the FA Cup, we made hard work of Peterborough in the third round, drawing at home before running out 2-0 replay winners. A draw at The Hawthorns against Burnley in the next round was followed by a 3-1 defeat at Turf Moor.

Away games had become a chore and we didn't win on the road again in the League after the trip to Middlesbrough in September. Our new loan recruit from Paris Saint-Germain, Youssouf Mulumbu, finally made his full debut in our 2-0 home defeat to Liverpool in May, having been plagued by injuries since joining us four months earlier. Most Albion fans still backed Tony Mowbray and I was one of them. I agreed with his principles and believed that he would eventually get it right. To show our support, through Mask-arade, we gave a Mowbray mask to every Albion fan as they entered the turnstiles at our last game, against Blackburn. A film crew from *Midlands Today* visited our offices on the Friday and Ian Winter broadcast live with the three of us lurking behind him wearing our Mowbray 'faces'. A message on the back of each mask requested fans to put it on just before kick-off. *Match of the Day* host Adrian Chiles was informed and the cameras zoomed in on thousands of Tony Mowbrays at Ewood Park as the teams warmed up. The players put in a good shift and deserved their 0-0 draw.

Dragons' Den

Mask-arade was going from strength to strength and the three of us appeared on TV's *Dragons' Den*. Although we didn't receive an investment, the programme was broadcast to an audience of over six million and our website nearly crashed. Our appearance effectively launched the business. It was on the Mask-arade stand at the Grass Roots football show where Jade met her future fiancé, Tom. He was a Birmingham City apprentice at the time and approached our stand in his club tracksuit. She had visions of being a 'WAG' and asked if she could leave her duties to meet him for a drink. I was pleased to discover he was actually an Albion fan and his parents are lifelong Baggies. All boxes ticked!

On June 16 2009, despite overwhelming support from fans, Mowbray left for Celtic. Two weeks later, we appointed our twelfth manager in twenty years, Roberto Di Matteo from MK Dons.

Croatia

A month later, I was at Luton Airport bound for Zagreb to see Albion play NK Varteks in Croatia. I was in the queue when Adrian Chiles walked past and beckoned me to join him on priority boarding. I sat next to him on the plane and he explained that his mother is Croatian and how pleased he was that we were playing in his 'other' country.

He also told me his Croatian friend was meeting him at the airport, so he offered me a lift to the game. We were met at the airport by Padraig and I commented on the Dinamo Zagreb pennant hanging from his car mirror. Next thing I knew, we were driving into Dinamo's Stadion Maksimir and being shown round the trophy room. I was also given a club t-shirt. Padraig needed to call at home before leaving for the game, so we were given a beer while he got ready. His wife was struggling with a newly delivered fridge as the door was on the wrong side. In a surreal situation, Adrian and I spent the next 30 minutes in the kitchen swapping the door around.

En route to the game, I was informed that we would first go for something to eat. Halfway through the 54-mile journey, we stopped at a lovely restaurant high in the stunning countryside. I have never seen so much food. There was enough to feed a coach-load, let alone the three of us. Our host also ordered copious amounts of beer and, as we sat in the sun, stuffing ourselves stupid and getting very drunk, I was thinking we weren't going to make the match. Neil Reynolds kept texting, asking where I was. All I could say was: 'Getting pissed with Adrian Chiles in the Croatian hills!'

Padraig settled the bill and we finally set off. We pulled up outside the Varteks Stadium just in time to meet Neil and the lads before they entered the ground. Adrian had media duties to attend to, so I thanked him and Padraig for the lift and quickly grabbed another beer before meeting our new manager on the stairs. He was slightly bemused when I asked for his photograph holding a Di Matteo mask.

As I was slightly inebriated, I can't remember much about the match other than Craig Beattie scoring twice in our 2-2 draw. The game was apparently watched by a crowd of 1,800. The beer continued into the night as I joined Stockbroker Dave, Long Haired Mick and other die-hards in a bar listening to Neil's ska and reggae CD which included The Liquidator.

2009/10

I travelled to Cheltenham for our final away friendly to see our new England international 'keeper, Scott Carson, make his first appearance.

In the Championship, our first game was at home to eventual champions Newcastle. Slovakian left-back Marek Cech made his debut in our 1-1 draw, a rare goal from Shelton Martis earning us a point. The following week at Nottingham Forest, we were often under pressure, but an own goal somehow gave us an unexpected win.

A 2-0 win at Bury kicked off our League Cup campaign, followed by the 4-3 defeat of Rotherham in round two. Once again, we came up against Arsenal and lost as usual, this time 2-0 in front of an incredible 56,592 at the Emirates.

Luke Moore, commonly known as 'Luke Warm', came out of his slumber to net two goals in our 3-2 midweek win at Peterborough. Home wins against Plymouth and Doncaster, the latter containing a goal from young Chris Wood, were overshadowed by an amazing 5-0 victory at Middlesbrough. Brunty (2), Bednar, Mulumbu and our new winger, Jerome Thomas, were all on target at The Riverside. The week after, in true Albion fashion, we lost at home to Crystal Palace.

My dad was a diabetic and had been suffering from dementia for some time. He was admitted to Stafford Hospital after going into a coma and sadly never came around. He passed away on 18 October, 2009.

Our promotion push was soon back on track and another new recruit, Simon Cox, bagged his first goal in our 5-0 thrashing of Watford. We were scoring for fun and our 2-1 win at Leicester was followed by a 4-1 win against Bristol City and a superb 4-0 romp at Sheffield Wednesday. Even the dreaded festive period couldn't slow us down. Two more good wins, over Peterborough and Scunthorpe, saw us keep the pace at the top with Newcastle.

A huge Albion army descended on Huddersfield in the FA Cup and goals from Dorrans and Wood saw us comfortably through. A fine 4-2 round-four home win against Newcastle had us dreaming of Wembley again. We were a minute away from exiting the competition at Reading when full-back Joe Mattock equalised to force a replay, which we lost 3-2.

We hit a run of good form from late January, winning eleven of our fifteen games including three points on my first visit to Swansea's new Liberty Stadium, where Dorrans and Miller scored without reply. On 10 April, I drove to another new ground, Doncaster's Keepmoat Stadium. My mate Silve had returned for the game from his home in Spain and I had the kids with me for a game that we needed to win to secure promotion. We arrived early and spent a pleasant lunchtime drinking in the spring sunshine. The atmosphere was excellent and, once again, Albion fans came together when it mattered, roaring the lads to a 3-2 victory and another stab at the Premier League. The players all came over afterwards and we celebrated as one.

Second place was ours with three games to play but we were too far behind Newcastle to be crowned champions again. However, unlike 2004, when we switched off with promotion secured, we remained unbeaten and it was Hawthorns party time against Barnsley as a 1-1 draw brought the curtain down on a super season. We had certainly become a yo-yo club and I wondered how long we could stay up for this time. Boing Boing, indeed.

32

Thank You, Roy

World Cup in South Africa

In the pub before the Barnsley game, Dubsey mentioned that he had two sets of tickets available for England's games at the World Cup in South Africa. So after clearance from Ruth and a quick call to Steve, I relieved him of his spares.

We flew into Johannesbourg, via Mauritius, landing on the day of England's game against the USA. We hired a car and headed straight for the nearby city of Rustenburg where the game was due to take place. However nobody in the city seemed to know where the stadium was. It was hard to believe a World Cup was taking place. Eventually, we found it and had to use the park-and-ride facility.

Compared with the immaculate new grounds I had encountered in Japan and Germany, the Royal Bafokeng Stadium was a bit of a dump. There was no real organisation, just semi-trained, barely interested locals. The seats hadn't even been cleaned. On the plus side, the lack of security enabled us to walk around freely inside, so we headed for the dug-outs and had some fun with my masks opposite the TV cameras. Our phones were going crazy as friends texted to inform us we were live on television. After Steve Gerrard put England in front, a catastrophic mistake by 'keeper Rob Green gifted the USA an equaliser.

It took us ages to get back to the car, and then to find our campsite. When we did, it was all locked up. It was almost getting light when we finally set about getting some sleep. It had been a very long day.

A couple of detours were made before we headed south. We called into Sun City, where we bumped into the England team playing golf and a visit to Botswana. At the border, we were informed we didn't have the required insurance to allow us in. But, if we agreed to give the cleaner a lift on our return journey, we would be allowed to enter illegally. Deal done! On our way back a few hours later, the cleaning lady jumped in and we dropped her in Rustenburg.

After a 282-mile drive taking five hours, we made it to Bloemfontein. We obtained tickets for Japan v Cameroon that evening and I was fascinated at the culture clash between the two sets of fans, mixed with some Europeans. It was a right melting pot. The Free State Stadium was a massive step up from Rustenburg as Japan won 1-0. On our drive out of Bloemfontein, as we waited at traffic lights, a guy opened the back door and attempted to steal a bag off the backseat.

Another diversion next day took us on foot into Lesotho, a taxi showed us round Maseru – the capital of this poor country, including a visit to the Setsoto Stadium.

Over 1000 miles after leaving Johannesburg, we made it to Cape Town and had a terrific few days leading up to the England v Algeria match. Unfortunately, I broke a bone in my foot descending Table Mountain after revisiting the scene of my proposal to Ruth.

The atmosphere on the Waterfront on match-day was brilliant as England fans converged on the bars. My Albion flag of St George and Steve's Exeter flag were both prominent at the entrance and TV personality Danny Baker and ex-Albion reserve Bruce Grobbelaar were two of the celebrities we encountered.

After an all-day drinking session, it was time to walk (hobble) to the game. The new Green Point Stadium was more like a proper World Cup venue, but England's performance was woeful and the 0-0 draw was greeted with boos from the thousands of travelling fans. Wayne Rooney famously reacted to camera at the end.

The trip had nevertheless been another fantastic experience. Travel and football ... you can't beat it.

Netherlands

A pre-season match against VVV Venlo presented me with the opportunity to see the Baggies play in the Netherlands. I decided to drive there with Ollie, Neil and Chris making up our car load. We headed via the Channel Tunnel and stopped overnight in Eindhoven, calling at PSV's excellent Philips Stadion, where a fans' day was taking place. We met up with other travelling Albion fans and enjoyed a few beers on a warm evening.

Next day, we located our guest house and explored the city of Venlo in the south-east of the country, near the German border. Albion fans were everywhere and a convenient bar soon acted as a magnet for the thirsty Baggies. We had taken an assortment of Albion player masks and had lunchtime fun arranging 'team' photos.

The game was played at the tiny Sportpark Dijckerhof, home of VV Reuver. In the lovely afternoon sunshine, a crowd of 3,112, around 300 of them Baggies, saw us squeeze home 2-1 over a team that had finished twelfth in the Dutch Premier League the previous season. A first-half goal from Ishmael Miller was cancelled out before Gabriel Tamas's strike won it.

Our hosts had laid food on in a marquee afterwards and a great time was had by all as two sets fans got on well together. So much so that Venlo's fans have adopted Albion as their English team and vice versa. Their supporters have since come over for several games and Albion fans have been to see our Dutch friends play. Sadly, this side of football makes the papers.

2010/11

Another Premier League campaign began. Could we stay there this time? The omens didn't look good on our manager's return to his old club, Chelsea, who reminded us of the gulf by hammering us 6-0 on the opening day. Nigerian international Peter Odemwingie, our new signing from Lokomotiv Moscow, scored the only goal on his debut against Sunderland in our first home game. He scored again four weeks later in our 3-1 home win against Blues.

On our visit to Arsenal, the unthinkable happened. We raced into a 3-0 lead. Although the Gunners pulled two back, it was still an amazing win. Another good result followed in our next away game, our new striker Somen Tchoyi scored his first goal in a 2-2 draw at Manchester United. Yet another new forward, Marc-Antoine Fortuné, was on target in our 2-1 home victory over Fulham. In a crazy game at Blackpool, our Spanish centre half, Pablo Ibanez, was sent off early on, then our feisty Chilean, Gonzala Jara saw red following a ridiculous tackle that put his opponent in the stand. Our nine men couldn't hold on and we lost 2-1.

In the League Cup, we were progressing well, beating Orient away (2-0) and Manchester City at home (2-1) before a brilliant 4-1 win at Leicester saw us through to the quarter-finals. Most of the big clubs had been knocked out, so we really fancied a good result at Ipswich. I lost all respect for Roberto Di Matteo at Portman Road. We were clear of the relegation zone so in my opinion we should have played our best team and gone all out to win it. Instead he 'rested' most of our regulars and we wimped out 1-0. Unforgivable.

After our regular defeat to bogey side Stoke, 3-0 at home, we went to Everton fearing the worst. Surprisingly, we turned in an excellent performance and secured a 4-1 victory, Mulumbu grabbing our fourth goal before being ridiculously sent off for over-celebrating. New fans' favourite, Austrian Paul Scharner, also scored. We made it six points out of six with a 3-1 home win against Newcastle but crashed out of the FA Cup at the first hurdle, losing 1-0 at Reading with Jonas Ollsen sent off.

We were in a bad run and, to me; Di Matteo had clearly lost the plot. Our 3-0 defeat at Manchester City on 5 February proved the final straw for the board and, within hours, he was relieved of his duties. First-team coach Michael Appleton was placed in charge on a caretaker basis but the experienced Roy Hodgson was appointed head coach in time for the Black Country derby at The Hawthorns on 20 February. Our loan signing from Arsenal, Mexican Carlos Vela, scored a dramatic last minute equaliser against Wolves – a bit of a turning point and he saved another point at Stoke the following week, this time in the 87th minute.

The team seemed to have new confidence, which was evident when goals from Mulumbu, Morrison and Scharner nailed a 3-1 win at Blues. A good draw at Arsenal was followed by more success; a very rare 2-1 home victory against Liverpool, with Chris Brunt putting away two penalties, and a 3-2 win at Sunderland.

My highlight of the season came in late April; we were down to ten men against Aston Villa after Paul Scharner had seen red with the game poised at 1-1. Then, with the minutes ticking down, Mulumbu set The Hawthorns alight with a well-taken winner. Sadly, we were still in dreamland at Molineux the following week and went down 3-1. It was only Hodgson's second defeat and another three points were added to our tally in our last home game, with Mulumbu on target again in our 1-0 victory over Everton.

Newcastle Brown Day

Things had been going really well at Mask-arade. The Royal Wedding had generated record sales, with over 250,000 William and Kate masks being shipped around the world. The BBC had contacted us regarding a feature for a Dragons' Den follow-up series and despatched a film crew to follow us to St James' Park for our last game. We were giving out Bomber Brown masks for the 'Newcastle Brown Day'. The fans' general theme was a tribute to the Baggies legend.

Chris, Ray and I travelled the day before and spent a very drunken night in Whitley Bay before meeting the BBC team at the ground on Sunday lunchtime. Newcastle had given us permission to set up a stand inside the ground, so we covered the perimeter fence with 'Bomber' masks. The great man even paid us a visit for a photo-shoot and an interview for the cameras.

We were so high in the stand that the players looked like Subbuteo figures. At half-time, we felt like leaving as the 'Toon' had raced three goals clear. We then witnessed a remarkable comeback, with Somen Tchoyi helping himself to a hat-trick in front of Albion's fans to rescue a draw. Our eleventh-place finish was our highest in five seasons of Premier League football. We also topped the fifty-goal mark for the first time as well as attaining over forty points.

Do you know the way to San Jose?

Albion's pre-season announcement presented me with a chance to see the Albion in the States. Due to other travel arrangements, I was only able to get to the USA for the first of our three matches – against San Jose Earthquakes. I flew to San Francisco for the first time since 1981 and spent an enjoyable two days reminiscing and also drank at the legendary Mad Dog in the Fog pub that used to be run by Albion fanatic Roger Howell. In addition, I went to my first and last baseball game, The Giants were playing New York Yankees at the AT&T Park and I obtained a black market ticket. The build-up was pleasant enough, with a few beers in a pub garden among friendly Giants fans. But I was totally confused by the game. It appeared to finish, then start again and the fans went crazy over nothing. It was a glorified game of rounders to me and I spent most of the 'ball game' watching the ships on the sea behind the open end. Stupid game!

I caught the train to San Jose and met Neil and Joan. On match day, I called at the ground and the staff kindly presented me with an Earthquakes shirt. Later, we located the rest of the Albion fans, including regular travellers Chris Ward, Sauce, Kevin Wainwright, Norman Bartlam, Dave Bending and Duncan and Emma Holman, spending the afternoon sampling the local brew in Teske's Germania beer garden and other excellent bars.

A useful crowd of 6,872 turned up at Buck Shaw Stadium in the grounds of Santa Clara University. We were one down after three minutes as the Earthquakes' keeper hit a clearance from the edge of his area that caught Boaz Myhill out as he stared into the sun. On the stroke of half-time, the hosts scored again but Jerome Thomas reduced the deficit and Morrison, Fortuné and Miller then all went close. Unfortunately, it wasn't to be and we lost 2-1.

Word had got round that the fans were heading to Trials Pub back in San Jose afterwards. We entered to find it packed with thirsty Baggies, the majority USA-based, all with stories to tell regarding their allegiance. Some were ex-pats but most were American citizens who had adopted the Baggies for various reasons. This was the first time many of them had seen their heroes 'live'.

2011/12

Hungarian star Zoltan Gera returned from Fulham. Shane Long came in from Reading, Gareth McAuley was recruited from Ipswich and England goalkeeper Ben Foster joined us from Blues, initially on loan.

The fixtures weren't kind. Our opening three games were against champions Manchester United, runners-up Chelsea and our perennial bogey team, Stoke. Sure enough, we lost all three, albeit by the odd goal; though new signing Long scored in the first two. I was on holiday in Zanzibar for the Chelsea game and watched on TV in a Jambiani bar.

We despatched Bournemouth 4-1 in the League Cup before losing 2-1 at Everton. A Peter Odemwingie goal put our first three points on the board (at Norwich) but we were taken to the cleaners when thrashed 3-0 at Swansea.

Mid-October was a period to remember as we beat both our main Midlands rivals in six days. Goals from Brunty and Odemwingie did the damage against Wolves at The Hawthorns, then Olssen and Scharner scored on a memorable afternoon at Villa Park. Scharner lifted his shirt after his winner to reveal a t-shirt bearing his son's painting of the Albion crest. I was in corporate hospitality and, when our goals went in, there seemed to be as many Albion fans as home ones in the Trinity Road Stand. What a week!

I had the hospitality treatment again at the Emirates in our next away game. Unfortunately, there was no repeat and we went down 3-0. Just before Christmas, we put six points on the board with successive wins at Blackburn (2-1) and Newcastle (3-2), McAuley netting his first Albion goal in the latter. Consecutive League defeats against Everton, Spurs and Norwich meant 2012 didn't start anything like so well, the run being ended at Stoke of all places, where 'Mozza' and 'Dozza' netted.

A Simon Cox hat-trick helped see off Cardiff 4-2 in the FA Cup but we disappointingly went out then when Norwich won at The Hawthorns for the second time in a fortnight.

12 February, is a date that still sends shivers down the spines of Wolves fans. They were already struggling when Albion arrived to put a big nail in their coffin. The Dingles were simply blown away, a superb Odemwingie hat-trick and goals from Olssen and new loan signing Keith Andrews giving us an amazing 5-1 victory and our best win against them since 1964. Wolves were humiliated and reacted by sacking Mick McCarthy. Relegation also followed.

Black Country bragging rights boosted confidence and there was more success; a fantastic 4-0 win against Sunderland and a 1-0 victory over Chelsea in March that was our first against the

London club in thirty-three years. It also ended a run of thirteen successive defeats against them. Hodgson's team broke another hoodoo in late April, when Odemwingie's goal secured our first win at Anfield in forty-five years.

Leamington Baggie Steve Skidmore was a new car mate travelling with me to Wigan. Steve is an excellent guitarist and well known for his CD recording of 'Baggies Battle Cry'. It's also fair to say that 'Skidders' is partial to a drink. On the journey up the M6 he polished off several cans and a small bottle of whisky, around six more pints followed in the pub before the game. After a Paul Scharner goal had given us a 1-1 draw, I got back to the car in good time hoping for a quick get away – no Skidders! I eventually made contact via phone, however all he could say in a very drunken voice was 'I don't know where I am' and 'where's the car'. This was no help whatsoever, I was on a housing estate in Wigan without any redeemable features and I had absolutely no idea where Skidders was! Half-an-hour later he miraculously appeared, staggering down the road with a pint glass in his hand – he had managed to find a pub easy enough!

Hodgson was offered the England job and duly accepted, so our last away game, at Bolton, was given an England theme. Mask-arade knocked-up some Roy Hodgson masks to underline the tribute. The away end was a mass of England shirts and St George flags. Memories of 2001 came flooding back with Albion fans in full voice. Bolton looked to be party poopers by scoring twice early but Brunty and Mozza grabbed a goal apiece as we staged our second end-of-season comeback in successive years, this time making it 2-2. We actually aided Villa's survival by denying Bolton three points.

We signed off at home to Arsenal, our Hungarian keeper Marton Fulop making a debut that turned into an absolute nightmare as all the Gunners goals in our 3-2 defeat were from his mistakes. Fulop sadly died of cancer in November 2015.

Our tenth-position finish was a slight improvement on the previous season and we were definitely 'Pride of the Midlands', with Wolves bottom and Villa just staying up. Thank you, Roy.

Mugged in Colombia

During a week away with Steve Conabeer and Phil Kennedy, we were strolling round Bogota on our first day when a guy jumped out on us, wielding a knife. We immediately scattered and Steve slipped over. The mugger held the knife to Steve's throat and relieved him of his money and camera. I felt helpless. I wanted to kick him off but that might have made the situation much worse. Instead, Phil and I got help and the police arrived in minutes. We joined them, chasing the thief through the streets, eventually catching him. At the station, Steve claimed he had lost his camera, pesos and US dollars. The camera and pesos were returned, but not the dollars, so the police stripped him and punched him endlessly, asking where they were. He denied all knowledge. Later that evening, in the bar, Steve put his hand in his back pocket and found the dollars!

33

We Know What We Are

Albion appointed Steve Clarke as head coach on 8 June and he took his squad to Scandinavia for a mini-tour to prepare for the new season. I enjoy that part of the world, so decided to go to both games.

Malmo

The first match was in Sweden against FF Malmo but not in the ground I visited in 2000. The hosts had moved next door to the new 24,000-capacity Swedbank Stadium. I flew with Billericay Baggie, Ian Tinsley, meeting him in the Stansted Airport bar, which soon filled up with familiar faces. In Malmo, we went out with a large group of Scandinavian Albion fans, Olle, Torbjörn and Stian being joined by new Swedish faces including Robert Jensen, Geir Anreassen and Henrik Skaalvoid. They were all great guys and a good evening's drinking was had as we acquainted ourselves with the 'Scandies'.

On match day, we joined hundreds of Albion fans in completely taking over Harry's Bar in the city centre. As well as the usual suspects, it was good to see Dutch Baggie Duco van der Veen again. The outside of the bar was soon covered in Albion flags and the biggest, friendliest policeman I had ever seen helped fasten the banners to the awning. He must have been nearly 7 feet tall and was christened 'High Tower' and 'RoboCop' as he joined in with the banter.

At the stadium, we met a local that Dubsey had once encountered on his travels. Hubert Sarnandt was a Malmo supporter who arranged to meet us again after the game, watched by a 3,128 crowd including nearly 1,000 Albion fans – the biggest overseas Baggies following I had seen since Zurich in 1981.

Malmo scored the only goal after eight minutes, although it looked a good yard offside. We had our chances, especially in the second half, with Saido Berahino and Peter Odemwingie having efforts saved. Liam Ridgewell headed over and new loan signing from Ghent, Yassine El Ghanassy, should have done better with only the keeper to beat. It was good to see youngsters Saido Berahino and Kemar Roofe in action.

Hubert kindly chauffeured us afterwards, pointing out the city sights before taking us to the excellent Malmo Brygghus, where numerous Albion regulars were getting stuck into the strong beers brewed on the premises.

Copenhagen

I flew home on 20 July, then, five days later, flew from Stansted to Copenhagen for the second game. It was my first visit since Albion's game there in 2001. After reacquainting myself with the lovely city, I joined up with a few fellow Baggies in familiar central bars and was soon joined by my old mate, Benny Andersen, the first Dane I met on my first visit in 1999. I hadn't seen him since my wedding, so we had several beers while catching up, before the game.

Outside the Parken Stadion, I bumped into Adrian Chiles and his daughters. There were fewer than a hundred Albion fans this time in the 3,197 crowd but we still made plenty of noise. In a fairly even game, a 25-yard Steven Reid free-kick gave us a 20th minute lead that we held until the final three minutes, when a Shane Long penalty and magnificent effort from Gabriel Tamas gave us a flattering 3-0 victory. At the end, we had a right laugh with Ben Foster, who came to the away enclosure to be greeted by two fans wearing masks depicting his face. Benny and I then spent the rest of the night, drinking into the early hours.

Tunisia

On holiday in Tunisia, I attended a cup game between rivals Etoile Du Sahel and Esperance De Tunis. It was mayhem! Ollie and I shared a taxi to the Stade Olympique with two guys from our hotel. It was the last day of Ramadan and we were greeted at the ground with scenes of fans climbing the walls and general chaos. We were informed the game was a sell-out, so we offered a copper a few quid and were immediately taken to the front of the queue and pushed through the turnstiles.

The atmosphere was incredible. Half the stadium was engulfed in red smoke and massive banners. I had never witnessed anything like it anywhere. There were only around twenty-five Tunis fans behind one goal and their coach was parked inside the ground. Apparently, it was agreed that only a small number of away fans could attend. The home fans didn't seem at all interested in the tiny Tunis contingent, but constantly threw missiles at the police and became more and more excited. At half-time, with the hosts trailing 1-0, I said: 'The worst thing that could happen is for Tunis to score again.' Sure enough, they went two up before the hour. All hell was let loose. The fans stormed on to the pitch, causing the players to run for cover and the referee was left with no choice other than to call an abandonment.

We had no idea what was going on or what to do. The police started to baton-charge the fans on the pitch and then on the terraces. All of a sudden, the whole crowd raced out of the ground in unison, like water going down a plug hole. We stayed inside, in the hope it would die down, but the police decided otherwise and started firing tear gas at the few of us left inside. We were forced to leave, with our eyes stinging. Outside, we were faced with thousands of wild fans pelting the police with rocks. It was decision time. Do we stay with the police and risk getting hit, or run across the road to join the fans and cop some more tear gas? As the police had protective riot shields and we had nothing, we held our heads and ran.

It was as if war had broken out, with sirens wailing, flashing lights, tear gas and flying rocks. We started walking quickly away from the stadium and got talking to some fans who appeared normal. Then, after around twenty minutes, a police car drove past and our new friends stopped our conversation to pick up rocks and throw them at the vehicle. We continued for about half-an-hour until we eventually found civilisation. A good hour after the match was abandoned, with our eyes still smarting, we managed to get a taxi back to the resort. What a night!

2012/13

Back to the normality of West Bromwich, we started off spectacularly. Liverpool came to The Hawthorns and were thrashed 3-0, our new loan signing from Chelsea, Romelu Lukaku, netting on his debut, along with Odemwingie and Gera. We followed up with a decent 1-1 draw at Spurs.

The good old League Cup presented me with a new ground to visit, Yeovil. Steve from Exeter joined me at Huish Park on a cold August evening to see us progress with a 4-2 win. Unfortunately, we couldn't repeat our first-day heroics against Liverpool in round three, going down 2-1.

We were getting nose bleeds in the League, a 2-0 home win over Everton and 1-0 win against Reading putting us in the top three. Only one defeat came in our first seven League games, 3-0 at Fulham, and, after beating Chelsea at home for the second season running, I had a tremendous fifty-second birthday present with a 4-2 win at Sunderland; Gera, Long, Fortuné and Lukaku all helping themselves to a goal. Steve Clarke was named Manager of the Month. Then our usual home defeat to Tony Pulis's Stoke was sandwiched between another two losses.

For the midweek trip to Swansea, Chris and I decided to make a night of it. We played shite with The Swans going three up after just 30 minutes, Lukaku eventually made it 3-1 but it was still awful. After the game we headed off into town to drown our sorrows. I couldn't believe how busy it was in Wind Street, it was student night and everywhere was packed. It was a bitter cold evening and we were wrapped up in coats and scarves, however the youngsters were queuing up to get in the bars wearing next to nothing. In fact one young girl trying to beckon punters into one particular club was actually topless. The match was soon forgotten and I didn't have to look too far for somewhere to hang my coat up!

Director of the Year

As construction and marketing director at Alumet, I had been heavily involved in making the company more sustainable. Our success led to numerous awards and celebrity visits from David Bellamy and Brian Blessed. I also had to show The Duke of Kent around the premises and met more royalty when I was introduced to Prince Charles at Millennium Point. My efforts were rewarded when I was named West Midlands Environmental Director of the Year 2012. I went on to represent the area at the grand final in London and was proud to have Jade with me at the glittering ceremony. To my surprise, I collected the National Director of the Year award for Leadership in Corporate Responsibility. I was also named runner-up as Overall UK Director of the Year, collecting my trophies from Michael Portillo.

Christmas was kind to Albion for a change and we clocked up six points with good 2-1 wins at home to Norwich and at QPR. We were back at Loftus Road in the FA Cup third round, in which we stupidly allowed QPR to equalise with virtually the last kick after Long had put us ahead. We lost the replay 1-0.

At Villa Park on 19 January we were dreadful in the first half and Villa raced into a 2-0 lead. But we came out a different team after half-time. A 20-yarder from Brunty pulled one back and Odemwingie bagged a dramatic 83rd minute equaliser to give us a point. Transfer-window deadline day in January, made us headline news for all the wrong reasons. The want-away Odemwingie drove down to QPR in the hope of signing for them. We refused to sell and Albion fans pretty much lost faith with him after that. He was even given time off following the ridiculous saga.

We completed the double over Liverpool in February, 'GMac' and Lukaku scoring as a terrific 2-0 victory made it 5-0 'on aggregate' against Brendan Rodgers' team. We continued to win the odd game to keep us well placed and we all headed to Norwich for our last away game for a party. Mask-arade offered free to provide Lukaku masks to travelling fans, but we received a torrent of abuse on message boards with accusations of hijacking the theme game. In the end, we cancelled the print run.

I joined my mates for a weekend in Great Yarmouth and we attempted to drink the place dry the day before. Albion's performance on the Sunday was disgraceful. The players looked as though they were already on the beach and were deservedly walloped 4-0.

And so to The Hawthorns for the season's finale to see Sir Alex Ferguson's 1,500th and final game in charge of Manchester United. Nobody in the capacity crowd could have predicted what we were about to witness. The champions went 3-0 up after 30 minutes and we sat back to suffer the rout. Then, just before half-time, James Morrison reduced the deficit and, when substitute Lukaku was unleashed, he soon found the net from 20 yards before Robin van Persie made it 4-2. When Hernandez added a fifth, it looked all over but Lukaku scored again on 81 minutes, then Mulumbu made it 5-4. Our astonishing comeback was completed when Lukaku completed his perfect hat-trick (right foot, left foot and header) with four minutes remaining. We even went in search of a winner as United hung on at 5-5. What a game!

The players came out for a lap of honour after their eighth-place finish – our highest ever in the Premier League. The crowd sang: 'We know what we are, we know what we are, pride of the Midlands, we know what we are.' And we were right.

RIP Richie Brentnall

I received some devastating news on 21 May. My good friend and legendary Baggie, Richie Brentnall, had died following a freak accident in Spain. Richie had been on the Costa del Sol for several years but kept his season ticket in our section of the Brummie Road End. After watching Albion play Man City on TV in one of his local bars, he caught a taxi home and argued with the driver over the fare. After a minor scuffle, Richie stumbled, fell and banged his head. He went into a coma and tragically never recovered.

He had no next of kin, so Dubsey and Bill Ahearne sorted out his apartment in Spain, got his body home and arranged the funeral. I offered to do the eulogy at Sandwell Valley Crematorium seven days later. It was one of the hardest things I have ever done. I had an endless list of funny stories – he was such a character. But to tell them with his coffin next to me was tough. Seeing as he had no family, the turnout was impressive, with Albion fans from all over the country turning up to pay their respects. Everyone sang 'The Lord's My Shepherd' and left the building to 'Rat In Mi Kitchen' by UB40 – one of Richie's favourites. This surely must be the first time this track had ever been played at a funeral. There was also a touching tribute from the Pena International branch of the Malaga FC supporters club. Richie attended most Malaga home games as they had become his adopted Spanish team. The wake was in the Horse and Jockey, West Bromwich, and the evening was spent exchanging stories about our lost friend. It seemed everyone had a Richie tale to tell.

Seat HH 69 in the Brummie is much quieter these days. RIP big fella.

34

Oh, Vienna

Austria

I was really pleased when Albion announced their plans for the summer of 2013. Games in Austria and Hungary were scheduled, providing me with another two countries where I had yet to see us play.

Ollie and Jade were desperate to join me, but the first game clashed with school and university, so I made arrangements for them to fly out for the second game and meet me in Vienna.

I hired a car in Vienna to get to the game against Hannover '96 in Gleisdorf. Neil Reynolds and Norman Bartlam joined me for the 109-mile journey. It was a lovely little town, dominated by a large church and array of solar panels. The quaint ground was actually called the Solarstadion. I had a photo taken wearing a mask of our new signing, Nicolas Anelka. I held a beer and 'tweeted' the picture, it received loads of derogatory comments such as: 'He should have more respect for his club' and 'It just shows his lack of interest in playing for West Brom'. Obviously, the mask was so life-like that people really thought Anelka was having a lunchtime session before the game. The fact he is a Muslim and doesn't drink never occurred to them!

The Gleisdorf staff kindly let us in for nothing among a crowd of 512, including around 150 Baggies. It was weird seeing Anelka in an Albion shirt but he displayed some excellent touches and it looked as though he could be a good signing. Hannover took the lead on 28 minutes before Markus Rosenberg equalised 15 minutes later. He hadn't scored for us in the League but this was his second goal in two friendlies. He left the pitch at half-time to a chorus of 'He's Markus Rosenberg, he scores when he wants' – a smile and wave showed he appreciated the irony. An unfortunate deflected own-goal by Craig Dawson gave the Germans an undeserved victory.

Back in Vienna, we had a brilliant night celebrating Albion fan Warren Stephens' thirty-second birthday. I discovered I had been at school with his mom, which made me feel very old. A large group of us, including Warren's mates James Rennie, and Southampton Baggie Graham Bartlett met in the Stern Brau bar and tried all sorts of weird and wonderful ales including a revolting chilli-beer. Cue severe hangover next day!

On a free day, I went to Austria Wien v Admira in the Austrian Premier League. It was a lot better than I expected. The Vienna fans created a fantastic atmosphere in the Generali Arena. The home end was a mass of maroon and white flags bearing messages such as 'fanatics' and 'no surrender'.

The kids flew in and I met them at the airport. I was chuffed to see them and relieved they had made their connection and remembered to adjust their watches. We spent a smashing day sightseeing in Vienna in glorious sunshine.

Hungary

Our second game was over the border in Hungary, against the Ferenc Puskas Academy in the town of Sopron. The kids were excited about visiting a new country and the 75-mile drive soon passed. We checked into our hotel at the same time as Dutch Baggie, Duco, and soon located the Albion contingent outside a bar in the market square. A lot of new faces had appeared and the beer was flowing nicely.

The 5,000-capacity Varosi Stadion was the former home ground of FC Sopron, who dissolved in 2008. In front of a thousand spectators, Albion comfortably eased past some of Hungary's enterprising youngsters, Anelka scoring two and Graham Dorrans with a penalty as we ran out 3-0 winners.

Some of the noisy Albion fans took it upon themselves to wind up the hired security stewards around the pitch. It started as a bit of a joke but got quite serious once certain Baggies started flicking peanuts at them. The 'hired muscle' were Arnold Schwarzenegger lookalikes, dressed in tight black t-shirts, combat trousers and army boots. One of the Albion lads, Peachy, gestured to them that he would take them all on. I have known him personally for years as we have worked around the world together.

Once Jade saw what was going on, she said: 'Tell him to stop it, Dad.' I had seen him in this situation too many times before to intervene. Outside the ground, he ran at the stewards with his fists flying. They rolled him up like a carpet and threw him in the back of their van. That evening, he entered the pub unscathed. Hungary had become just the latest country that he had been arrested in.

Cork

Less than two weeks after returning home, I was off to Ireland to see Albion take on Cork. I flew from Bristol and joined Neil at a small guest house above The Welcome Inn, one of the city's oldest and last remaining traditional pubs. The bar provided the perfect start for a pub crawl to the compact Turner's Cross ground. When ordering a Guinness, I was politely informed that everyone in Cork drinks the local Beamish Irish Stout – fine by me.

Several hundred Albion fans were among the crowd of 3,000, with plenty of St George flags on display. The in-form Anelka netted a hat-trick, Dorrans scored twice and ex-Cork player Shane Long made it a convincing 6-0. A great trip was concluded at the excellent Franciscan Well brewery, where we were joined by a dozen travelling Baggies.

Belarus

Steve and I managed a weekend away in Minsk and visited the magnificent Dinamo Stadium just before the main stand was demolished. All went well until our journey home. We both thought our return flight was 4.30 p.m., so we arrived at the airport (26 miles from the city) at 2.35 p.m., only to discover our plane had just taken off. The flight was 14.30, not 4.30! We couldn't get a refund so searched the Internet and booked on another flight, via Russia, leaving at midnight. There was absolutely nothing at the airport, so we spent a boring eight hours before attempting to board. We were stopped at the gate and asked for our Russian visas. We explained that we would only be in transit and therefore didn't need a visa, but the official informed us the flight was to the domestic airport in Moscow and the international airport was across the city. We were turned away.

No refund again and we spent another hour on my iPad searching for yet another flight. We found one leaving at 5.00 a.m. and booked it. By the time it was boarding, we were pretty much living at the airport and were almost sleep-walking as we went to the gate. Our passports were inspected and we were ushered into a room. We had no idea what was wrong this time until a burly official informed us that our Belarus visas ran out at midnight and we were in the country illegally! Just when we thought we were never going to leave, he felt pity on us and we were allowed to board. It had cost us £1,000 in flights to finally get home a day later than scheduled.

2013/14

Southampton were our visitors for the first game. They looked better than us and it was no surprise they took all three points thanks to a 1-0 win. Next up was Everton away, and I was on a family holiday in Albania, desperately trying to find a bar to watch the match. I located one with a television and talked the landlord into showing our game, much to the annoyance of the regulars, some of whom came in, muttered something about Man United and Chelsea, then left in a huff. There was only me and the kids left in there by the end of the 0-0 draw. We finally managed a goal in our fourth League game, GMac heading an injury-time equaliser to secure a point at Fulham.

Saido Berahino burst on to the scene in the League Cup. He bagged a hat-trick in our 3-0 win against Newport with loan signing Matej Vydra making his first starting appearance. We went out, as usual, against Arsenal, finally losing 4-3 on penalties.

After raising expectations with his pre-season promise, Anelka looked distinctly ordinary in the real world of the Premier League and continually failed to deliver. Our goals in a superb 3-0 victory over Sunderland came from full-back Liam Ridgewell, new loan signing Morgan Amalfitano and Stephane Sessegnon.

Mask-arade had secured licenses with the top five Premier League clubs and we were invited by Manchester United as their special guests for the Bayer Leverkussen, Champions League game. It turned out to be an Albion reunion as we were joined by Bryan Robson, Mickey Thomas and Arthur Albiston for a drink before kick-off. Thomas was a right character and told us endless stories from his incident-packed career. At half time, we were instructed to wait in the executive box for a special surprise; in walked Robson, Lou Macari and Gary Pallister with the Premier League trophy and the Community Shield. United won 4-2 on what turned out to be a memorable evening.

One of the most remarkable victories of recent years came on 28 September. I had to miss the match at Manchester United as John Challis (Boycie from Only Fools & Horses) was opening the new Mask-arade distribution centre. I couldn't believe the news coming through that goals from Amalfitano and Berahino had given us a 2-1 victory at the champions – our first win at Old Trafford since the legendary 5-3 in 1978.

Our mini-revival against Liverpool was abruptly ended in October when we were brushed aside 4-1 at Anfield. I sat with the home fans and it was difficult to hear a Scouse accent; the fans around me all seemed to be from Scandinavia or Asia. Suarez was on fire and basically unplayable.

Another huge disappointment came in the shape of Scott Sinclair, signed on loan from Manchester City. I remembered seeing him rip us apart when he played for Swansea. However, he never appeared interested wearing the famous stripes. He was a complete waste of space.

At Stamford Bridge on 9 November, we were minutes away from a historic win that would have ended Jose Mourinho's undefeated home record. But Villa-supporting referee Andre Mariner awarded Chelsea a farcical injury-time penalty to give them an underserved draw. It felt like a defeat as I stood in disbelief at the end of the game. A further draw and four straight defeats followed and Clarke was placed on 'gardening leave' on 14 December after a dreadful 1-0 loss on my first visit to Cardiff's new stadium. This defeat left us two points above the relegation zone in sixteenth place. Keith Downing was placed in temporary charge.

Anelka finally did something useful at the end of the year, scoring two of our three goals in a 3-3 draw at West Ham. But the game was broadcast live across Europe and the controversial Frenchman made the anti-Semitic 'Quenelle' salute on camera. His claims that it was in support of his French comedian friend fell on deaf ears. He was banned for five games and eventually sacked by Albion.

A poor performance in the FA Cup third round against Crystal Palace saw us lose 2-0 at The Hawthorns. We urgently needed a new boss and Spaniard Pepe Mel was the surprise choice, watching our terrible 1-0 defeat at Southampton from the stands before officially taking over as head coach before the home draw with Everton on 20 January.

He introduced a brand of all-out attacking football, but our defence was not good enough to adapt. Uruguayan international Diego Lugano was particularly exposed at Villa Park of all places as we let a 2-0 lead slip before embarrassingly losing 4-3.

Mel had to wait eight games before his first victory, with Mulumbu and Sessegnon on target in our 2-1 win at Swansea. Ruth and I stayed in South Wales for the weekend and, coincidentally, shared our hotel with Albion's players. It was interesting to see Sessegnon sitting alone and not mixing with his team mates.

Another loan signing, French/Congolese striker Thievy Bifouma, was introduced and he initially looked the part, with his Mohican hair-cut and his trickery on the ball, however he flattered to deceive and was soon released. Despite the football being easy on the eye, we were struggling and in grave danger of relegation. Our 3-3 home draw with Cardiff was a classic example of our gung-ho approach. We were leading 3-2 as the game entered injury-time when Berahino naively crossed instead of holding it in the corner to run down the clock. Cardiff broke away and equalised. Berahino's attitude allegedly led to a punch from James Morrison in the dressing room afterwards.

Another 3-3 draw, this time against Spurs, sounds useful but we were leading 3-0 before our defensive frailties were again too easily exposed. Fortunately, wins at Norwich and at home to West Ham brought us enough points for safety and I breathed a sigh of relief. I met Pepe Mel at a Hawthorns event and thought he came across really well. He was very likeable and his philosophies made him popular with most fans. Our game at Arsenal on 4 May was designated as a tribute to the former Real Betis manager. Various Spanish outfits were on display, including bullfighters'. Our supporters showed more fight than our players and we lost 1-0.

We finished with another two defeats, 2-0 in a non-display at Sunderland and then our predictable loss at home to Stoke. We finished seventeenth, simply not good enough, and Mel left by mutual consent less than 24 hours after the final match.

Spain

During FA Cup final weekend, a group of us went to Spain to raise a few glasses in memory of Richie Brentnall. On the Friday night, we went to Malaga v Levante at the Rosaleda Stadium. I met Richie's mates from the Pena Supporters Club beforehand and we shared stories of our mutual friend.

Next day, we met at midday in the Tahiti Bar and greeted my old mate Silve, who now resides in Spain. We went on a pub crawl of Richie's old haunts. It was good to see an Albion flag stating 'RIP Richie' on the wall in the London Bar. When we showed a photo of him in some of the bars, the locals often recognised him and were unaware of his death. It was good to toast his memory and I think we did the big man proud. We pledged to make the memorial weekend an annual tradition.

On the Sunday, Tony and I drove to the Seville v Elche match. The hosts had just won the Europa Cup and there was a party atmosphere in the Estadio Ramon Sanchez Pizjuan. We also called in at the Estadio Benito Villamarin, home of Pepe Mel's former club, Real Betis.

For the first time in years, I missed the pre-season tour. Two games were arranged at the same venue in Sacramento, USA. But I had just returned from a week at the International Licensing Expo in Las Vegas, so I reluctantly declined.

35

Up the Junction

My reaction on 14 June when Albion unveiled Alan Irvine as head coach was: who? To say I was underwhelmed was an understatement. His previous job was as boss of Everton's youth academy – hardly the experienced figure we required. He soon became known as 'AFI' – Alan Fuc**ng Irvine!

He immediately looked to strengthen our defence, signing Belgian international Sebastien Pocognoli, World Cup stars Cristian Gamboa (Costa Rica) and Jason Davidson (Australia), Northern Ireland's Chris Baird and Andre 'Norman' Wisdom on loan from Liverpool. Our major signing was England international Joleon Lescott.

Our new strip was horrendous. It was mainly white with a very thin navy pinstripe that wasn't visible from a distance. I'm a traditionalist and, to me, Albion wear proper navy blue and white stripes.

The Desi-Junction pub in West Brom High Street had now become my regular pre-match haunt and having a lunchtime drink with the lads in there, was often the best part of a home game.

2014/15

We got the new season underway with a 2-2 home draw against Sunderland, Saido Berahino bagging a brace. Our new boss had to wait until 21 September for his first League win, 1-0 at Spurs. Due to problems with trains for this Sunday lunchtime game, I had to drive to London's outskirts, then catch the train to White Hart Lane. It was well worth the hassle though, as Mozza's goal gave us three points.

In the League Cup, we made hard work of it against Oxford in round two, eventually triumphing 7-6 on penalties. A good 3-2 win over Hull put us into round four when Bournemouth knocked us out 2-1 at Dean Court.

One of our best performances came at home to Burnley, another two goals from Berahino helping us to a 4-0 victory. A good 1-0 win over Leicester came at the newly-named King Power Stadium. The highlight of AFI's tenancy, though, was on 13 December, when a spectacular Craig Gardner strike gave us three home points against Villa.

Defeats over Christmas (nothing new there) against QPR, Man City and Stoke left us sixteenth and perilously close to the relegation zone. The QPR defeat was particularly painful. Goals from Silvestre Varela and Lescott had us comfortable at 2-0 ahead but we relaxed and a Charlie Austin hat-trick gave Rangers victory. Irvine was duly sacked on 29 December, having won just four of his nineteen League games. This time Jeremy Peace acted swiftly in appointing a replacement … step forward Tony Pulis; the previous season's Premier League Manager of the Year who had performed heroics at Crystal Palace. I must admit I wasn't a fan of the football Stoke played during his spells there, but, if we needed someone to keep us up, he was the man.

His first game was against Gateshead in the FA Cup and we won in style, 7-0. Tickets were in high demand for the fourth-round clash at St Andrew's. It had been a few years since we had played the Blues and Cup fever swept the Midlands. Big Victor Anichebe turned on the style, scoring both goals in our 2-1 win.

Scotland midfielder Darren Fletcher had been recruited from Manchester United and was immediately instated as captain, making his debut in our 2-2 draw at Burnley. Back in the Cup, we performed brilliantly at home to West Ham in a tie I missed due to being in Brussels with Ruth. Normally, fifth-round weekend is blank, so I had booked a few days in Belgium. I watched our scintillating display in a city bar. Brown Ideye had suddenly started to look the part and helped himself to two goals in our 4-0 victory.

After a sound 1-0 home win over Southampton, we entered probably the worst week of my football life. First up was a midweek League game at Villa Park. As the game entered injury-time, it looked all over a 1-1 draw, only for Ben Foster to inexplicably fumble, then concede a stupid penalty to gift Villa an undeserved victory.

That defeat was hard to take, but just four days later we had a chance to make amends; we were back in Witton for the FA Cup quarter-final. This was the big one for me, although when a 5.30 p.m. kick-off was announced, it was a recipe for disaster. I went with the kids for a pre-match drink in the Hare of the Dog near the university but, as we walked towards the stadium, it resembled a war zone ... riot police on horses, dogs, sirens and a helicopter. It was a throwback to the 1970s and could easily have been prevented if fans hadn't had five hours' drinking time before the game. Our fans were bizarrely split into two sections, with home fans at the front of the Witton End. On the pitch, Villa were there for the taking and I expected us to go for it. Unforgivably, we didn't and they took advantage. Scott Sinclair, of all people, scored their killer second goal, causing a mass pitch invasion by their deluded fans. Albion's followers retaliated by ripping up seats and hurling them at the enemy. It was chaos. Worst of all, we were out of the Cup and Villa were going to Wembley for the semi-final.

We were dangerously close to the relegation places again and our run-in hardly inspired me with confidence. The next two games were critical and we completely messed the first one up by losing 4-1 at home to QPR. Then came Astle Day against Leicester. The game was dedicated to my hero and our players were given a special one-off dispensation from the Premier League, to wear the 1968 FA Cup final strip. It was emotional to see the team in the famous white shirts, shorts and red socks. They even wore replica tracksuits beforehand with 'WBA' on the back. In the ninth minute, everyone in the Brummie Road held up placards spelling out 'ASTLE KING'. Unfortunately, Leicester hadn't read the script and, despite Fletcher's first Albion goal and another from Gardner, we crashed 3-2. Our two home 'bankers' had gone and we had a nightmare run of games ahead. Relegation was a distinct possibility.

We went to Crystal Palace expecting nothing and came away with three points, Craig Gardner scoring the goal of the season in our 2-0 victory. A valuable point against Liverpool followed before we had a great day in Manchester. I was given four hospitality seats, so along with Chris, Ollie and Tom, I caught the train for the 5.30 kick-off. I love Manchester pubs and there are a couple of classics in the city that we always go in: The Circus Tavern (smallest bar in England) and the Grey Horse Inn next door. By the time we got to Old Trafford, we were well oiled and, when Boaz Myhill saved a penalty, we all jumped up despite being surrounded by Reds. A steward advised us to keep quiet and sit down, then showed us his Albion stile-card. He was student in Manchester, earning some extra money. When Olsson scored the winner, we couldn't restrain ourselves and leapt up in celebration again. The steward just looked at us, nodded his head and smiled. Our 1-0 win completed a fantastic day. If Carlsberg did away games!

The points pretty much ensured our survival and a good draw at Newcastle left us with only games against Chelsea and Arsenal. Chelsea had already secured the title but our performance was still very impressive and we earned a memorable 3-0 Hawthorns victory, with two goals from Berahino and one from Brunty.

Finally, we travelled to the Emirates and another positive result proved too much to ask. We caught Arsenal on one of their better days and were well beaten 4-1. Fortunately, the Gunners carried this form to Wembley the following week, embarrassing Villa 4-0. We watched the final during Richie's memorial weekend at Fuengirola's London Bar.

USA

Having missed the 2014 USA tour, I was determined to go to the States this time. I was unable to attend the first game, in Orlando, so I flew to Charlotte to take in the games against Charleston (South Carolina) and Richmond (Virginia). Charlotte was conveniently situated between the two venues, so I hired a car for the five days.

Due to my flight to Newark being delayed, I only just made my connection to Charlotte. Unfortunately, my bag didn't and I drove the 209 miles to South Carolina with just the clothes I was wearing, arriving at my hotel in the early hours. I had previously contacted Charleston Battery FC and their helpful staff sorted out a discounted hotel rate for me. Next morning, still with no sign of my bag, I drove into town to buy some essentials and called at the Blackbaud Stadium, the venue for that evening's match. I thanked the staff for sorting the hotel and received some VIP passes for the Three Lions members-only pub at the ground.

I visited the Emanuel African Methodist Church, where a gun massacre three weeks earlier had left nine dead. I laid some flowers on behalf of Albion supporters. Downtown Charleston was lovely. I walked along the waterfront and the Battery, admiring scores of historic, brightly coloured buildings. Later, I received a call from fellow Albion travellers: Stockbroker Dave, Long-haired Mick and Keith Whitehouse, who were drinking in Tommy Condon's Irish pub in town. It was lashing down, but I jumped in the car and drove the 12 miles to meet them. I pulled up at some lights and BANG! A truck ran straight into the back of me, skidding on the wet surface and causing the airbags to inflate on the rear seat. What could go wrong next?

I gave the lads a lift to the ground, where we accessed the superb Three Lions pub inside. The club owners showed us round the facilities that doubled as a museum. It was the best collection of football memorabilia I had ever seen, with everything framed, including Stanley Matthews' England caps and Maradona's signed World Cup shirt. There was even a signed Albion shirt and a great collection of rosettes and pennants from the 1960s. We were invited into the bar for a free meal – the hospitality was first class.

I was still wearing the clothes I had travelled in, so was delighted when I heard that the first thousand fans entering the ground would receive a free match t-shirt. I gratefully accepted, put it on immediately and said: 'Thanks – you don't happen to have any pants, do you?'

An estimated 3,500 crowd saw our new Irish signing, James McClean, refuse to acknowledge the flag of St George during the national anthems, causing controversy back home. The game was played in intense heat and humidity and Berahino played a neat one-two with Victor Anichebe for our 42nd minute opener. Brown Ideye headed the winner eight minutes from time after Charleston drew level. The decent numbers of Baggies were mainly ex-pats or American citizens and we appeared to be the only group, along with Mike and Linda Thomas, who had travelled from England. In the pub afterwards, we said our thanks and farewells and I left the lads to hit town while I went to my hotel for some much-needed sleep.

Due to the time difference, I woke in the early hours and decided to start my 424-mile jaunt up to Richmond for the second game. As I checked out, I was so pleased to be given my bag, which had turned up an hour earlier. I was able to change into fresh clothes for my mammoth seven hours on the road.

The other lads travelled by train, so I met them in The Penny Lane pub in Richmond centre for the evening session. Dubsey had again put me in touch with one of his mates, Simon Wilson, a Man United fan he had met during the Mexico World Cup. Simon turned up with his sons and joined us for the evening. It was such a good pub that we stayed for the duration. Among all the British paraphernalia was the obligatory Albion scarf pinned to the ceiling. Simon kindly gave me a lift back to the hotel and agreed to meet us at the game next day.

The match against Richmond Kickers was played in the lovely Careytown district. I got a taxi a few hours before kick-off and explored the area, predictably ending in a bar, where I met Gene O'Connell and the Pittsburgh Baggies. We were joined by another two groups who had travelled down from Canada. I jumped in Gene's car and arrived at the ground in time to set up a tailgate party. A gazebo was quickly erected, decorated with Albion flags and out came copious amounts of food and beer. The flags acted as a magnet for other Baggies and our group soon expanded to around twenty, all swapping stories about their Albion addiction. We were surrounded by dozens of 'Kickers' fans, all having their own tailgate parties and offering us more beer. It was a shame to have to go to the match as we were getting nicely settled for the afternoon.

The party atmosphere continued inside the City Stadium, with a band blasting out popular songs on a stage next to the main stand and beer tents everywhere. We were joined in the 6,832 crowd by more Albion exiles; Alister, Will, Rebecca and Lisa Collings, who now reside in Maryland, and Peter Hodgetts, who had driven from Ontario, Canada. Before kick-off, all eyes were on James McClean. This time, he toed the line and faced the flag.

In temperatures hitting 91.4 degrees Fahrenheit, huge forks of lightning brought an abrupt halt after just six minutes. The referee took the teams off for the best part of an hour as a torrential storm threatened. The players may have been safe, but we were sat on steel benches! Luckily, it blew over and play eventually resumed.

McClean opened the scoring with a fabulous long-range strike in the first half. Our new signing from Wigan, Callum McManaman, and substitute Adil Nabi both went close before Richmond equalised on 85 minutes. With 90 seconds remaining, Ideye scored his second winning goal in two games with an excellent far-post header. Simon gave me a lift into town afterwards and we had another good night at The Penny Lane.

After driving back to Charlotte Airport, I checked in to discover my flight to Newark was delayed 'indefinitely'. When I finally reached Newark, my connecting flight had already departed, so the airline put me up in a New York hotel and booked me on the 7.00 a.m. flight next day. Back at the airport the morning after, everything seemed fine until I looked at the board to see that the word 'cancelled' had suddenly appeared next to my flight. I started to think that I was never going to get home and had visions of living at the airport like Tom Hanks in 'Terminal'. The customer relations desk was twenty deep, so I called United Airlines and, to my surprise, got through. As luck would have it, there was a plane from Houston bound for Heathrow making an unscheduled landing at Newark because a passenger had been taken ill. They got me on the flight and I eventually made it home.

Apart from losing my bag, having a car crash and missing a flight or two, I had a great few days. The joys of following the Albion!

Postscript

It's 2016 and life is good. Ruth is happy, teaching primary schoolchildren in Warwickshire. Jade is now engaged to Tom, she has graduated and is a school teacher in West Bromwich. Ollie has secured a plumbing job at University of Warwick and he and Jade are Albion season-ticket holders.

Chris, Ray and I sold Mask-arade last year and I have retired from Alumet. I'm travelling more than ever and, despite being held up at knifepoint in Colombia, getting lost in the Andes and left stranded in Belarus, I continue to explore new destinations. I still attend every Albion home match, most away games and pre-season tours.

Thanks to football, I have been to most towns and cities in the UK. It has also enabled me to visit many places around the world that I had not heard of or would otherwise have had no reason to go to. I have met some incredible people on my travels. There truly is an international West Bromwich Albion family and the hospitality offered to me in countries such as Australia, New Zealand, Japan, Belize and Denmark enforces the power of Baggies 'brotherhood'.

The ninety minutes every Saturday afternoon (or whenever) is purely a side-show to the camaraderie that exists between like-minded supporters. Players, managers, coaches and directors come and go but friendships developed through our common interest last forever. I have kept the same seat in the Brummie Road End at The Hawthorns since the new stand was built and it's great that the next generations have joined us in recent years; Davel's daughter Sophie, Andy's daughter Ellie and Jade now give our section a female presence. We still miss dear old Richie. His sudden shouts of ALBION when all around was quiet was part of my match day. We will continue to go to Spain every year to raise a few glasses in his memory.

Until writing this book, I hadn't realised how many of the 200 or so football grounds that I have visited had sadly disappeared. In 2015, I saw Albion play West Ham at the Boleyn Ground for the last time, another classic football venue that will be lost forever. To me, the new all-seater stadia have taken the atmosphere away. I still get a 'buzz' when visiting new grounds for the first time but give me freezing cold terraces with a pie and Bovril any time!

About The Author

Dean Walton was 'Born to be a Baggie'. He has followed his beloved West Bromwich Albion all of his life, rarely missing a home game in the past fifty years.

Since leaving school in 1977, he has worked in the construction industry, installing glass facades on landmark buildings around the world. He had a personal audience with The Queen at Buckingham Palace in 2004 after Alumet had received the Queen's Award for Enterprise. He went on to be named as UK Director of the Year for Corporate Sustainabilty in 2012, before hanging up his hard hat and boots in 2016.

In 2009, Dean appeared on *Dragons' Den* with his colleagues from Mask-arade, pitching their personalised card masks, a product that was first trialled at an Albion match and went on to be a hugely successful business.

He is a West Bromwich Albion shareholder and a member of the Albion Assembly. He lives near Leamington Spa and is married with two grown-up children who, in keeping with the family tradition, are both Baggies' season-ticket holders.

His love for travel has seen him visit 125 different countries, including eighteen with the Albion.

Bibliography

Matthews, Tony, *West Bromwich Albion – The Complete Record* (Derby: DB Publishing, 2012)

Wright, Simon, *Flight of the Throstle*, (Marston Gate: Amazon.co.uk, 2011)

Wills, Terry, *From Flat Cap to Bronx Hat – The First 40 Years*, (Marston Gate: Amazon.co.uk, 2015)

Matthews, Tony, *Baggies Abroad*, (Durrington: Pitch Publishing, 2015)

Acknowledgements

I would like to thank the following for their valuable time and assistance:
   Tony Brown, Bob Taylor, Adrian Chiles, Andy Hunt, David Instone, Chris Lepkowski, Andy Payne, Tony Jones, Steve Conabeer, Eileen Baty, Julie Harley, John Stringer, Dave Holloway, Jeremy Barnes, Ian Richards, Dave Bowler, Danny Jones, Laurie Rampling and everyone on the Look Back in Albion Facebook page.
   Thank you to my non-football loving and very understanding wife, Ruth.
   Special thanks the family of Sir Bobby Robson www.sirbobbyrobsonfoundation.org.uk

Email: borntobeabaggie@gmail.com
Please like the Facebook page: www.facebook/BorntobeaBaggie
Follow on Twitter: @BornToBeaBaggie
Follow on Instagram: BorntobeaBaggie